WALSINGHAM

WALSINGHAM

Elizabethan Spymaster & Statesman

ALAN HAYNES

SUTTON PUBLISHING

First published in the United Kingdom in 2004 by
Sutton Publishing Limited

This paperback edition first published in 2007 by
Sutton Publishing, an imprint of NPI Media Group Limited
Cirencester Road · Chalford · Stroud · Gloucestershire · GL6 8PE

British Library Cataloguing in Publication Data
A catalogue record for this book is available from the British Library.

ISBN 978-0-7509-4771-8

Typeset in Photina MT.
Typesetting and origination by
NPI Media Group Limited.
Printed and bound in England.

For N L K
My eyes on the Internet

'A court is a conspiracy.'
M. Bradbury, *To the Hermitage*, p. 139

'His thoroughness was compulsive and regenerative, a pathological condition.'
Don DeLillo, *The Names*, p. 46

'Am I politic? Am I subtle? Am I a Machiavel?'
Shakespeare, *Merry Wives of Windsor* III, i

'I know of no disease of the soul but ignorance.'
Ben Jonson

CONTENTS

ACKNOWLEDGEMENTS

For indispensable help with the preparation of this book I am beholden forever to my exceptional research assistant Nicolas Keen who provided a blizzard of new material. Over several years he saved me vast amounts of time, and much money.

Living in a Somerset village, far from research libraries, I deluged my local branch library with requests for difficult-to-obtain books. The ladies of the library were very helpful. They would have had an easier professional life if I had researched this book while abroad – as I had hoped – but that did not happen. Nor did I get to spend long periods enjoying the hospitality and polite interest of the owners of any Elizabethan houses. No one was generous with provision of the family archives. Just my luck!

Writing outside the academy can be lonely and somewhat daunting. I have been very fortunate in my chosen general reader, Emeritus Professor Park Honan, a distinguished biographer in his own writings.

I am also grateful to Dr Simon Adams (Strathclyde University), a specialist in the period, for reading, commenting and correcting. If, from time to time, he recoiled 'as at a bad smell' I hope he thinks still that it was a task worth doing. Dr M. Leimon must be thanked since he kindly allowed me to use material from his Cambridge PhD thesis.

Funding from the Oppenheim–John Downes Memorial Trust greatly relieved the cost of preparing a handwritten manuscript for publication.

Since a crushing conjunction of events in 1998 I have had wonderful support from the Royal Literary Fund and its administrators – help that has been critical to my well-being and so to the writing of this book.

Finally, the Hélène Heroys Foundation (Switzerland) helped immeasurably by funding the last stages of writing, before becoming defunct.

INTRODUCTION

The nineteenth-century fashion for two- or three-volume biographies was sliding exhausted towards a temporary oblivion, when early in the twentieth century a graduate student at Yale – Conyers Read – began studying the life and work of Sir Francis Walsingham (1530–90). After completing his doctorate Read went on to achieve a rare mastery of the political and diplomatic history of Elizabethan England. His appetite for the manuscript sources available then, and subsequent printed material, was almost unlimited, and at length he produced *Mr Secretary Walsingham and the policy of Queen Elizabeth*, published in 1925. These acclaimed three volumes, with copious references and often lengthy quotations from documents, are rightly still recommended for student reading, and gratefully pillaged by them for essays. But even Read ignored or scampered over elements of Walsingham's career, and the possible fourth volume was not written.

After publication the behemoth biography broke down, collapsing under the weight of its research effort and the light, voluptuous kicking delivered by an entirely different kind of writer – the lean and not very learned Lytton Strachey. Few now bother to read him, while in marked contrast the academy has constantly and rightly cited Read on Walsingham. Even so, I suspect that the text has been as much dozed over in airless university libraries as pored over with gratitude. And Read had another effect; three volumes effectively smothered any later historian's inclination to take on the same subject. Now, after eighty years, the first single-volume biography of the redoubtable statesman and spymaster is here available for students and the general reader, placing the life it sets out within the rich historical and social context. For Read, the diplomacy of the Elizabethan Secretary of State was more significant, and dignified by detail, than espionage, but recently historians have been less fastidious, and Walsingham's activities and direction of the clandestine world have once again been scrutinised to greatly rewarding effect.

Those who served under him as intelligencers and spies were just as he was – men of the age. His subtle authority over the greedy, the feckless and the nervily patriotic stemmed from his candid purpose – to protect Elizabeth I and advance the Protestant cause when she fumbled the politics. Although desperate for employment spies could be scathing about their place of work; so Henry Wotton considered Florence 'a paradise inhabited by devils'. Yet he seems to have relished the challenge of posing for years as a German Catholic, and was 'able to penetrate areas of religious controversy undreamt of by other spies'. Walsingham put together and consolidated with gold a spy service that mesmerised European rulers, especially as like a great swordsman he developed a startling instinct for when to pause, when to catch brief breath, and when to lunge for the heart. No wonder his enemies feared him, and the unknowable number of his agents.

Was that a snort of derision from his Queen? She was never comfortable with the tireless intellectual, and creative dissonance centred their dealings. No doubt beside the man in black she felt gaudily frivolous, and his unremitting loyalty could seem like pressure or a challenge. However so – in their frequent meetings, argued exchanges and letters galore, the one could test the other almost to breaking point. Yet the possible even probable rupture never came, and though the haughty arch Tudor could rail against him, once deflated even she had to admit that his breadth and vigour of mind were irreplaceable; a proven fact when he died exhausted in 1590. For his part, as the years passed he grew in confidence, and he found ways to achieve an essential elasticity in government policy. Also pressed into service was the element of the apocalyptic in his imagination, as a result of his time as ambassador to France. Elizabeth must have been unaware of it when she appointed him, and although reluctant to go to such an expensive, corrupt place, he became the resident ambassador to the Valois court. So it was he who had the shocking misfortune to be in Paris during the Massacre of St Bartholomew in August 1572.

Thousands of French Protestants (Huguenots) were murdered in Paris and in towns across France by French Catholics. Among the mutilated dead were friends and acquaintances of Walsingham, whose own life was at risk. The depravity of what happened left the little cluster of Englishmen and foreign nationals in the locked and guarded embassy, aghast. The horror was psychologically overwhelming, yet when Walsingham emerged early in September for meetings with King Charles IX and the Queen-mother, Catherine de Medici, he seems not to have faltered – the diplomat in him prevailed. What had prepared him to show such strength under pressure? The answer must surely be his reading and his education abroad. Exiled from Marian England, Walsingham had furthered his intellectual expansion by time spent at the University of Padua. He had become a stoic – a crucial psychological prop for survival and sanity. Moreover, in the time of exile he became a cultivated *homme du monde*; humanistic learning in a multi-national centre made him less brittle. Not, by his own admission, less choleric – but then, as he also averred, choleric men make the best husbands.

Little chance to prove this to his first wife, except through his kind treatment of her son after her premature death. When he was vetted for a second marriage to a wealthy widow, somehow Walsingham's constant bouts of ill-health escaped them, as he escaped later sickness through the loving attention of Dame Ursula, who bore him two daughters. Mary Walsingham, second born, died in childhood; Frances, their first born, survived and made eventually three remarkable marriages: first to Philip Sidney, then to the Earl of Essex, and finally to the Irishman who looked strikingly like Essex – the Earl of Clanrickarde. Since the first two marriages aroused the extreme exasperation of Elizabeth, it was fortunate for the young wife that her father could not be alienated by Elizabeth, who could lash out at those who thought to flout her objections to a marriage. Walsingham was the second most important man in the kingdom, a shade behind Lord Burghley, and surely the equal of Leicester, whose position was eroded by Tudor hatred of his countess, Lettice Knollys, the piling up of debts, and the mid-1580s debâcle in the Low Countries when he took an army to assist the Dutch rebels. All this happened as Walsingham's career reached its peak with the destruction of the Babington Plot.

The reader will get a deliberate steer from me that is contextual and detailed because coherence in a biographical life often emerges by allowing the life to slide off-centre, placing the subject back in the crowd as well as picking him out from it. There are times when like Polonius in *Hamlet* Walsingham seems to disappear behind an arras. But while the sententious statesman in the play falls to the stabbing sword of Hamlet, Walsingham moves in and out of the court, driving himself to work harder, constantly reading and writing letters, and the pulse of the work strongly suggests a controlling hand and a brilliant authority. Hence my defence of the contextual strategy I have adopted; it seems to me the only secure way of following the complexities of the late career. Reflect too on his powerful, unnerving presence, dressed in black with the gleaming white starched neck ruff setting off the trim black beard. An interview with a man not above average height could still make the most confident sweat, forced to meet the serious, dark-eyed gaze; and consider being Babington when in their private meetings he sought to hide treachery.

In midlife Walsingham moved out of the retired anonymity of a country-living gentleman. First he became an MP, returned in 1562 for two places, Banbury and Lyme Regis, and choosing to sit for the Dorset constituency in the former seat of Sir Nicholas Throckmorton. His brothers-in-law Robert Beale and Peter Wentworth later entered the House of Commons nominated by Francis Russell, 2nd Earl of Bedford, and it seems very likely that Walsingham did the same. With dizzying speed (as it seems now) he became a diplomat and then a key minister of Elizabeth. It put him beside the throne of England to guide, correct and even defy one Queen, bring another to execution, and eventually help to defeat the might of an overbearing global empire. These career triumphs came late in life and were in every respect hard won. But the effort involved does not diminish, in my view, his strong challenge for the accolade, 'man of the century'. And if the reader of this biography allows Walsingham to nudge aside contemporaries – Burghley, Drake or perhaps even Ralegh – what will happen to the myth of the personal greatness of Elizabeth I? I say let that rickety notion be dumped forever into the dustbin of history.

Chapter 1

THE STUDENT STRATEGIST

In the decade after the death of the adipose and sinister King Henry VIII, his realm, especially the court and Westminster, was a tense, nerve-jangling place. His child successor, Edward VI, was surrounded by self-seeking senior noblemen tenaciously engaged in power struggles for wealth and advancement, and when the boy died the apparently nerveless John Dudley, Duke of Northumberland, had the temerity to place Lady Jane Grey on the throne, a young woman married to one of his sons. This coup speedily collapsed under the weight of public disfavour. Mary Tudor, Catholic half-sister to the late King and herself half-Spanish, took her throne. Though generally welcomed to her royal inheritance as a relief after greedy, disruptive factionalism, she was the embodiment of the old faith so ruthlessly plundered by her father and his loyal cohorts. Mary purposed the full restoration of Catholic rites, and by February 1555 her thrust was a choking fact with the first public burnings, the terrible consequence of resisting the ultra-zealous Marian government and church. Her marriage to the Spanish Philip II was resisted by Sir Thomas Wyatt who during his rebellion appealed for patriotic support. He failed and was executed; other Protestants fled abroad from what they felt was an increasingly alien court. Philip arrived with courtiers galore and even his own confectioner, Balthazar Sanchez, who settled in Tottenham. Yet her husband and Cardinal Pole could not persuade Mary to proceed with more caution and moderation.

Tiptoeing away from the brutality was a princess. She was Elizabeth, stepsister of a queen wedded to government by faith, but who in a benign gesture allowed her out of the Tower. The arch-pragmatist Elizabeth said jittery prayers on knees perhaps still knocking at All Hallows, Barking, and then it was on to nearby Fenchurch Street for a celebration lunch of pork and peas at the King's Head. Mary had little to celebrate, as it became clear that to consolidate Catholicism she had to provide hope of a Catholic succession, and when her reproductive system failed her the survival of Elizabeth 'created an automatic and Protestant reversionary interest'. Even so, Elizabeth's peaceful accession was not a foregone conclusion, but when it happened late in 1558 there was at large a feeling that Protestantism had retrieved the high ground and Catholicism was again in retreat, with 'Sweet Sister Temperance' as Edward VI had called her, in charge of the realm.

The lingering, sour reek of the burnings went away, and even the once *papabile* Archbishop of Canterbury, Cardinal Reginald Pole, involuntarily aided Elizabeth I by dying within hours of the now unlamented Mary, generously buried with full Catholic ceremony. The new queen was young, in her prime, not beautiful but certainly eye-catching; a woman who would frequently ignore or deliberately fumble conventional royal preoccupations such as the dynastic; who looked balefully on war and ideological passions, and who gave space to active men in her court and government to master political concerns, but not her in her privilege. Pole's legacy to her was an ecclesiastical vacuum; alienate Rome by harshness and she might be excommunicated, leading to a possible civil war with a host of enemies. But her title to the throne being essentially Protestant, doing nothing was not an option for Queen Anne Boleyn's daughter, and by the time of her mid-January 1559 Coronation, she had actually made religious changes that, as she was advised, almost brought her beyond what was possible without Parliament's agreement, and this did not open until 25 January. The Elizabethan church settlement included statutory recognition that the Bible, the works of the early fathers and the decrees of the first four councils provided the basis for Anglican belief.

The revamped Privy Council was emphatically Protestant and dominated by university-trained laymen, not clerics. A Marian privy councillor like Sir William Cordell was shunted off, but retained the office of Master of the Rolls until his death in 1581. Elizabeth had a key trusted adviser and Principal Secretary – Sir William Cecil – the second most influential person in the realm during most of a long reign. During 1558–9 the political landscape was given its specificity by the return to government and high influence of the group of Cambridge University men who had been taught by, or felt the gale of influence of, the late humanist Protestant scholar of lowly birth and brilliant reputation, Sir John Cheke, one of whose sisters was briefly married to Cecil. Their mother, wife of a beadle who died and left her with little to raise a family, kept a wine shop in Cambridge where as a student Cecil took a glass. Cheke was a scholar in Greek and a Marian exile, first in Italy and then in Antwerp. Like his great predecessor, William Tyndale, translator of the Bible into English, Cheke overestimated his personal safety from the agents of Catholicism. Tyndale had been arrested and burned; Cheke was a little more fortunate, being seized and shipped to the Tower of London. Fear drove him to recant – and then he seems to have resolved to die, an end probably aided by the unhealthy environment. His widow Lady Mary also had a vinous connection, being the daughter of the sergeant of the wine cellar to Henry VIII, and wealth from the wine trade laid too the foundations of the Walsingham family fortune which allowed Francis Walsingham to go to King's College, Cambridge, for years Cheke's domain.

Vineyards were part of England's ancient history, but the red wine for the mass of converted Christian England was too rosé for Christ's blood. Hence imports (French), and from the time that King Edward (the Confessor) gave the monopoly of its carriage to the ship masters of Rouen, it was brought to England by French vessels which sailed *en masse* during the more settled Channel weather of April to early October. Winchelsea has still surviving medieval wine vaults built for storage on a vast scale to match the huge number of hogsheads being imported. The wealth of vintners like generations of Walsinghams is well illustrated by a story of the famous Henry Picard, who as Master of the Guild of Vintners had five Kings dine at his table: Edward III, David of Scotland, John of France and the rulers of Denmark and Cyprus. In after-dinner cards Cyprus lost heavily and Picard, in a sweeping gesture, handed back to him the gold he had forfeited in play.

James Walsingham (d. 1540) had seven daughters and four sons; the eldest, Edmund, became Lieutenant of the Tower, was knighted, and when he died in 1549 Scadbury Manor in Kent, long in the family through a mid-fourteenth-century marriage, passed to his son, Sir Thomas Walsingham. One of the uncles of Sir Thomas, William Walsingham, had a career in law and probably resided at Footscray in Kent with his wife Joyce (née Denny), the daughter of Sir Edmund Denny of Cheshunt, Herts, a Baron of the Exchequer, an advantageous position wherein lay opportunities to increase the family fortune. In his will the pious Denny asked for twenty-eight trentals of masses to be said for his soul, and the souls of his father, mother and three wives. The brother of Joyce Denny was Sir Anthony Denny who married Joan Champernowne, the aunt of Walter Ralegh, whose mother was a Champernowne. Along with Sir William Herbert, Sir Anthony was chief gentleman of Henry VIII's privy chamber, and then its head following the dismissal of Sir Thomas Heneage. Denny did less well in land grants than his colleague Herbert, and after Waltham the most valuable property in his portfolio was Sibton, Suffolk, once the property of the Duke of Norfolk. Denny helped to put in motion the sweeping religious changes of the later part of Henry's reign which were to deprive his own father of his devout wishes.

When William Walsingham, a former under-sheriff of London, died soon after the birth of his son Francis in the early 1530s, Joyce Walsingham sought to protect her five daughters and her son by a prompt remarriage, and she selected Sir John Carey of Pleshey as her new spouse. He was an uncle of the Henry Carey who became Lord Hunsdon, and was widely assumed to be an illegitimate son of Henry VIII from the adulterous relationship with Mary Boleyn. The younger sister of Anne, Mary had married Sir John Carey's brother, William, a gentleman of the bedchamber. William Carey died in 1528, and Anne Boleyn had the wardship of young Henry granted to her by the King. This Carey–Boleyn connection was always a restraint later on Elizabeth I when she and her kinsman Francis Walsingham disagreed profoundly about foreign policy. Family mattered. Sir John moved his to Hunsdon (Herts) after his appointment as royal bailiff of the manor.

Unless sent away for a self-improving period in a great household, Francis probably lived with his mother in the Carey home, while Scadbury remained the home of his first cousin, Sir Thomas, who married Sir John Guldeford's daughter, Dorothy. Of the early life and education of Francis we know nothing other than it would have given particular attention to Latin history and the liberal arts – grammar, rhetoric, logic, geometry, arithmetic, music and astronomy; then, in his late teens, he went to King's College, Cambridge, which he left without taking a degree after being a Fellow Commoner for some two years. Quite soon this could signal an inclination to Catholic recusancy, but Walsingham was always a sincere Protestant, and he made no hurried decision about his future. Like rather few before him but many since, he chose to travel from September 1550 (heading who knows where), before returning to London in 1552 to study law at Gray's Inn, one of the Inns of Court where increasing numbers of commoners studied law, not necessarily to follow the example of his long-dead father. Still, it was a litigious age and any gentleman could reasonably expect that at several points in his life he would indeed be in court as a plaintiff or defendant. Certainly his prospects for advancement were not diminished by such studies, although many students found them acutely boring. It was Nicholas Bacon, also of Gray's Inn – which then stood by itself, north of cottage-lined Holborn, in Gray's Inn

Lane – who urged Henry VIII to employ his common lawyers in diplomacy, replacing the hitherto indispensable churchmen. If the intellectually gifted Francis did find the law boring, at least the country-dweller in him should have been satisfied, and when he wanted to quit his books he had only to walk a few yards from the Inn buildings to be in the countryside.

Nor was he any great distance from the booksellers around St Paul's. There were books appearing at this time – the mid-century – to fire his imagination, among them a *History of Italy* and *Italian Grammar* – the last dedicated to John Tamworth, who married Christian, Walsingham's sister. Both were the work of William Thomas who years before had fled to Italy with a large sum of money stolen from his noble employer. Having made belated restitution and been forgiven, Thomas still remained in Italy, a place of civilised delight. Back in England, he was at length favoured by Edward VI and became Clerk of the Council of the Duke of Northumberland, which was also joined by John Cheke.*

Under Queen Mary both these salvationist Protestants lost favour, and after a period in the Tower Cheke went into exile in Italy; Thomas was executed. The scholar administrator travelled south in company with Sir Richard Morison, a civil lawyer trained in Padua, who had adapted Machiavelli's writings for the use of Henry VIII in the 1530s and 1540s.[1] Italians had become diplomatic mercenaries in service to Henry; travel by Englishmen to Italy seeking advancement acquired a cachet. Cheke and Morison lodged with Sir Thomas Wrothe and Thomas Hoby, translator of Castiglione's *The Courtier*, after 2 November 1554, and when the following year Walsingham arrived in Padua, it may be he fell in with this little academy. Before enrolling at the university of Basle, Walsingham's Denny kinsmen Anthony, Charles and Henry were in Padua in August 1554, and it was there that he met Pietro Bizari, advocate of the Reformation, who the following year met Francis Russell, earl of Bedford in Venice, later becoming tutor to the Russell children. By December 1555 Walsingham was the chosen *consularius*, the official representative of the students comprising the English 'nation' in the faculty of Civil Law at the ancient university of Padua. However, this was an oddly abbreviated honour, because some four to six months later he abruptly quit Padua with other Englishmen following the

* Principal Secretary in 1553.

exposure of the Dudley plot in the spring of 1556; at the same time Cheke himself had become thoroughly disenchanted with foreigners and their manner of conducting themselves in daily exchanges.[2] The constant irritations occasioned by exile did not readily evaporate; threats, shortages of money and an almost fatal illness cast a pall over Italy for Cheke, and in turn Walsingham may have drifted into the same frame of mind. Or, and perhaps more importantly, he was becoming seriously uneasy at the decay of Venetian-Papal relations, which threw up the problem of where to go for safe exile. Southern Italy and Spain were too dangerous, so a more obvious path of retreat would be to Strasbourg, where Thomas Sampson fetched up, or Switzerland, where in Basle, Zurich or Geneva many more exiles were secure. (Robert Beale went to Strasbourg, where he lived in the house of Sir Richard Morison (d.1557), before moving to Zurich. Morison's widow would marry the 2nd Earl of Bedford.) Walsingham may even have been inspired by the *peregrinatio academica* – visits to the most famous Reformed seats of learning. He was reading deeply in theology, and the impulse to embrace it elsewhere may have been hard to resist. At length he reached Basle and seems to have spent time there with William Temple, a King's College Fellow. Does this help to explain why the library of King's would later give Walsingham one of its Bibles for presentation to Philip II of Spain?

Walsingham had quit England to defend his life and beliefs. Along with the other 800 or so who fled the Marian terror, he had never, in the words of John Knox, 'bowed to idolatry', so on his return he was untainted (in some eyes) by collaboration, unlike Sir William Cecil, against whom the accusation was boldly made as late as 1579 by a parish priest of Barton upon Dunsmore – Mr Prowde. The unspoken sub-text to this may have been the more dangerously held notion that Elizabeth had also 'bowed to idolatry' in the time of her half-sister, but then she might have done this anyway without any pressure – it was anyone's guess. Walsingham had not prospered in exile, but he had gained a rare level of maturity for a young intellectual. He returned to his father's Footscray estate; his stepfather had died in 1552 and his influence had gone. The Walsingham sisters were married (save for one at this time) and their mother Lady Joyce would herself die in 1560. Once re-established in Kent, the dark and eligible bachelor landowner needed a wife, preferably comely and rich. Within two years he had met and married just such a woman, Anne Carleill, formerly married to the late wine merchant Alexander Carleill (Carlyle?). The daughter of Sir George Barne (Snr), the former Lord Mayor of London and Alice Brooke, Anne had a son already, and money. The young couple settled at Parkebury Manor in Hertfordshire, leased by Francis, and shortly before her death he had disposed of Footscray. He was her executor and in her will she left him £100 (*c.* £50,000 today). Even though she died within two years of their marriage, Walsingham stayed put until in 1565 he remarried, having proved his honest intentions. This second marriage was to another widow, Ursula (née St Barbe), whose father was a Somerset landowner, and one of her uncles, William St Barbe, was a gentleman of the Privy Chamber, where access to the queen was strictly controlled and most appointments conferred courtier status. Ursula St Barbe had made her first marriage to Sir Richard Worsley of Appuldurcombe (IoW), and when he died in 1565 Walsingham became a candidate second husband to a lady with property in Lincolnshire at Boston and Skirbeck. To prove his honest intentions the widower had to promise to settle lands to the yearly value of 100 marks on Ursula, for which he was bound for 2,000 marks. To Ursula's brother-in-law he had to convey Parkebury, and in July 1566 was bound to 1,000 marks for this transaction (the cause of litigation). If he pre-deceased Ursula she was promised plate worth £500, and by a still later deed she would also get a manor valued at £100 per annum.

Neither Walsingham nor his second wife had strayed out of social demarcations. He got a housekeeper of good standing for him, little Christopher and his older sister Alice Carleill, who would later marry Christopher Hoddesdon of the Muscovy Company; a mother already of two sons John and George, who would both die soon, accidentally blown up by gunpowder held in the porter's lodge at Appuldurcombe where the newly-weds lived, a boat and lengthy horse ride from London, Windsor, Nonsuch, Richmond or Greenwich. (With the death of the two boys, Ursula's first brother-in-law took possession of Appledurcombe, and Walsingham and his shockingly reduced conjoined family had to console themselves with Carisbrook Priory and the manors of Godshill and Freshwater. The restored priory evidently served as their residence, and what remains today is incorporated into a farmhouse.) She got a dark-haired, dark-eyed, slender and good-looking bearded man in his mid-thirties, spiritual, intellectual, a man of substance and temperate habits, albeit, as he noted of himself, 'choleric' – when, as he also said, choleric men made the best husbands – and a protective, loving future father of two daughters, Frances and Mary, who died very young in 1577.

When Elizabeth became queen it was Sir William Cecil who became her chief adviser and minister. If like Walsingham he had been a Marian exile, or plotted more extreme resistance, she would not have picked him. He was married to the sister of his Cambridge tutor, Sir John Cheke, and on her death married Mildred, the eldest of the highly educated Cooke sisters, three of whom married men who had strong careers at Elizabeth's court – Sir Nicholas Bacon, Sir Thomas Hoby and Sir Henry Killigrew, who was to become a strong follower of Lord Robert Dudley, the accomplished, preening royal favourite who got him an Exchequer office. Any government office remained outside possibility at the moment because Walsingham, like the Earl of Bedford,[3] had been a Marian exile – this choice was like an invisible badge of former hostility to the Crown, worn by Bedford since his implication too in the Wyatt plot. His flight abroad had been first to Geneva, then Venice, where the fork-bearded nobleman listened to continental church reformers. Some people attached much hope to this, but apart from minor diplomatic assignments the young privy councillor did not get a specific office until 1564, when he became governor of faraway Berwick and Warden of the East Marches. He never ceased to work towards a Calvinistic solution of England's problems, and echoing his views was the Earl of Huntingdon, whose own claim to the throne remained and effectively kept him out of high office. All his Plantagenet blood ancestry made Elizabeth wary of this loyal servant who on his father's side was a descendant of Edward III. I believe it was the intimate links to Bedford – one of those who with Sir Henry Sidney had linked Lord Robert Dudley to Sir Nicholas Throckmorton – that got Walsingham, kinsman to Elizabeth, sidelined for so long. In the case of Throckmorton, a former Wyatt ally and Protestant firebrand, he had narrowly avoided a treason indictment through a technical loophole. When Mary had died he was soon panting for a post, but when the ambassadorship to France happened he urged aid for the Huguenots and got himself captured in the fighting that was supposed to lead to the re-annexation of Calais, so recently lost to France. To attain power Throckmorton needed an energetic supporter, otherwise his career – beyond being the ablest intelligencer of his day – would be inconsequential – no wonder he attached himself to Dudley's cohort. That he did so in the mid-1560s indicates the strength of the favourite at court. A favourite who dared to look to Mary, Queen of Scots, nine years younger than Elizabeth, mother of the recently born Prince James, and a prime candidate for the English throne in the event of Elizabeth's early demise. To Cecil the notion of an accommodation with Mary, a Catholic and a Guise, was impossible, and this turn of events may well have suggested to him the utility of having Walsingham within his affinity, this at a time when Henry Killigrew became Cecil's brother-in-law, and the Earl of Leicester's older brother, Ambrose, Earl of Warwick, married Anne Russell, daughter of Bedford.

Was it marriage to Ursula Worsley that made Walsingham more ambitious? Was he actually keen to advance or did it just occur as a result of increased contacts with Cecil? Pietro Bizari in Venice by 1565 was writing to Cecil and Walsingham with information. Hostility to Cecil in council was led by the Duke of Norfolk with other nobles following, antagonistic to an upstart commoner; nominally Protestant when Cecil was strongly so, 'they naturally leaned for support towards the Roman Catholics'. Cecil would need a quiet, staunchly Protestant aide, a man of intellect and integrity, and he found him in Walsingham who 'was already at the very outset of his official career an earnest co-worker in the cause of militant Protestantism'. By August 1568 (if not before) the long pause in his career was over.

Chapter 2

HANDLE WITH CARE

The years 1568–9 were vastly important ones for Elizabeth and her government. The challenge came from the coiled support for the cause of Mary, Queen of Scots, the Catholic claimant to the throne of England, who had been ousted by her Scottish enemies for exile in May 1568. Instead of passing through England to her former home in France, Mary was placed under house arrest in the very country whose throne she coveted. Despite her lamentable (even murderous) record as a wife, the premier Duke of England, the 4th Duke of Norfolk, himself a Catholic-leaning Protestant, was soon ruminating on the possibility of marrying her, despite a warning from Elizabeth in October 1568 that the notion of nuptials must be dropped. Mary's Scottish subjects charged her with many errors and crimes, so that after weighing the matter Elizabeth decided to establish a commission of enquiry, nominating Norfolk, the Earl of Sussex and Sir Ralph Sadler to meet in York with representatives of Mary and her half-brother, the Regent of Scotland, the Earl of Murray. Mary recoiled from such a procedure as beneath her regal dignity, especially since her complicity in the murder of Lord Darnley, her former husband, was bound to be raised. The Casket Letters, documents incriminating Mary, when shown to Norfolk at York, for a time made Mary seem utterly repugnant, but Murray denied the Casket letters open circulation without Elizabeth committing herself to give judgement against the accused. Not likely – so the York Conference petered out, and to end the stalemate Elizabeth decided to appoint a much larger London-based commission that would sit in Westminster where she could get at it.

When this conference also folded after the revelation of the Casket letters by a bumbling Murray, who caught wind of a rumour that his throat might be cut as he made his way north, he decided it was politic to make a grovelling apology to Norfolk before departing. They met in Hampton Court Park, with Sir Nicholas Throckmorton supervising the renewal of amity and Norfolk maintaining that he was resolved to marry Mary, and even hinting that his own daughter might one day wed the boy king James VI. Sworn to secrecy, Murray revealed all to Elizabeth before he left London and she agreed to support him as Regent; a £5,000 dole would help.

With the Casket letters available to sway domestic and European opinion, Elizabeth's position had been strengthened. She had ample evidence to justify her treatment of Mary to Philip II, a self-preening expert, as he thought, on English affairs. But contacts between the King of Spain and his former sister-in-law were not helped when he loftily refused further audiences to the English ambassador to Spain, John Man. It may be this mattered less than his appointment of an opinionated bigot as his own ambassador in London, Don Guerau de Spes, who arrived in September 1568. De Spes was under orders by Philip to carry out the directions of the Spanish governor-general of the Netherlands, the Duke of Alba. Yet within a very few weeks in a foreign country, where he lacked for the moment informed contacts, de Spes was behaving with an arrogant freedom that marked him down as dangerous. He told Alba in December 1568 that Elizabeth had confiscated the five shiploads of silver sent from Spain to Alba's bankers in the Netherlands, when the ships carrying this cargo of bullion had taken refuge in Dover before landing it in Portsmouth and Plymouth. Actually, she had not, and virtually single-handed de Spes managed to spark a trade war. Alba ordered the prompt seizure of all English goods in the territory he ruled for Philip. Trade as such was to cease, and this disaster forced Elizabeth to counter with her own responses in January 1569. Blame for the embargo fell on Secretary Cecil, whose dominant position in the court government seemed sinister to some, and his unpopularity among city merchants was matched by a loss of confidence in him by the Privy Council. Elizabeth's reaction to Alba was to mimic his policy thrust and to have de Spes placed under house arrest, a restriction lasting until July 1569, while the captains and some of the ships' crews were imprisoned.

So Philip had no diplomatic representatives to resolve the problem other than Alba, a grandee who had lived in England during Mary's marriage to his prince, and had his own intelligence cluster *in situ*, and who even before receiving royal instructions was sending envoys to England. Although Elizabeth was unaware of it Alba was not her principal enemy; he saw no point of advantage in seeking her overthrow to be replaced by a French catspaw, and he opposed any policy that jeopardised Anglo-Dutch trading. Alba, by his resistance to royal inclination and his frankly expressed realism, started to repair the damage done and Chiappino Vitelli (Marquis of Certona) was sent to England to establish how the restoration could be effected. Vitelli found a positively friendly Privy Councillor in Robert Dudley, Earl of Leicester, who spoke Italian and was chief among Cecil's opponents at this time. Elizabeth's handsome favourite was sure that Cecil had thwarted the wooing and winning of the Queen. Others taxed the minister for the severity of treatment of recusant Catholics since the arrival of Mary. Criticism of an anti-Spanish drift in English foreign policy came from still others who feared a dirty little rapprochement with France, the enemy of historical choice. Cecil was faced by enemies on all fronts save one – he had the confidence of the Queen. Finding that they could not heave him out of power, a number of malcontents rallied round the *fainéant* Norfolk to promote his marriage to Mary. The Duke and the Earl of Arundel took the complicated issues of matrimonial and foreign policy to the house where de Spes was currently in quarters under guard, using as their emissary the Florentine money-dealer Roberto Ridolfi, who delivered what was considered to be a 'safe cipher' for key correspondence.

Ridolfi had settled into business in London in 1562, and within five years he was handling the secret funds sent by Pope Pius V to English Catholics. In January 1569 the French ambassador to London, La Mothe Fénélon reported to Paris that Ridolfi was now offering himself as a bridge between rattled London and angry Brussels, and when he got to meet de Spes late in February of the same year he gave the assurance that the snatched treasure would be returned to Spain. In his isolation, de Spes had time to ruminate on a plan that went beyond anything Ridolfi had secretly communicated in March to La Mothe Fénélon – the papal commission to overthrow Protestantism, the restoration of Catholicism, with Elizabeth worked by the puppet masters Norfolk, Arundel and Lumley. By late May the brooding de Spes had even come to the view that Elizabeth had to be removed, and Philip II should either claim the throne or support Mary. Details, together with Ridolfi's plan, were smuggled to Alba, who despite his deep unease did forward them to Philip for consideration. This was '*the Enterprise of England*'.

In the summer of 1569 the jitteriness that had once assailed Elizabeth as she looked to her future returned like an avalanche. Norfolk had quit the court – to do what? Raise the standard of rebellion, rescue Mary and advance on London? As yet Cecil knew nothing about possible aid to Mary's cause from Philip II or Alba, but he too feared the worst. In fact when the rebellion came it was relatively localised, and led by the northern religious malcontents the Earls of Northumberland and Westmorland, proclaimed traitors by the Lord President of the Council in the North, the Earl of Sussex, on 28 November

1569. The military response of the government was sharp; the rebel earls fled to Scotland as a preliminary to European exile. Alba's scepticism about the 'Enterprise' was enhanced and he sent rude letters to de Spes, and a detailed letter to Philip on the latter's invasion plans which is saturated in sarcasm. Startled by the withering tone and content Philip stalled any policy he might have had in mind to allow Alba to make decisions. His error (as we will see) was to allow – even require – de Spes to maintain contact with Ridolfi. Not lacking in confidence he offered his services again to the Privy Council as an intermediary with Alba, but paid out *c.* £3,000 from de Spes to John Leslie, Bishop of Ross and spokesman for Mary in Elizabeth's court. Ridolfi's disinclination to remain obscure in the shadows led to his arrest with a clutch of Englishmen, Italians and Spaniards. Twenty-five charges were made against him and he was interrogated by the Italian-speaking aide to Cecil, Francis Walsingham, who was mastering the craft of counter-espionage. Being questioned in his own language just before the Northern Rebellion seems to have smothered any resolve he might have had to lie and resist. At some point Walsingham achieved the psychological mastery he required to 'turn' Ridolfi into a double agent.[1] In November the new recruit to the government side was released on bail of £1,000 (rough equivalent today to £500,000) and by the beginning of 1570 Ridolfi had been discharged unconditionally because Walsingham and whoever assisted him could find nothing of substance against the immigrant while his freedom might well lead to an indiscretion.

The rebellion of the Northern earls had repercussions too for Mary and Norfolk, who both experienced close custody. Elizabeth had hoped to deal with him with a charge of high treason, but found to her chagrin that he had not infringed the Treasons Statute. In due course, as the estates of the defeated earls were settled on her men, Elizabeth allowed his release from the Tower to his own property at the Charterhouse in August 1570. Norfolk set about improvements to his house (for a time renamed Howard House), and even while he had the builders in, renewed his dealings with the ebullient Ridolfi, who was edging into plotting again. Presumably he felt immune to any *mauvais* interpretation by the surveillance of the great building, and seems to have thought Englishmen too untutored in revolution to make their own plans. He prepared the Bishop of Ross and de Spes for his notion of a general rising, given its ideological thrust by the Papal Bull *Regnans in excelsis*, which attacked in vivid language Elizabeth's authority. Ridolfi grandly exaggerated figures for those Englishmen who were willing to resist Elizabeth through contacts with Norfolk's secretary, William Barker, the elderly lawyer George Ferrers, and Edmund Plowden, a famously distinguished common lawyer whose Catholicism barred him from being a judge. When Mary's bishop was questioned in October 1571 he disclosed that Ferrers had long favoured the Scottish claim to the throne, and it was perhaps miraculous that Ferrers and Plowden emerged unscathed from the implosion of the Ridolfi plot.

In Europe Ridolfi had the support of Philip II, whose willingness to marry his sister-in-law of years before had long abated. He was actually alarmed, and not a little displeased, with the papal bombshell, fearing reprisals by Elizabeth on the Catholic community – still a substantial element in the population. Instead he looked approvingly on the more devious schemes of Ridolfi, skilfully concealed hitherto, who slid out of England in late March 1571. It has been averred that Cecil (now Lord Burghley, to signal Elizabeth's esteem) had no suspicions about the wily Florentine who remained on excellent terms with Walsingham (in whose house he had been confined). It is possible to be both wary and willing to employ a man with such a stack of contacts, and Burghley may actually have been more cautious about Ridolfi than his junior aide. After an audience with Elizabeth on 25 March the banker left for Europe, taking with him a commission to open talks aimed at ending the damaging trade war. Were Walsingham and Burghley aware of Ridolfi's authorization from Norfolk and Mary to get plot assistance from Spain? Not immediately perhaps – though they may have had suspicions – but Ridolfi's deciphered letters to Mary, the capture of the code used by Ridolfi, and the testimony of his English contacts and de Spes revealed everything. Such bungling may (or may not) have been deliberate; certainly in the autumn of 1571 when Philip sent him to see Alba, he was briskly cross-questioned. It emerged that de Spes was the overseer of business and according to Alba, Ridolfi was 'a man of limited understanding'.[2]

The principal components of the plot were fourfold: Alba was to send between 6,000 and 10,000 men to Harwich or Portsmouth as an invasion force, but not before Norfolk and his sympathisers took Elizabeth captive or even murdered her while she was making her annual progress through the south of England. This piece of brigandry would be followed by a general rising in the country against the remnants of her government, presumed to be disorganised or paralysed, and then it was a free Mary who would marry Norfolk. She would be queen and he would take the crown matrimonial. Consider this now and the flaws betray themselves. Despite Philip's passion

that the enterprise should go forward too few troops were allocated, and given
the totally unrealistic time of six weeks for preparation. Nor was Philip
beyond making organizational changes that Alba would regard with
incredulity; the King wanted men scheduled to reinforce the army of Flanders
to take part in the invasion, and the force itself was to be commanded by a
recalled Vitelli. Moreover, Ridolfi's geographical knowledge of England was
ignorantly casual – he did not even know the whereabouts of Harwich – and
his reliance on the temperamentally limp Norfolk was also misplaced. The
Duke and Mary had never met, and she was still married to the renegade Earl
of Bothwell, then rotting in a Danish gaol. Even so, a papal annulment might
remove that impediment, and if three marriages each could betoken anything
it might mean both making an effort to achieve a harmonious relationship.

Harmony was not high on Alba's list of ends desirable. As far as he was
concerned the chronology of the Enterprise was wrong; Norfolk should lead
the rising and prompt the invasion. Nor was he greatly impressed by the
chatty Ridolfi who to him seemed a volatile mixture of subtlety and childish
indiscretion. The man talked too much, but this was a personal habit that did
not seem to bother Guerau de Spes excessively. On 25 March 1571 he wrote
to the King's Secretary of the Council of State, Gabriel de Zayas, reporting the
departure of Ridolfi and requesting that the secretary should arrange an
audience between the Italian and Philip. De Spes used his official cipher for
the conspirator's correspondence. If he wanted to contact Mary, then like
Ridolfi and Norfolk he had to do it through her representative in Whitehall,
the Bishop of Ross, who passed items to her in Sheffield Castle, where she was
quite comfortably close-watched by the Earl and Countess of Shrewsbury. Not
closely enough, however, to prevent her written commission to Ridolfi passing
to him via the Bishop.

Just before Ridolfi made passage, de Spes received a visit from the
representative of the boldly unscrupulous sailor, pirate and larcenist, John
Hawkins of Plymouth, son of one of Henry VIII's most esteemed West Country
sea captains. The agent for Hawkins was George Fitzwilliam, a distant relation
of Lady Burghley, whose brother Hugh Fitzwilliam served as chargé d'affaires
in the Paris embassy from mid-1566 to January 1567. Speaking for Hawkins,
Fitzwilliam, a former Spanish captive held in prison in Mexico, gave a stirring
diatribe on the anger Hawkins (supposedly) felt about the failure of Elizabeth to
support him in his efforts to get released men captured, in September 1568 at
San Juan de Ulua. The battle there ended a voyage of almost unredeemed

disaster for Hawkins; 400 men had sailed with him and in all about seventy returned. In August 1570 he had told de Spes of his alienation, and early in 1571 he scattered further bait when he spoke openly of defecting to Philip II with all his ships if the King would release the captive twenty who had fetched up in a Seville gaol. It is now impossible to ferret out whether Walsingham was the artful source of these alluring gestures. Certainly Hawkins was a senior member of a cluster making periodic snatches against Spanish trade in the Channel, and they were hand-in-glove with the increasingly powerful French Protestants – the Huguenots. As Hawkins made his move on de Spes in August 1570, Walsingham had royal instructions on 15 August to go to France to act in conjunction with the resident ambassador, Sir Henry Norris, in the negotiations between the Huguenots and Charles IX of France. But La Mothe Fénélon informed the Queen before Walsingham went over that the treaty of St Germain had royal and Huguenot assent, so in appearance at least Walsingham's mission had ebbed in importance to one of formal congratulations. But the French ambassador himself took the view that Walsingham was sent to discover the effect of the peace on the attitude of Charles towards Elizabeth, and especially how he would view Mary and the Scottish problem. As for the Huguenots – if Walsingham did have any dealings with them he was immensely guarded about them; by the end of September he was back in England to report, and by October he was dealing once again with Ridolfi.

Hawkins, as far as we know, never did meet Ridolfi, although it is just possible they had a chance meeting at the Spanish embassy in Winchester House, Southwark. In February 1571 Hawkins was in London as a Plymouth MP, shortly after Walsingham had gone reluctantly to France as Elizabeth's new permanent ambassador, the private cost of the appointment making him clearly unhappy. Walsingham had seen how the embassy drained the pockets of even someone like Norris, 'whose living is known to be great' and who was allowed £280 a quarter for living expenses. Walsingham got £3 6s 8d a day 'for his diet', payable two weeks before his arrival at his point of embarkation. This was Dover, and on 1 January 1571 he landed at Boulogne after a little campaign in wining and dining La Mothe Fénélon in London, thereby hoping to make his own Paris reception more cordial. De Spes, ever dour, wrote to Philip II that the English ambassador was sent to France because Elizabeth calculated he would cause dissent there. This was perhaps a little unkind to the Queen and her diplomat, who only reached Paris on 16 January; certainly she wanted him in close contact with the Huguenots, and he had too a role as cupid, for Elizabeth was once again marriage-minded (or so pretended) and Henri, Duke of Anjou, was her sighted prey.

So, by the spring of 1571 Walsingham was in Paris; Ridolfi was in the Low Countries and George Fitzwilliam was in Spain where he met with his relative, the English-born wife of the Duke of Feria, Lady Jane Dormer, and piecemeal presented the Hawkins proposal of disengagement from Elizabeth and re-engagement to the Catholic cause there. With the interest of the Duke snared, Fitzwilliam was to return to England to secure credentials from Hawkins and Mary, Queen of Scots. Feria sent rings to them both and the Duchess and Philip also prepared gifts for her.[3] When Fitzwilliam got back to England he went to de Spes to explain his travels and ask for a meeting with Mary, which was not within the ambassador's remit. So Hawkins asked Burghley, who arranged it for early June, and out of that meeting Fitzwilliam got a missal dedicated by Mary to the Duchess, as well as letters to Feria and Philip asking for the release of Hawkins's twenty English sailors. He and Burghley were shown these items, and the latter (who now knew what Ridolfi was orchestrating) was also told of the offer of service to Spain, with the rider that this might be used to uncover all the clandestine effort being made by England's enemies. In his baiting of de Spes Hawkins concealed the fact that Burghley was now fully appraised of what was going on, and the ambassador and his royal master, although suspicious, found Hawkins and Fitzwilliam convincing enough that hope triumphed over intelligent reflection. If the Ridolfi plot and Hawkins's transfer of allegiance and ships chimed together it would be a royal flush. The English would be severely deflated, a significant part of their marine power lost to Spain, and this in turn would cripple Dutch resistance to the colonial power by removing English support for the Sea Beggars in the Channel.

The resistance fighters of Prince William of Orange, at sea under their designated admiral, Adrien de Berghes, *seigneur* de Dolhain, formed a fleet. It got limited recognition in England – although Walsingham would surely have urged more, since their militant Calvinism so neatly matched his – and shelter by the Huguenots at La Rochelle. Dolhain was not a success in William's eyes, unwilling or unable to control the violent excesses of his men and reluctant to share the spoils of war. Eventually Dolhain was imprisoned in England with the connivance of the Dutch prince. Perhaps it was the absence of Walsingham as their advocate that led to a much tougher attitude among Elizabeth's Privy Councillors towards the Sea Beggars under an eccentric Liègois, William de la Marck, Lord of Lumey. By mid-1571 they were becoming exasperated with these wilful belligerents, who had found shelter in English ports such as Dover and attacked any vulnerable shipping. Louis of Nassau came to realise how dangerous to the Orangeist cause it would be if Elizabeth became too exasperated, as indeed some of her subjects were – most notably Sir John Hawkins. Very likely it was the strong presence in Dover of the Sea Beggars that set him off, because the port was about to become pivotal in his own dealings with Spain. Even more important was the return of Fitzwilliam to Spain to meet with Feria. Their agreement for the use of Hawkins's ships (sixteen) for six weeks, at Spanish royal expense, was the key item signed up for on 10 August 1571. In return, those English prisoners still held in prison in Seville were to be freed, and when a few subordinate matters had been settled Feria expounded the Enterprise to Fitzwilliam, who was sent back to England carrying explanatory letters for Hawkins, Mary, Queen of Scots and de Spes. From Philip, Fitzwilliam received 500 gold ducats, a ring and, for Mary, a ruby.[4]

Back in April a servant of the Bishop of Ross, the active spokesman for Mary at Whitehall, one Charles Bailly, was arrested at Dover and a packet of letters taken from him. Given his position in Paris, then the hub of espionage, it seems realistic to suggest that Walsingham had been given his name and in turn had contacted Burghley. He was probably waiting for the packet, but the Warden of the Cinque Ports, Lord Cobham, was sympathetic to Norfolk, and he allowed the Bailly packet to be seen by Ross, who went by night to de Spes. The ambassador removed two letters from Ridolfi, substituted two others in cipher, and then enjoyed reports that the Lord Treasurer had a clerk working for weeks on breaking the cipher. Ridolfi's attitude to Hawkins was recorded in a brief memorandum now lodged in the Simancas archives; he was blithely optimistic that there was nothing the mariner could (or would) do to endanger the plot. But as has recently been pointed out by Geoffrey Parker, adding another fleet to the 'Enterprise of England' made it bottom-heavy, and it was these foreign vessels that Philip II intended should transport the battalions of Alba across the Channel; and a trio of forces in Plymouth, Santander and Zealand had to be sandwiched together before the invasion could become a reality.[5] Seepage of the grand plan was evident in Paris (of course) but also Florence and Rome. When the Florentine Vitelli heard that he was the intended commander of the invading force he was both gratified and aghast, since by the summer of 1571 he was utterly negative about the whole operation. So was Alba, who thought the King's intention a muddle, de Spes inexperienced in public affairs, and Ridolfi a soft-handed banker without the required military experience. He reiterated in a letter to Philip that he had made no preparations, and Philip responded with an ardent declaration of intent. The safety of English Catholics was at stake.

The future of one man we can identify in government hands certainly was. Charles Bailly was held for a time in the Marshalsea, and a stooge was locked up with him to get the truth about the papers he had been carrying. Burghley's agent for this was William Herle, who on 11 April 1571 reported Bailly was 'the most secret minister of all ill-practices in Flanders'; a huge exaggeration but enough for Bailly to fetch up in the Tower. Here he was tested by torture; 'more frightened than hurt' according to de Spes. Eventually Bailly fell to a little government ruse, the advice of another government spy, to surrender the cipher key. This he did. With Burghley and government agents trawling for details of what was proposed on all fronts, Fitzwilliam arrived back in England early in September to tell Hawkins of the planned Spanish invasion. Hawkins sent Fitzwilliam to Burghley with telling details of the involvement of Norfolk as one prop of the plan, and very soon the Duke was also back in the Tower. When Philip sent Ridolfi back to the Netherlands at about this time, Alba cross-questioned the Italian to find that he had no contacts in England and that this burden had fallen on de Spes. No doubt this was noted with a wry smile by Alba, who had nothing but contempt for him.

That was not yet the end of the matter, although some of the nervous apprehension felt by Elizabeth, and perhaps some of her councillors, was dissipated. Burghley had come out of his dark days as the single man of honour in her service; virtually everyone else was touched in some way by Norfolk's wretched lack of intellectual clarity and his scheming. Very soon the cultured Lumley was in the Marshalsea; Southampton, the vehement papist, was back in the Tower; Arundel was under guard in Arundel House; and Cobham was under arrest in Cecil House on the north side of the Strand. Yet even so Philip II sought comfort in the freedom of Ridolfi and Hawkins, and he was buoyed up by the stunning victory of Don John of Austria over the huge Turkish Ottoman fleet at the battle of Lepanto. A few weeks later when Ridolfi was in Rome, he too still spoke as if the plot for which he had connived, lied and fumbled, still existed to threaten Elizabeth. This was absurdly optimistic and likely based on a fantasy of huge reward if it ever succeeded, while if it failed then perhaps he would escape blame and his confiscated property, which he valued at nearly 15,000 escudos, would be restored to him. Alba's brutal realism about the plot and its adherents lately became clear to Ridolfi, who blamed the Duke for not supporting it, or beyond that actually sabotaging it. Alba's brisk view was that the engaging but noisily vocal Vitelli and his master in Florence had 'revealed the whole plot to the Queen'. Philip II took an altogether milder view even as the full extent of failure hit him hard. The miseries that he anticipated for English Catholics were not immediate, even if the premier Duke of England did have to go before his peers in Westminster Hall in January 1572, arraigned for treason. The verdict of guilty was inevitable and the vultures began to gather for the spoils: Hunsdon mentioned to Burghley his ambition to be Keeper of Howard House. But before that could happen the Queen's prolonged bout of procrastination had to end, and it happened in two ways. On 10 February 1572 the Privy Council instructed its agents to summon William de la Marck and inform him of the Queen's desire that he 'prepare to depart and so remain no longer on these coasts'. When the grey-robed, dishevelled tormentor of priests and monks had not left some eleven days later, the Mayor of Dover was ordered to get rid of him by any means short of force. Finally, on 1 March 1572, Elizabeth issued a proclamation ordering 'all freebooters of any nation to depart, and not to return, on penalty of confiscation of goods and imprisonment'.[6]

This effort at dealing with an unpleasant situation was modest preparation for the decision on Norfolk, so long delayed that some thought he would emerge in one piece from the Tower. Burghley told Walsingham that when Elizabeth reflected on the danger to herself the execution seemed an essential end to the drama; then she would recall his social position, title and blood, and once again stall the inevitable. Yet as the months passed it became clear that no more information about Mary could be chivvied out of Norfolk, and as a witness of State he had indeed became redundant. Burghley remained steady in his application of pressure on the Queen, and he was fortunate that a plan to have him assassinated was punctured by the resourceful Herle. The plan emanated from de Spes and aroused such indignation that the turbulent ambassador was at last expelled to the Low Countries. This was an uncomfortable billet given the animosity of Alba, who believed that de Spes was saved from trial and imprisonment only by the intervention of brigands who murdered the former ambassador as he made his way back to Spain. When the English Parliament met at the beginning of May the clamour for the death of Norfolk might have been heard by him and the Earl of Arundel in the Tower. A month later and Norfolk was executed. The Earl survived the unseasonable freezing wind of disfavour blowing out of the court, and his reconciliation to Rome was delayed until 1584.

Chapter 3

DIPLOMATIC SCARS

F rancis Walsingham made a notable advance in his career when appointed ambassador to the Valois court of France. He resisted taking the post for a time because he anticipated the hit his own fortune would take when Elizabeth was so careless of paying her diplomats. However he could not stall for too long: an absolute 'no' was unthinkable. Not only did he have a total mastery of Latin, the key language of diplomacy, but also he spoke excellent French and Italian. So in many conversations with King Charles IX and his Italian-born mother, Catherine de Medici, and French courtiers both Catholic and Protestant, he was never tongue-tied. Alberico Gentili, specialist in international law and later an Oxford professor, may have had the example of Walsingham in mind when he wrote that an ambassador should have command of at least three foreign languages. So to the leased embassy building on the quai des Bernardins on the Left Bank, just across the Seine from the expanding palace of the Louvre, went the new permanent ambassador with his assistants, in a modest entourage. After Walsingham a key figure was Robert Beale, who married Edith St Barbe, Ursula's sister, and acted as secretary to his brother-in-law. Even for comparatively minor tasks Walsingham needed men of experience, men he could trust. One such was his messenger, Walter Williams, cheerfully called 'Wat' by his employer, and an altogether more unbuttoned fellow than he. Literate, French-speaking, something of a chancer, Williams was a Welshman who drank, but was not the toper clown. Certainly a decade after this a Catholic prisoner in England made him out to be a figure of fun, but he was surely more than that, as John Bossy has noted, for Walsingham employed Williams for over fifteen years.[1] This service record suggests that Walsingham found him trustworthy and useful. Perhaps very useful if Williams spoke Welsh, for Walsingham would sometimes use it fully to bamboozle letter thieves and secret agents when his own secret service was functioning. Williams had a seven-year stint as a letter carrier, and then in 1577–8 he was back in France to escort the younger brothers of the Earl of Oxford, before taking off to serve under the Earl of Leicester in the Netherlands campaign.

Walsingham went to foully stinking Paris with instructions to foster the interests of the Huguenots. His alacrity in seeking them out as soon as he arrived in the city was remarkable, 'and he was discussing the question of a league with them before he had been in France a fortnight'.[2] He was particularly often in the company of Jean de Ferrières, vidame de Chartres, who had spent some years in England, along with Gaspard de Coligny's brother, Cardinal Châtillon, now of the reformed faith but strangely clinging to his title. It was these two French Protestant aristocrats who had lobbed into Anglo-French consideration the possible marriage of Elizabeth to Henri, Duke of Anjou. Walsingham also talked at length with François de Beauvais, Sieur de Briquemault, who remained in Paris as a semi-official guardian of the Huguenot interests. He wanted especially to know the English view of any proposed Anglo-French league against Spain, and within days Walsingham replied (not waiting for London to instruct him) by urging the desirability of bilateral hostility against overmighty Spain in talks with *la reine-mère*. This was presumptuous and had to be squared with Burghley. Charles IX and his mother found impediments in the Elizabeth-hating Guises. Charles would not set course to help them, but he created few hindrances, and merely dawdled when Walsingham pushed at the matter. The King's anti-Spanish stance was encouraging and it gave Walsingham a little *frisson* of pleasurable self-regard to note Charles's cordiality to him, in contrast to his cool, even curt, reception of the Spanish ambassador. But when the King did nothing to hinder the sneaky activities of the Guises, Walsingham began to distrust the King's intentions, while the heir-presumptive to him was likely to be of service to them. He wrote to Leicester about Henri, Duke of Anjou, and moved to the conclusion that he could be eased out of the role of royal cuckoo by marriage; Leicester, writing to Walsingham, perceived Elizabeth 'more bent to marry'. The marriage of Charles IX provided her with an opportunity to send a message of congratulation through a special envoy, Lord Buckhurst, and if an opportunity arose to treat with Catherine de Medici on the Anjou match he had secret instructions to do it.

These led to a secret meeting with Catherine in the gardens of the Tuileries. A written offer of Anjou's hand for Elizabeth was drawn up and delivered to Buckhurst on 13 March 1571, and the next day he left Paris for England. This left Walsingham able to give his attention to other matters, with his paid agents in France sourcing him with information, and one of those in service to the French ambassador in Spain was bribed to provide news. He also took on Pietro Bizari, who made the journey to Paris in spring 1571. As for the Spanish ambassador in Paris, Walsingham experienced a particular problem – Don Francisco de Alava spoke only Spanish and refused to communicate in a language Walsingham directly understood. That, could be by-passed, but in the marriage negotiations, with both sides reluctant to make any sort of commitment, Walsingham had real problems; Anjou was losing any ardour (however synthetic) he may have felt, having been slyly tutored by the Guises, and his mother and brother were growing tired of Elizabeth's delays. If Walsingham mentioned the pivotal matter of religion then the whole thing would surely collapse, and as he wrote to Burghley he was 'very much perplexed'. It was critical to the very idea of her marriage that a foreign husband be one of great standing, and a union with Anjou would squash residual discontent in England that she had wilfully neglected her dynastic duties. Walsingham declared that he would set aside his own opinions 'to think only of her Majesty and of her safety'. He would emulate the Roman citizen forbidden by law to loiter on the town wall. Seeing the enemy about to scale it he does not seek permission to be where he should not be, because a crisis takes him to the spot to repulse the enemy.

So Mr Ambassador conveyed the wary message of a queen to a less-than-pleased queen mother, who declined his invitation to send a formal representative to London to open negotiations. No, she would send Giovanni Cavalcanti, who lived near Walsingham in the suburb of St Germain des Prés, to state the definitive French requirements, which meant that Walsingham had won this trick by forcing Catherine to declare her hand. Cavalcanti met Elizabeth on 13 April with a clutch of particular points to be resolved and, remarkably, within eleven days he was back in Paris with her responses. Religion, as Walsingham learned from the letters London sent to him, was the sticking point, and he was not to shift at all in any future talks with *la reine-mère*. In fact his immediate talks were with Paul de Foix, the diplomat representing the King, and both sides presented beautifully ordered and inflexible responses. Walsingham stoutly maintained that Elizabeth could not allow her husband to be a practising Catholic, and four days later he was saying the same to Catherine in conference at St Cloud.

Walsingham wrote at once to Elizabeth and sent a private letter to Burghley following the effort by Catherine to convince him that Anjou might quickly become a Protestant while newly wed. Walsingham at this point believed that the French would swallow the fly rather than allow the nuptials to wither, and he had support from senior Huguenots who had spotted increasing friction between Charles IX and his brother. Certainly Franco-Spanish relations were strained, and a close alliance with England was very desirable, since it would have the added benefit of removing Anjou from the country to a glittering marriage. Perhaps the problem really was in London, with a queen using the marriage to her own ends; a powerful minister (Burghley) who favoured it, and a powerful courtier (Leicester) who secretly did not. Walsingham of course knew their respective standpoints; as for his own, he would go along with the marriage until concessions were required to accommodate Anjou's religion; on that point he remained implacably against 'being myself not persuaded that an evil may be done whereof good may come'.[3] As it was, in subsequent talks at the French court about the letter from Elizabeth of 11 May, he found hints of movement at the top, and on 20 May he paid a visit to Anjou to speak of the reasons why he could not be a Catholic in England. He handed over a copy of the English Prayer Book and asked the Prince to consider its correspondences with the Roman one. Anjou again put up the notion of private worship that would not offend, but Walsingham cared not a jot for this idea and said so. Later exchanges with de Foix convinced him of the correctness of his own attitude, when the Frenchman swore in secret that within a year of arriving in England Anjou would be fully taken over by Protestantism. Taking soundings from other sources encouraged Walsingham, who risked a letter to Leicester clearly endorsing the marriage, which chimed with French Protestant wishes.

But not now the wishes of Elizabeth. As time passed and Leicester eloquently declared to her his reasons for resisting the proposal, she too shifted away from any positive action, and set out sturdy counter-proposals. Elizabeth would not admit Anjou's right to be crowned King as Catherine demanded, and above all she cited religion. While Walsingham and Catherine and others toiled over problems great and small a French envoy, the captain of Anjou's guard, visited London and met with Elizabeth at Hampton Court early in June. These meetings reiterated the old arguments, and nothing advanced. Leicester suggested in a letter to Walsingham that the alliance might be forged on some other basis, and Elizabeth said he should remain silent on the matter unless it was put to him directly. L'Archant returned to France in July, and despite mild words the marriage proposal had realistically been talked out. Catherine and Charles IX were greatly displeased, and Anjou took much of their personal blame for his obstinacy. Those who had secretly nudged him to this end would pay for it, and this appears to have been the fate of de Lignerolles, who within a short time was murdered.

Walsingham had been in talks with Huguenot delegates for several months about an offensive league against Spain – France, England and the German princes. Although Catherine de Medici held back on it, Charles IX seemed in favour, and in July at the Château de Lumigny en Brie he had a secret meeting with Count Louis of Nassau, who had to be fetched from La Rochelle. As Walsingham reported of his own subsequent meeting with the Count to Leicester, he was a likeable man, and the summer prospects for the league seemed only to improve, and Charles grew ever more favourable to the Huguenots. He had their leader Gaspard de Coligny travel from the west coast stronghold to join him, and Coligny won over Catherine before the proposed conference at Blois early in September with the ambassadors of all the foreign powers. Walsingham, who had been ill for some time, was dosing himself with 'physic', homemade remedies, apparently opium based, which might not have been the safest preparation for diplomacy and caused him to delay his departure for a few days. En route for Blois he met a secret agent called Michel de la Hugnerye, working for Sieur de Briquemault, the spokesman for the Queen of Navarre, Jeanne d'Albret, whose own mother Marguerite of Navarre had encouraged Catholic humanism without excluding Protestants at her court. Hugnerye put the imagination and diplomatic skills of Walsingham to the test by making an altogether startling suggestion – that the Queen of England should marry Jeanne d'Albret's son, the 18-year-old Henri of Navarre; a shock proposal coinciding with Huguenot intentions that he should marry Marguerite de Valois, sister of Charles IX.[4] Walsingham, under medication, did not dismiss this possible union of age and youth. Happily for all parties Jeanne d'Albret had a greater sense of realism, and though there was a faint flicker of royal interest in London nothing developed out of it. Perhaps it was simply a prod to bestir Anjou. De Foix had done his best in England flourishing a ducal portrait, but returning to France in early September he confronted its hopelessness, the same view as Walsingham who had privately long thought the league a better option.

For months he had worked when sick, but by mid-September he was so unwell he wrote to Burghley for the speedy sending of a stand-in, so that instead of dying he might just recover. Robert Beale was there and was considered, but then Henry Killigrew was selected and left England on 20 October with orders to Walsingham to get well soon so that he could continue in service. At some time Dr Rodrigo Lopez, his London physician, also went over, perhaps armed with his infamous enema pump. Walsingham finally left Blois for Paris on 30 October and got to the embassy five days later, where Killigrew awaited him. The treatment began not long after, and although Walsingham growled about fees to quacks he may have listened to diet recommendations; but did his cook?

When news came through of the victory of the Spanish fleet over the Turks at Lepanto, Coligny and his friends constantly urged a forward policy against Spain in the Low Countries. Walsingham and his old friend Killigrew now felt that Anglo-French amity (such as it was) might thrive if a special envoy was sent. London was repeatedly told this, and then everyone had to wait for Elizabeth to decide. Finally, with Burghley unmovable, Sir Thomas Smith was sent, and reached Paris on 24 December 1571. In his baggage were Latin and English copies of George Buchanan's polemic against Mary Queen of Scots and these were widely distributed at the French court. Killigrew himself personally delivered copies to M. de Foix and Michel de Montaigne. Catherine de Medici sought to have the book suppressed, but with all the diplomats of the embassy giving out copies it did great damage to the public reputation of Mary. It was a further measure of Elizabeth's obtuseness that Smith was supposed to renew the Anjou marriage negotiations, even allowing that he might worship as a Catholic in private. But he had been lost to the Protestant cause in France, proving it in a very localised dispute over the foundation of a Jesuit college in Bordeaux. The Huguenots sought to block it, but it was Anjou to whom the Archbishop of the city directed his appeal for help, and he got the nod of royal assent.

On 4 January 1572 Smith went with Killigrew to a royal reception at court, leaving Walsingham to be nursed by his wife. The usual formal pleasantries were exchanged and Smith presented evidence that confirmed the complicity of Mary, Queen of Scots in the Ridolfi plot. Two days later the marriage question was allowed, and Catherine declared her son was now so devout that his weight had sunk dramatically and his skin colour was horrible to behold – it was all fasting and vigils, vigils and fasting. Would the Duke then be satisfied to make his worship private?, enquired Smith. The Queen replied that Henri would require high mass with all the attendant public ceremonies. 'Why, madam, then he may require also the four orders of friars, monks, canons, pilgrimages, pardons, oils and creams, relics and all such trumperies. That in no wise can be agreed.' This sardonic outburst came from Smith, a man keen to see the ageing Elizabeth married as each year would make her less attractive: 'the more hairy she is before, the more bald she is behind'. Catherine de Medici was almost equally realistic, and now found a late substitute for Anjou – his younger brother the Duke of Alençon who had for some years been leaning to the Huguenots. Smith was rather taken with the idea. For the time being the treaty of alliance took precedence, and in April 1572 the recovered permanent ambassador was working with Sir Thomas in the negotiations for the Treaty of Blois, which sought to replace the historic antagonism between the two nations with a mutually advantageous, albeit weak, defence pact. Viewed with approbation by Catherine as a substitute for the failed Anjou marriage plan, the treaty was a device to advance trade and good relations, and on the English side there was some comfort to be taken from the total silence in the treaty with regard to Mary. Charles IX was actually rather unflattering about her – the poor fool would not cease plotting until she lost her head.

Normal trade with Spain by the English was still not possible, but some repair work had been done with this in mind. Spain was told that the treaty of Blois was not directed against them, and even before it was signed the new-found Anglo-French amity was severely tested. English benign acceptance of the Sea Beggars, led by de la Marck under the flag of Orange, had evaporated during the first months of 1572, as we have noted. To find a haven after being required to leave England, de la Marck settled on the little Zeeland port of Brill. Subsequent to the April ultimatum and seizure, it surprised de la Marck and William of Orange that a series of risings followed across Holland and Zeeland, becoming an insurrection against the rule of Alba. Elizabeth had not intended this – rebellion always dismayed her – but the extension of either Spanish or French power in the Low Countries was anathema to her. So hundreds of Flemish exiles, armed and supplied, went home; better to have them there than the French, for the forward-thinking Admiral Coligny had persuaded Charles IX to aid the rebels. When English volunteers, including Christopher Carleill, went to Zeeland in May to aid them too, they had instructions that if the French seemed likely to annex the revolt, the English battalions should go to Alba's assistance. As it happened Catherine de Medici was the primary force that ruined Coligny's intention, and when Count Louis of Nassau launched an Orangeist attack on Alba from French soil, the rebels were swamped.

In Paris the political marriage proposal of Alençon to Elizabeth was little more than a cream-filled pastry that threatened to go stale, despite spirited attempts by such as M. le Mole, the Duke's representative in England, to keep it appetisingly fresh. The key marriage for French Protestants, the Valois court and the Guises was that being prepared for the son of the late Jeanne d'Albret, Queen of Navarre – Henri, King of Navarre – to the King of France's sister, Marguerite de Valois ('la reine Margot') who, alas, was in love with Henri, Duke of Guise (1550–88). Paris was heaving with partisans of both sides, so how is it that Walsingham, with many friends and aides to advise on the minutiae of French politics, did not remark the gross over-heating of confessional attitudes? The majority Catholic population, ever ready to snarl at outsiders, choked on the new bold self-confidence of the Huguenots; they were heretics who would burn in hell. To the Guise family the only solution was the murder of Coligny, a proposal that Anjou favoured. Although such deliberations as were held were in secret, rumours of clashes to come passed from *quartier* to *quartier*. Catherine de Medici probably knew the plans made by the Guise by mid-July, and gave her consent during the week before the wedding.

Paris in August is well-known for its *chaleur* and violent rainstorms, but the 'infernal' marriage raised the temperature among Parisians even more. Walsingham's failure to remark on the stormy rumblings about the city was very likely because, as a diplomat, he had a privileged position in viewing with his wife Ursula the elaborate masques and festivities that followed the wedding on 18 August. For example, on Thursday 21 August all the diplomatic corps (except the Spanish ambassador) had window seats at a mock battle between Amazons and Turks, and the following revels went on long into the night. Despite this exhausting frivolity Coligny, now so close to the King, was about very early for a meeting of the Royal Council on the morning of 22 August, and afterwards he walked from the Louvre to his residence. On the way, on the rue de Béthisy, the assassin hired by the Guises shot at him with a tripod arquebus[5] from a barred window of a just vacated property of Madame de Nemours, mother of the Duke of Guise. The three bronze balls which damaged both of his arms missed his chest only because, while reading a petition that had been handed to him seconds before, he paused to spit. Hustled home in great pain he was soon attended by the shocked King's surgeon, who cleaned the wound in the left arm and amputated the admiral's blasted right index finger. The news spread, and Walsingham heard it at about 9.00 pm. Once it was clear that Coligny was far from dead, an apparently endless stream of well-wishers climbed the stairs to his bed-chamber. It seems very likely that Philip Sidney was one such.

Meanwhile the immediate investigation of the assassin yoked him to the Guises, and there were rumours that the Duke was himself to be arrested. If in his self-defence he named Catherine de Medici as privy to the plot, then her throne and life were in danger; in turmoil she was now convinced that all eminent Huguenots had to be violently removed. After frantic deliberations and a private meeting with Charles IX, the intention was decreed and then preparations made with fierce urgency. Early on the morning of Sunday 24 August Guise raced to Coligny's quarters with Swiss mercenaries, who hacked the Admiral to death before defenestrating his remnant body. Raids on the lodgings of other leading Huguenots (such as Peter Ramus, the philosopher) accounted for many more deaths of men Walsingham had been talking to, but within the silent embassy a handful found refuge. So violence had arrived smiling and unannounced, and within days of calamitous horror it was reckoned that thousands of Huguenots died in France. Of the Huguenot hierarchy only a clutch survived, including Henri of Navarre for the first time forced by circumstances to abjure his faith, the vidame of Chartres and Count Gabriel Montgomery. The latter was certainly one of the principal intended victims, and he escaped with armed retainers only by a headlong dash out of Paris on a route to the west of France. He got to Jersey and for several months sought aid from Elizabeth for the relief of La Rochelle, now (like the less important Sancerre) under siege. She was cautious about official efforts, not wanting to lose so soon the Treaty of Blois. But she did allow private initiatives and some four hundred Englishmen responded, including Martin Frobisher.[6] Some within the coastal city so desired religious freedom they were willing to renounce allegiance to France for English rule. The siege finally ended in July 1573, and although the terms of the royal edict of pacification were not generous there were no immediate complaints from the people busy eating and drinking. Local Protestants in Normandy at length persuaded Montgomery to lead them in 1574 in a revolt that led to his execution in Paris, 'to the great content of the people'.

Also among the escapees was Philipe Duplessis-Mornay (b. 1549), a gifted young aristocrat who was to become an outstanding defender of French

Protestantism. He returned to France in 1573 at the fervent request of Walsingham's friend, the Huguenot commander François de la Noue. Also in flight were foreign Protestants such as a group of merchant families from Lucca in Italy. The Calandinis, Burlamachis and Diodatis had quit their hometown between September 1566 and March 1567.[7] Now most of them fled to Sedan. Some Huguenots, like Briquemalt, along with Englishmen in Paris, naturally sought refuge with the Walsinghams at the embassy, which was shuttered and barred and apparently under an armed guard led by the Duke de Nevers, who seems to have secured not only the building but also individual Englishmen staying outside of the embassy: Philip Sidney (later Walsingham's son-in-law), Philip Wharton (3rd baron), Dr Timothy Bright, one John Watson, a son of Lady Lane, and possibly Nicholas Faunt. They got to the building on the quai des Bernardins only after a trail of horror which Nevers rather revelled in. How long they remained in the house with Pietro Bizari is not known, although Walsingham did not venture out until 1 September, when a dozen gentlemen-at-arms arrived to escort him to the Louvre. At least three Englishmen were killed during the days of terror; unfortunately we do not know even their names. Dr Watson in company with Philip Sidney soon in haste quit Paris, and surely his reward came early in 1573 with the deanery of Winchester, and later a bishopric.

Walsingham had arrived in Paris under protest, and after the time of killing he spent another eight months anxiously awaiting his recall. While he carried on his diplomatic tasks with fortitude, I believe he took a serious psychological wound from the events and took months to recover his equilibrium. Those who found refuge with him praised his courage and kindness, and certainly a special bond of affection and admiration was formed between him and the young Philip Sidney. But the man (rather than the ambassador) had lost friends and acquaintances to unspeakable barbarism, and for a godly man there was the spiritually wrenching thought that God through his providence controls all human activity; this would mean surely that the Lord had allowed what had happened. Was God a Catholic? For this 'most sharp maintainer of the purer religion' such a thought was anathema. Still, some Huguenots now worshipped as Catholics, including Condé and Navarre, whose first abjuration came some twenty years before the one that gained him such notoriety. It may have been partly Walsingham's effort not to give way to grief and shock, to work until recalled, that saved him from a nervous collapse. Certainly Burghley wanted him recalled immediately the news was delivered at the court by

Nicholas Faunt, where in hours it was the only topic of conversation pitched at various levels of distress. The alliance with France was in jeopardy; the English court wore mourning black; Fénélon was to deliver his government's account of the events, and after was subjected to what was essentially house arrest until it was certain that Walsingham and company were safe.

The skimpiness of Anglo-French diplomatic relations was something from which Elizabeth wanted to avert her eyes until relations with Spain had been shored up. Yet Walsingham at the French court was powerfully dignified, and Catherine wrote to Fénélon, now back in London, 'je vous assure qu'il est bien affectioné (a ce que j'ay cogneu) a entretenir la bonne paix et amitié d'entre elle et nous', so that it may be that his public face suggested less through inscrutability than he actually felt. Writing to the Privy Council on 24 September when Condé and Navarre were at court under surveillance, he composed a sentence that the Huguenots might have written of the Valois: 'I think less peril to live with them as enemies than as friends.' And enemies they seemed ready to be again, despite the besmirched Treaty of Blois, for the Guise faction had asserted their power and Mary Stuart's Paris envoy was two days in conference at the court. An attack on England, while unlikely, did, even as a rumour, feed an appetite. And while the Spanish ambassador now dressed fourteen new servants in velvet-trimmed cloaks for conspicuous consumption and his master gleefully reflected on the Massacre, Walsingham was pondering his own rapid impoverishment.

Back in March he had written to Burghley that a third of his savings had gone; in amplifying this in a follow-up letter he noted expenditure of £1,600 beyond his income, land sold to the value of £60 yearly, and debts of £730. By June his expenses amounted to £200 per month, despite economies in food, numbers of servants and a stable reduced to twelve horses. By July he had to borrow from Catherine de Medici's personal agent, Guido Cavalcanti, in anticipation of his salary. Writing to a friend in London he noted that he owed Cavalcanti £373 15s and so would have to borrow in London to pay off the debt.[8] While her ambassador was facing a bumpy financial future, aided only by the settlement of a suit he had brought against his wife's brother-in-law, John Worsley, Elizabeth was to be godmother to the daughter of Charles IX and his wife, Elizabeth of Austria. Asking her was the rather smart idea of a French courtier (Marshal de Retz), even though it promoted a fit of pique in the papal nuncio and made for complications in the baptismal arrangements. But it seemed likely to stall English aid to Montgomery in La Rochelle, and it might even smooth things sufficiently to allow the French to seek loans from England. Leicester was to have deputised for Elizabeth, but the crossing was thought too hazardous with pirates at large. And so it proved, when the Earl of Worcester's ship with the christening gifts was indeed plundered; although a gold salver, the queen's gift, was saved, her noble representative lost £100 and a dozen or so of his retainers were killed or wounded in the melée. Worcester had to make the crossing early in February 1573, and lost much of his own finery, so he deserved the lavish entertainment put on by the French court. On 7 February Walsingham and he had an audience with the King, and then with Catherine, at which were discussed all the stale topics of marriage to Alençon, his appearance, Elizabeth's need to see him, his religion, and of course the matter of La Rochelle. All familiar and repeated, so that Worcester had not to remain long in Fence.

For Walsingham, an anxious, coin-counting father-to-be, this was the penultimate discussion on the usual subjects. By April, when he wrote at length to Burghley, he was blunt about Alençon's pockmarked appearance and general demeanour; there was little or no chance of Elizabeth becoming enamoured of him. As for the French, 'they are altogether persuaded that her Majesty hath no intention to marry'; if she was not the heavenly Virgin, perhaps she was a virgin made there in Heaven by God. Nor could Alençon go to England and then be rejected, since it would leave him dishonoured. Above all, he would have to be allowed in religion 'some secret exercise for himself'; the most hopeless proposition of all. How remarkable that Walsingham managed not to convey signs of *ennui* as these topics were reiterated, and even caused Catherine to stumble in his last interview with her late in March. For by then the extremely long drawn-out process of finding his replacement had reached a satisfactory conclusion for all the parties. Walsingham had nearly got free of his posting in the immediate aftermath of the Massacre, but Charles IX had warned that the withdrawal of the English ambassador would lead him inevitably to recall Fénélon. Sir Thomas Smith, Leicester and Burghley all made the case for their friend and colleague Walsingham, and for a time it seemed that Francis Carew would replace him. However, Carew organised his defences among the Queen's ladies and managed to get a late deflection. Smith wrote to Walsingham about the efforts being made by his wife and friends, and then made a nudging reference to the Queen's pernicious habit of changing her mind. Carew begged off; Sir John Hastings made his plea sickness and was excused, and then Burghley looked into the crowd and spotted Dr Valentine Dale, MP, who was pressed into accepting the post. He had made all his preparations, including taking on servants and buying horses, when Elizabeth went into one of her sustained pirouettes. She was in the middle of secret negotiations with Alençon and required a man fully informed and tremendously discreet to be on the spot. Walsingham signed his agreement; although his funds were so low he could not follow the court when it moved from Paris to Moret. Then in mid-March came good news from the determined Smith, who got Elizabeth to sign the authorization for his return. Dale, on the orders of Smith, was to leave immediately, and he reached Paris on 15 April 1573, with his presentation to Charles IX four days later by the outgoing envoy. The King was warm in his thanks, and having expressed his satisfaction handed to Walsingham a gold chain worth 1,000 crowns. After a hitch that required him to return to Parish for a final diplomatic interview with the King at Fontainebleau, Walsingham got presents for his wife and newly-born daughter Mary from Catherine de Medici. She even offered the use of the royal coach for his comfort as he journeyed to Boulogne. Walsingham reached London about a week after leaving Fontainebleau, and on 10 May was at court to make a direct report to Elizabeth. Even she could not find fault with his diplomatic deportment, attention to detail and clear devotion to duty. No wonder that in the future he got other delicate missions on her behalf.

Chapter 4

IMAGO MUNDI

B y the mid-sixteenth century, within the vast palace of Whitehall with its apparently endless enfilades of rooms, there was 'the little study called the new Librarye'. This nerve centre of the kingdom was where the King if he chose worked on his papers and consulted his ministers. There were maps galore and globes here, while in the keeping of Walsingham's uncle, Sir Anthony Denny, were the oversize items whose dimensions excluded them from the little study – items that were very likely too political and military to be allowed into a public space. By this time, awareness of the utility of mapping was unremarkable in educated circles, but some ministers were keen even beyond mere interest, and it was through his close links with John Cheke, that Cambridge teacher and mentor of so many important men, that the Duke of Northumberland, father of the Earl of Leicester (born *c.* 1532), came into contact with one of the cleverest men in Tudor England, the remarkable polymath John Dee, undergraduate at St John's and then a fellow in Greek at the newly founded Trinity College. From 1548–51, Dee studied at Louvain University with Gemma Frisius, a friend of the great cartographer and map publisher Mercator (Gerhard Kramer). In 1551 Dee was introduced to William Cecil by Cheke, and Cecil became an avid collector of maps, including an early edition of Mercator's atlas. Maps became an important element in serving the needs of the state, part of the sustained process of devising policy, and Cecil became a notable annotator of maps and papers. The future spymaster Walsingham was altogether more demure, and only his signature is to be found in his copy of the first edition of Saxton's 1579 atlas of maps of the English counties.[1]

Walsingham's marriage in 1566 to Ursula St Barbe made him the son-in-law of Henry St Barbe, one of the magnates of the Muscovy Company, and within a few years the younger man himself had a financial interest in its future and potential growth, as one of its 'assistants' or directors.[2] This remarkable trading conglomerate employed consultants such as Richard Eden, translator of *Arte de Navigar* by Martin Cortés, a copy of which was brought back from Spain by Stephen Borough after a visit to the *Casa de la Contratacion* (Seville's House of Trade) in 1558. The Casa had made a huge impression on him, and to try to emulate what he saw Borough persuaded the Muscovy Company to put up the funds for the translation of the house manual of navigation and chart making. Eden produced *The Art of Navigation*, published in 1561 – a text of tremendous importance which it has been said 'held the key to the mastery of the sea'.[3] Alongside Eden as consultant was John Dee, strong advocate of the advantages to England that would accrue from seeking the north-east passage to Asia. The impetus came from the slant of the economy to the woollen cloth trade, the chief export, with Tartary and China supposedly offering fine prospects. In 1577 when, it has been suggested, Dee may actually have been giving thought to travelling to Asia, he published his text entitled *The Great Volume of Famous and Riche Discoveries*, now in the British Library in the badly scorched and fragmentary Cotton Ms. Vitellius. c.VIII art.3. With sublime optimism, he hoped that all the north-east part of Asia would become as well known to his countrymen as Denmark and Norway – the route to Russia around Norway having been found by British merchants in 1553.

Further advice was also taken from Richard Hakluyt, an Oxford MA who had set himself to the intensive study of the new geography which had grown out of the age of discovery; and he had been the first to lecture in the new knowledge at either university. Secure in his official post at Christ Church he had been able to devote himself in London to making important contacts among the expansionist movement's leaders, among whom was Walsingham. Just to make matters a little more untidy, we need to recognise that Richard Hakluyt was himself aided by Richard Hakluyt of the Middle Temple, his cousin, who was also a geographical expert who was called in to advise on the north-east passage expedition (1580) of Charles Jackman and Arthur Pet, which sailed on 1 July in two Muscovy Company ships. He was also taken up by Philip Sidney and Walter Ralegh, both of whom were taking a special interest in colonial projects. For Ralegh this stemmed from the efforts of his half-brother Humphrey Gilbert, then resident in Limehouse, to arouse interest in America. This land of unknown extent, which had Hakluyt and his colonising friends panting in anticipation, naturally divided itself into three regions: the south, a great Florida, then

Spanish; the north, Norombega or New France, claimed, though not yet settled, by both France and England; and the debatable middle region which from 1584 was claimed by England (never mind the native Americans) under the name Virginia.

The man responsible for generating enthusiastic speculation about the north-west passage was Gemma Frisius, whose delineation of it reappeared on Mercator's world map of 1538 and terrestrial globe of 1541.[4] Although Gilbert's *Discourse of Discoverie for a new passage to Cataia* was an academic treatise, it was published in 1576, and Gilbert found himself among a new coterie of sympathetic London intellectuals: Hakluyt, the historian William Camden, Thomas Hariot, the brilliant mathematician and later associate of Ralegh, also John Dee and the Antwerp merchant Emanuel van Meteren, cousin to the cartographer Abraham Ortelius, the friend of Walsingham and Christopher Carleill.

The publication of the *Discourse* was an advertising promotion for Martin Frobisher's first expedition intending to find the obsessively wished-for north-west passage. The investment coordinator for this was Michael Lok, a first-rate linguist, trader and London agent of the Russia Company, who had a deep interest in cosmography, cartography and their uses to advance English trade. Lok had bought a library of relevant books worth some £500, which was a hefty investment considering that he never secured more than £875 in ventured stock for the Frobisher voyage. Investors such as Burghley, Sussex, Warwick and his brother Leicester each put up £50, Walsingham £25, and there were various smaller amounts from Thomas Gresham and the Customer of London, William Burde.

In his accounts of his travels, Frobisher deliberately suppressed navigational details, but it seems he sailed to Baffin Island before returning to England to bolster the risk-taking appetites of the venturers with mineral samples and plant specimens. By October 1576 he was back in England and planning a follow-up expedition, and until Francis Drake, then preparing for his epic global voyage (1577–80) returned to England, Frobisher was the foremost figure in exploration. Hakluyt would later report that Ortelius actually came to England in 1577 for no other purpose than to pick over the details of what, where and why. Even in Moscow Mr Furbusher's (*sic*) voyage was reported in January 1579.

In the pleasing if improbable story recorded by George Best and printed by Hakluyt, the bags of rocks were treated sceptically by a wife of one of the investors. She supposedly heaved some of them onto her fire to see if they resembled coal in any of their properties. Then, in a quasi-scientific manner, the housewife doused them in vinegar (as you do), and they turned a golden colour. This set Michael Lok's investment nose twitching, and he bore samples to Will Williams, assay-master of the Tower, and George Needham of the Mines Royal. He may have been hoping after recent government encouragement to manufacture or source copperas, also known as green vitriol, from iron pyrite or 'gold stones'. The production of copperas, an important chemical used in the textile industry as a dye fixative and as a black dye, had begun on the north coast of Kent within the last twenty or so years. It also had uses in metallurgy, tanning, the preservation of ships' timbers, making printing ink and as a sheep dip. Resistance against the control of vitriols by the papacy or the Spanish Hapsburgs gave real impetus to the search for another source.[5] When the tests on Lok's rocks had been done, he was told they held gold and silver, and in no time the next Frobisher venture took shape as a mining and colonization enterprise. City and court put up the venture capital, and an ore processing plant was planned for Dartford in Kent. On the River Darent, Dartford was a port which in 1566 offered employment to fourteen seamen and seven boats of up to 15 tons, which carried goods in and out of London, and very likely provided the paper for the First Folio of Shakespeare.[6]

When Frobisher left on the second expedition his original notion of finding the route to China was abandoned – no doubt a disappointment to Lok, recently appointed life governor of the chartered Cathay Company. Elizabeth put up £1,000 to fund the first 'Canadian gold rush', old investors and new joined in – like Lady Anne Talbot, the Earl and Countess of Pembroke and Edward Dyer. If Walsingham's investment was £400, as has been tentatively suggested, then his personal fortune, so depleted by his time in Paris, was sharply in recovery. It made him the second-largest investor after the Queen.[7] The three ships toiled to Frobisher Bay on Baffin Island and in an inhospitable place used the window of opportunity to do surveys and to mine for more precious metal deposits. In the autumn of 1577, with 200lbs of black rock stowed away, they returned to London, and only two men lost. The estimate that only 900lbs of rock would, on reduction, pay the whole cost of the expedition, was especially exciting. So much so that the investors for the third expedition were ready for Lok to organise funds without any of the received ore being further tested.

In May 1578 a little fleet left Portsmouth with 400 people on board, heading for the Countess of Warwick Island, where the richest source of mineral rock had been found. Among them a spy was employed by the Spanish ambassador, Don Bernardino de Mendoza, who sent ore samples to Philip II and, more usefully perhaps, a marine chart of Frobisher's voyages which greatly pleased 'el rey del mundo'. The key proposition was that a mining settlement with 120 colonists would be established on the island (now called in Inuit, Qallunaat [White Man's island]) in the confident expectation that working for eighteen months the miners, carpenters, soldiers and mariners would find viable ore deposits.[8] Apparently no one had anticipated spring storms and free ice which took their toll of ships, men and equipment, and when they did reach their destination in mid-July there came the awful realization that the *Dennis* was one of the missing ships, and if it had gone so too had their pre-fabricated barracks. A stable colony was henceforward impossible, but they could spend the summer refitting the ships, assaying the ore and watching for Inuit. Most of them were suspicious and hostile, although three had gone to England with the returning second voyage. Now the venturers returned with 1,200 tons of ore, but after his September landing Frobisher learned the acutely disappointing news that the material was useless. This crushed many notions of further voyages and caused the bankruptcy and collapse of the Cathay Company; Michael Lok was also financially wrecked. There is some circumstantial evidence that Frobisher or the person in charge of the assaying may have sought to defraud the venture capitalists by losing the laboratory records of voyage three. The judge investigator did ask for them, only to be told that on the way home a storm wave had swept them through the porthole. More tragically lost to history was the clutch of men left behind on Qallunaat – men who might have put a different slant on the effort, seeing through the scam and threatening to reveal it. Frobisher came through the scandal, though not without difficulty, and at one point Mrs Frobisher and her children were found starving in a room in Hampstead. Desperate in the later 1570s, she wrote to Walsingham begging for his aid to recover a debt of £4.

As the Dartford works achieved nothing despite several years of unavailing effort, the Privy Council wanted explanations for the lack of revenue. The investors refused to pay and so creditors lost as well, and when the Crown auditors issued their final report in 1583 the entire debt of £2,796 14*s* 5*d* was dumped on Lok. There had been fifty-three stockholders and six of them women, yet none squawked as loudly as the Earl of Oxford who had bought half Lok's holdings before the third voyage, and when the end came complained he had been 'cozened'.[9] Of thirty-one court investors, only the Queen and one unnamed royal servant paid the subscriptions they had voluntarily made in the hope of a hefty gain. At length the Privy Council and its auditors settled the project's financial collapse by a practical if rather brutal means. They ignored Frobisher (who had some weighty court protection) and scapegoated Lok to face the opprobrium and the bills – the entire company debt of nearly £2,800. It was hard on him, and in a petition written several years later he claimed to have spent time in every London prison except Newgate. Even in 1615 a relentless creditor was using the law to try to secure his claim for financial recompense.

Despite the blemish on his reputation, the optimistic Frobisher, while hoping that the Earl of Leicester would underwrite another voyage to 'Meta Incognita', managed to find himself a captaincy on a royal ship. The appetite for finding the north-west passage remained unassuaged, and on 29 January 1583 Walsingham, the leader of the pack, visited John Dee at his home,[10] to confer with John Davis (or Davys) and Adrian Gilbert, and the next day Robert Beale, secretary and brother-in-law to Walsingham, was among them. The Principal Secretary listened to a lengthy discussion and was thoroughly apprised of the situation. In tandem Gilbert and Dee made a tactful approach to Humphrey Gilbert and he assigned to the Mortlake group his own claims to explore north of latitude 50° – that is, roughly to the north of the Gulf of St Lawrence. As a result Davis made three voyages in a comparatively short period – 1585 to 1587. In 1585 he sailed to the east coat of Greenland, before ice pushed him south. After two more efforts he left voyaging in the northern wastes, but his efforts are still marked by names such as Cape Dyer and Cape Walsingham. Just before this John Dee had thought to go on an expedition with Adrian Gilbert, but then abandoned this to hare off to Poland with Albrecht Łaski, Palatine of Sieradz, who had been taken up by the Dudley clan. It was at this time or just before that Humphrey Gilbert had a projected colony in mind to benefit land-hungry younger sons and the recusant Catholics increasingly beset by vexatious revenue raising. Yet the notion of exporting the faith through mass emigration did not sit well with the seminary priests who undermined the effort, as did Mendoza who threatened Catholic investors with death. There was also a rival project devised by Hakluyt's friend the stepson of Walsingham, Christopher Carleill (or Carlyle), the son of a London vintner, who had served the Huguenot cause at sea and serviced the Russia (Muscovy) Company. Carleill had too the backing of merchants in Bristol.

Despite failures and mendacities from her seamen Elizabeth still hoped for gain at the least cost to her own fortune. She wondered if Gilbert's proposition did warrant support, because he seemed to her to be unlucky, good fortune on the other hand, was the intangible bait that Drake had apparently welded to his showiest clothes when he met with her for six hours of secret talks after his triumphant return to England late in September 1580. 'The master thief of the unknown world' De Mendoza called him – perhaps half-admiringly, perhaps not. Gilbert lacked this mercurial element and, even if she allowed his expedition, it would likely be better to shackle him at home. With his patent running out of time he made another presentation in February 1583, setting out all the benefits to be derived from employing a dedicated servant. John Dee and Richard Hakluyt were both on his side, and the latter gave immense support with his 1582 *Divers Voyages Touching the Discoverie of America* dedicated to Sir Philip Sidney. Essentially it was an early draft of his great work dedicated to Walsingham – *Principall Navigations*. But it was Ralegh, the new court favourite, who moved Elizabeth to allow the departure of the expedition in June 1583, with Gilbert on the *Delight* (120 tons) and under the command of Richard Grenville. This time, sadly, the royal instinct had been correct, for although England's first colony in North America was set ashore (with Walsingham's support), the royal arms engraved in lead set up on a post, on the return journey to England Gilbert's ship sank near the Azores in a storm. The Gilbert patent was diverted in March 1584 to Ralegh, just after Walsingham sent Hakluyt to the embassy in Paris as chaplain to the new ambassador, Sir Edward Stafford.

At this time Walsingham had just exposed the 'Throckmorton Plot', another complicated and ill-conceived intention to depose Elizabeth in favour of Mary, Queen of Scots; it was the old 'Enterprise of England' again, and Mendoza and Mauvissière, the French ambassador, who had the right to communicate directly with Mary as a result of French pressure, and look after her interests, were both involved – the Spaniard as active as de Spes had been. Walsingham, now the master of an increasingly effective spy system, had a spy in the French embassy – Henry Fagot (who may have been, but probably was not Giordano Bruno). He wanted one in the English embassy in Paris because Stafford had strong links with the Bourbon household, having been a page to them.[11] As far as Walsingham was concerned Stafford was deeply untrustworthy, and having Hakluyt so close to him may have been to distract the equally suspicious envoy from a second spy. Even if the chaplain was not a true spy, he was certainly in France to gather information about America, and in Paris he was seeking data which would be useful to the colonisers. In April 1584 he wrote to Walsingham, who had been ill again and was swamped with work, 'I thought it not meet to trouble your honour with such things as I had carefully sought out here in France, concerning the furtherance of the western discoveries, but chose rather to impart the same with Mr Carlile.'[12] Moreover, not only had he been sending material to Carleill, he had even got the stepson a subscription sum of money from Horatio Pallavicino, then in Paris, for the proposed colony that Ralegh at great cost wanted shunted aside.

In the summer of 1584, as if in proof that Carleill had been superseded by Ralegh, Hakluyt began to write for the latter, and presented to Elizabeth a polemical piece called the *Discourse on the Western Planting*, intended to secure royal support for the colony of Virginia. The truth that was haunting policy makers like Walsingham and writers like Hakluyt was that England was a late entry to the race to secure global economic advantage, and Spain (fresh from gobbling up Portugal in 1580) had a huge advantage. The defeat of the Spanish and their great colonial empire seemed to many an impossible dream; Drake had only sailed once round the world, and how often could the huge treasure he had accumulated in the hold be replicated? And if war with Spain was immediately a popular cause, how long would this bellicosity last as general prices rose and the export of cloth faltered? One who knew the risks and embraced them was Drake himself, and Walsingham was one of those who had initiated his triumph and even put his name forward. With the overwhelming of the Portuguese, Philip II acquired a second navy, and to lead the resistance there was the pretender to the Portuguese throne, Dom Antonio, who found a refuge in England for his counter-plotting. Dark of hair and expression, Dom Antonio met those in England whose antipathy to Spain matched his own, and the plan that emerged from their little assemblies was in outline that Dom Antonio should seize Terceira, one of the Azores islands where the population remained on his side. An English fleet of eight ships and 1,000 men led by Drake would take the island and make it a naval base with a dual purpose: capturing the Spanish treasure fleet and the Portuguese carracks bringing spices from the Moluccas.

The Drake who was to do this was now Sir Francis, and the day before the Queen knighted him at Deptford, our Sir Francis rounded out the plan to capture Terceira and the alternative project of seizing all the Asian trading settlements of Portugal. Terceira got the nod of approval, and it seemed almost sure to succeed if the allied participants did not get embroiled in quarrels – which they did. Dom Antonio saw a rare chance to do something on a larger scale, which meant more funding. The men behind Drake argued with Frobisher's men. Elizabeth refused to help now without French assistance, and Dom Antonio, who had arrived in exile with a magnificent cache of jewels and given a huge diamond set in a ring to Walsingham as security for a loan, now sought its return. Mendoza may have heightened the truth for the delectation of Philip II, reporting that Elizabeth was suspected of gratifying her jewel fetish. In fact Dom Antonio was more at fault for a war budget far beyond that agreed. His furious response was to leave England and his diamond in settlement of all claims against him. He pitched his mobile court in St Germain, where the many naval officers about him engaged with the French. It was there that Hakluyt had many conversations with them and him. By the time of his first letter to Walsingham the chaplain had twice met with Dom Antonio, and talked to the captains and pilots – 'divers of them are lately come out of the East India, overland by Tripoli in Syria'. When Walsingham became vastly interested in trade with the Ottoman Empire he was not casting his bean into an empty pot. The Paris embassy was under instruction to lend Dom Antonio soothing, if insubstantial, encouragement, a task which could be neatly slotted in to geographical gossip with a minor official like Hakluyt.

Not all the Portuguese pilots had gone with Dom Antonio. There remained some in Elizabethan service, including Antonio Anes Pinteado, Francisco Rodriguez and Bartolomeu Bayão; but perhaps the most famous (or indeed infamous) was Simão (Simon) Fernandes, the Terceira-born mariner who was for the most part a Walsingham man, but able to freelance, hence his work as a pilot for Ralegh. Unflustered by vast distances to be sailed in little ships, Fernandes had been employed by the hard-up Humphrey Gilbert to sail a tiny pinnace with a mere eleven men aboard to the American coast, between roughly Nova Scotia and Cape Cod. He returned within three months, which was remarkable, and John Dee was one who perused his encouraging reports.[13] It was always hoped, overtly or covertly, that a smart investigation of the land there would produce evidence of precious metal ores. But there were also profits in the seas in the hauls of fish so beloved by the ever-greedy Spanish, and early in 1585 Walsingham wrote a position paper for 'the annoying of the King of Spain', declaring in favour of an attack on the Spanish fishing fleets on their way to Newfoundland. Approved in June by Elizabeth, after the Spanish embargo on English shipping ordered by Philip II the month before, Bernard Drake – instead of ferrying supplies in the *Golden Royal* for Virginia – was diverted to Newfoundland. Seventeen Spanish ships with hundreds aboard were corralled there, and as George Raymond turned up, sailing from Virginia, he and Drake combined their forces to sail to the Azores, where four more ships fell into English hands.

In March 1585, as Francis Drake was preparing for a new English sweep of the Spanish Indies, King Henri of Navarre wrote from Paris to Walsingham soliciting charts and the narrative of Drake's global exploit. His envoy Jacque Ségur-Pardaithan delivered the request and the richly ornamented map was sent; it was eventually to be found in the Bibliothèque Nationale – but no longer, for characteristically it was lost or very likely stolen. Richard Hakluyt, however, was vastly more alert, eager to prove his mettle to Walsingham. Not only had he picked up Portuguese data about the Far East, but also we have evidence, contained mainly in his *Discourse on the Western Planting*, that he gobbled up at least as much corresponding information on the western reaches of the enemy. Into his hands fell a survey of the Spanish possessions in the West Indies made by a first-rate French captain, of such value that it was included in the *Discourse* as sections 8, 9, 10.[14] The survey covered the Spanish coastal settlements, indicating their harbours and garrison strength and food supply. Just at the very time Hakluyt handed the text over, Drake's great expedition was being fitted out, and unlike the more circumspect Elizabeth, who would not purposefully expand her dominions east or west, Walsingham was so minded. Hence the recall from Ireland of his soldier stepson, Captain Carleill, to lead the twelve companies of soldiers, and he proved to be an excellent leader in the West Indies, where all things did not go to plan.

When Drake's fleet returned to Portsmouth late in July 1586, they had been absent for ten months, causing huge physical damage and psychological scarring that is beyond reckoning.[15] Only in one respect had this expedition failed, and that was money; after auditing the spoils the shareholder got a dividend in the pound of fifteen shillings (75p), which to a few seemed like a negative sum. So not a triumph, especially since the stately galleons of the treasure fleet escaped capture by a mere twelve hours – a fact that had Drake and Burghley plucking their beards in exasperation. Eventually governments would realise that war had achieved a partial success, but it failed to grind down Philip II, and it did not alarm him to the negotiating table. What was beginning to be exposed was the structural weakness of Spanish power in loci of decay. With an ease to shock the most complacent Spanish grandee, four of Spain's colonial settlements had been taken, with Captain Carleill[16] proving his military guile – in particular in the taking of Santo Domingo, third city in the Spanish empire, when to seize the Plaza Mayor he put up barricades made of larger items from churches, confident that the Spanish would be reluctant to fire on them. It was a story in which Walsingham could take quasi-paternal satisfaction, and which he could even repeat with a smile. An even grander satisfaction came within two weeks of Drake's return to England when Walsingham, by guile and fierce attention to detail, secured the arrest of Babington and his fraternity.

Richard Hakluyt came back to England in 1588 while working on his masterpiece *Principall Navigations*, and Walsingham, who had farmed out a number of documents to his junior employee, was also the senior figure who told him what he could and could not print about Drake. The corrector (censor) was Dr John James, Keeper of the State Papers and very exceptionally Walsingham himself certified the text to the Company of Stationers for publication. Furthermore, when he found that the account of Sir Jerome Bowes, passed by him or James, was considered prejudicial to future trade by the Russia Company, it was excised from the earliest printed copies, and a rather sanitised version put in its place. In this squeeze on material lies confirmation that Walsingham's interest in exploration and overseas discoveries was driven by the notion that it was the key to wealth, and, unlike Dee, Humphrey Gilbert or Ralegh, he had no vision of Empire beyond defeating the global ambitions of the vast Spanish collective.

Chapter 5

FUTURE FOES

The emotionally battered and physically debilitated former ambassador returned to England to find there that the scale of the horror of the Massacre of St Bartholomew was becoming clearer. For some individuals, like his brother-in-law Robert Beale, later Clerk of the Council, it presaged a global conspiracy of terror initiated by the Council of Trent to wipe out Protestantism. Lord Grey of Wilton was in shock with grief after the reporting of the events, and he prayed that Elizabeth would have the wisdom to do the things that would 'divert the same from hence'. Many writers wondered if Elizabeth was alert enough to see the dangers that surrounded her in a plot-riddled England.[1] Sir Thomas Smith noted that merchants were afraid to go to France for business, and the abundant ripples of unease had certainly reached Scotland, with James VI and his Protestant ministers cozying up to Elizabeth. For Englishmen outside government it was the arrival of thousands of refugees that reinforced the dramatic horrors of Paris, Rouen, Bordeaux and other provincial towns. Those seeking to escape from Dieppe began to reach Rye on 27 August, and the numbers made for some unease and friction – not always immediate, but enough that after a 'honeymoon' period the persecuted might decide to move on to Canterbury, Rochester, Sandwich and London. For a substantial group of fifty who quit Sandwich for Colchester, the initial stage of interest and good relations was quite extended, but by 1580 a request was made to London for their expulsion. Yet immigrants had friends too, and Dr George Wither, a friend of Walsingham, wrote on their behalf.[2] The Paulet family, who governed the Channel Islands, were also highly supportive. In the south of England educated Elizabethans welcomed refugees who shared their own faith, and Elizabeth allowed Archbishop Parker to write a special prayer, which remarkably even prays for the persecutors themselves.

Even before their blood-boltered involvement in the Massacre, the Guises had the hatred of most sections of English society, and one of the family was here, 'offspring, idol and instrument of Guise imperialism' – Mary, Queen of Scots. The fact that she was still alive irritated many to almost uncontrollable fury, and it was Edwin Sandys, Bishop of London who advised Burghley early in September that her head should be cut off. Despite the outrage that was felt widely there was not a sudden torrent of printed denunciations in broadsheets in English. It is as if the energies generated were directed to the refugees rather than their persecutors, and in any case the educated class, and not implausibly some below, had a good knowledge of French, and there were teachers of the language in provincial towns even before the calamity brought another wave of potential teachers (and possibly readers).

As they found homes and premises outside France, authors of writings on the Massacre, mostly French Protestant, began a propaganda response, networking in such a way that their writings spread across Europe. Huguenots naturally clustered together for worship and it was through these groups that English Puritan churches made links with Geneva. In London, the French church on Threadneedle Street founded early in the reign was Geneva in stone, wood and worship. Printers in the city saw a new subject emerge and they sought texts written, or brought over by the refugees. The publisher Henry Bynneman brought out five editions – three Latin, one French, one English – of *De Furoribus Gallicis* (anon.) as early as 1573. Its author was in fact François Hotman, a brilliant jurisconsult, then in Genevan exile, 'who detested both the Roman law and the Roman church'. His best-known expression of Huguenot resistance theory was in his *Francogallia* (1573), which was not translated into English. The other key works were Theodore Beza's *De droit des magistrates* (1574), also untranslated, and *Vindiciae contra Tyrannos* (1579), generally assigned to Philippe du Plessis-Mornay. He was one of those who fled to the Channel Islands before becoming an adviser to Henri of Navarre, and a close personal acquaintance of Anthony Bacon, whose extended stay on the continent was partly to serve Walsingham in his increasingly important role of spymaster.

London gained another important publishing house when the business of the refugee Thomas Vautrollier relocated. He produced many works by his countrymen, including Massacre pamphlets. To have all or any of this translated required the hiring of translators, most of whom were anonymous hacks, 'men in the game for wages rather than literary fame', keen to avoid the beady eye of Elizabeth, the Star Chamber ordinances of 1566 and the treason law of 1571, which made clear the statutory grounds for press censorship. A named translator like Arthur Golding, who was on Vautrollier's list, needed well-placed patrons, and he had the best: the political triumvirate of Burghley, Leicester and Walsingham. As translator of Ovid's *Metamorphoses* and Calvin's *Offences*, both dedicated to Leicester, it was not surprising when the Privy Council commissioned Golding to translate an attack by Bullinger on Pope Pius V, the Dominican who was later canonised. Golding was also the uncle of the Earl of Oxford, and both he and his nephew resided for some time in Burghley's home in the Strand. It was Golding and Vautrollier who produced the English version of Hotman's famous biography of Coligny: *The Lyfe of the most godly, valiant and noble Captaine . . . Colignie Shatilion* (1576). Another patron of Golding was Walsingham's brother-in-law, Sir Walter Mildmay, Chancellor of the Exchequer.

Far removed from metropolitan high politics, in Honiton, Devon was the wife of a local rector, Anne Dowriche. In 1589 her verse-oration *The French History* appeared, having used Hotman and Jean de Serres as its main sources, and at the turning point of part three Catherine de Medici is brought on for the first time to propose the Massacre. Her rhetorical energy and ruthless appeal to expediency surely suggest Lady Macbeth, or Marlowe's Barabas in *The Jew of Malta*. The queen mother of France is characterised as an ambitious Machiavel, and so associated with demonic powers by both sides of the confessional divide. The Machiavel was a malign spirit responsible for spectacular public crimes, and Protestant writers took it as axiomatic that Niccolò Machiavelli was the evil genius behind all the machinations of the Guise and the Catholic League. Dowriche prepared her readers for the linking of Machiavelli and Satan when, in part one, the latter alludes to several high-visibility ideas such as the difference between the lion and the fox. All classes of Catholics in England, and even in Europe later, regarded Francis Walsingham as the true Machiavel. James VI could not resist this demonising, nor other Protestants, who gaped at his Christian sincerity in private life and his Machiavellian finesse in international affairs. His reputation became tainted after his appointment to the Privy Council and his taking of office in the government as Principal Secretary, because in his self-appointed role as spymaster with a deep pocket he came to have dealings with men pitched into a foetid underworld, sometimes men of the underclass. Men like Charles Sledd, ex-servant of Michael Lok, and an ex-seminarist who found a niche as an informer for Walsingham and provided a deluge of detail on English Catholics abroad – presumably having mastered some memory system to mentally hold their details, or perhaps recalling under patient debriefing so that a logbook could be compiled. Sledd had no artistic dexterity to be able to draw correctly, as in some Renaissance photo-fit, but his lengthy descriptions and specific details must have been useful to pursuivants and port searchers. The contemporary copy of the logbook (not the original) is now in the British Library's Yelverton Mss.[3]

The black tableau mounted by the English court for La Mothe Fénélon could not be a permanent representation of Anglo-French relations. Murmurs began in the great hollow of disapproval. And when it became clear that the Huguenot cause in France had been hideously mutilated but that something survived, the flow of supplies began again. There were too important contacts between printers in London and La Rochelle: Du Plessis-Mornay spent time there and it became an important locus for literary exchanges.[4] The tone and direction of English policy, when it became part of Walsingham's remit as Principal Secretary in December 1573, had even before he was sworn into office caused ripples in France. The oath of office was administered on 21 December; the same day the Duke of Alençon wrote a personal letter to him soliciting his friendly offices and assuring him that any services he might render would be gratefully received and properly rewarded. As for London – the scrutiny of French policy was for signs of interest in the pro-Marian garrison holding Edinburgh Castle until May 1573. The passing of time allowed the conduct of relations with the French court to become asymmetrical as Elizabeth scooted from one expedient moment to another, including the nudging of the Alençon courtship. At this Burghley pursed his lips, while Leicester and Walsingham were quietly contemptuous. Responding to the cynical line that Elizabeth's marriage to Alençon would be evil but necessary for all that, the new Principal Secretary and his brother-in-law took issue with the proposition. Walsingham was utterly unpersuaded that it could be and good come of it, for he had the most profound conviction that Providence was working in European politics and that it had a fizzing tendency to confound human calculations.

Philip Sidney thought just the same and wrote to his political and intellectual mentor Hubert Languet in 1574 on the surprise death of King Charles IX: 'I am at a loss what to think of it, whether his death is a wound to our cause, or as I hope a healing salve. The Almighty is ordering Christendom with a wonderful providence in these our days.'[5] In fact, before the death of the King there had been a plotted alliance between Alençon and

Navarre's Henri, in which the English government had the temerity to get involved. It is hard to exclude the possibility of Walsingham being involved in the two princes of the blood royal planning to join the Huguenots at Sedan, which was beyond French control. There were whispers of a flight to England, but they were too soon prisoners. What sort of comfort did they subsequently derive from a visit made by Dr Valentine Dale? An English emissary was rushed to Paris to reconcile Alençon and Charles IX, but he became redundant with the King's demise, and there was nothing to do but wait for the arrival from Poland of the new King Henri III.

The Walsingham–Dudley axis that evolved and strengthened through the 1570s was undoubtedly influenced by Hubert Languet. Born in Burgundy, raised as a Catholic, and educated at the universities of Poitiers, Bologna and Padua, his first meetings with his contemporary Walsingham had taken place in Paris, where both were diplomats – Languet ambassador for the Lutheran Augustus of Saxony, a ruler who won the affection of his people by dedicating himself less to war than to economic development. The friendship of the ambassadors deepened as they became dining companions, and it was based in part on their shared perception that Protestantism was under severe threat and there was an acute need for international cooperation (like the Treaty of Blois) to haul it to safety. When Philip Sidney began his continental excursions, a worldly education beyond the academy, it was probably Walsingham who arranged for Languet to watch over the young man's progress. Newly ennobled by Charles IX as Baron de Sidenay in a mark of high regard for one so close to Leicester and Walsingham, the young man was also made a gentleman of the king's bedchamber. Both he and Languet subsequently fled the Massacre, meeting in Frankfurt as lodgers with Andreas Wechel, the printer of so much Protestant propaganda. The friendship of the serious young man and his immensely cultivated mentor was consolidated in 1573 when both were in Vienna – Languet was now ambassador to the Imperial court.[6]

Languet and the more cautious Elector Augustus fell out spectacularly over Protestant resistance in arms, and in 1577 he entered the service of the Count Palatine of the Rhine John Casimir, younger brother of the Elector Palatine, Ludwig VI, a strict Lutheran. John Casimir was essentially a high-minded, well-intentioned man whose strong resistance to anything papist led him to value friendship with England. He was well liked by Elizabeth and became one of her foreign Garter Knights. It has been suggested that

Languet, in matchmaker mode, tried to get one of John Casimir's sisters as a bride for Philip Sidney, whose marriage potential caused so many jolts at the English court that it was not settled until 1583 when he and Frances Walsingham were married. John Casimir had a high regard for Sidney, much less pinched than that of Elizabeth, and he was keen for the young man to enlist in his army with a high rank. Indeed, it was the fighting spirit of the sometimes hot-tempered Casimir that led to a split with Languet, who passed to advising Prince William of Orange in the late 1570s. He was joined by Philippe du Plessis-Mornay, whose life he had saved in August 1572. Mornay was in England four years later pressing the case for giving more money to the Huguenot cause, advocacy then wasted on the stubborn Queen. He returned the following year to put the case of their ally Henri of Navarre, and with Sidney and Walsingham had, of course, a meeting of minds. The misery of the time was the stiff reluctance of Elizabeth to do anything meaningful for Protestantism after the collapse of her relationship with Archbishop Grindal. Mornay wept when reporting her 'hard speeches' to Walsingham.

Worse was to come. Elizabeth, in a pre-menopausal flurry, was reviving the possibility of her marriage after the collapse of Spanish power in the Low Countries. If English influence there shrivelled, 'the resulting vacuum would almost certainly be filled by a French prince,' formerly Alençon, but now Duke of Anjou, and was he truly an independent or a puppet for the King of France? 'If the latter were the case, his emergence was as worrying a contingency to English policy as a restored Spanish hegemony.'[7] While Walsingham and Lord Cobham spent an unhappy and pointless summer of 1578 negotiating in the Netherlands, where in January Don John had won a victory over the rebels at Gemboux, a-wooing went the Queen. Leicester warned Walsingham to deal discreetly in any reference to the Duke, and wondered if she had been nudged into favouring him with her unwanted attentions again. Through gritted teeth, Walsingham wrote generously of the Duke's appearance and bearing, although interestingly, in a comparison of Anjou with Don John, the Hapsburg prince won all categories. But by September a fatal fever had killed Don John, Anjou and the Estates-General fell out and John Casimir's forces were stalled, unpaid, even after a visit to England sponsored by Leicester. The replacement for Don John – Alessandro Farnese, Prince of Parma – stepped in to buy off John Casimir's soldiers before sending them home.

While Walsingham was abroad the courts in London and Paris considered the proposed marriage with bemused amusement, or unease, or outright horror. Neither side took seriously the other's intentions. But when Jean de Simier, Master of the Wardrobe to the Duke, arrived in January 1579, the English court was galvanised. To seduce him into believing Elizabeth's matrimonial intentions, he was constantly entertained by dinners, jousting and masques as the entire court danced the Frog galliard, and the Queen urged pantingly that she should meet the Duke. If they could chime with each other the details of the marriage treaty could be quickly drafted, based on the terms granted Philip II when he had married Mary Tudor. Wooing by proxy seems a bizarre notion, but Elizabeth, with encouragement from some courtiers like the Earl of Sussex, went at it with almost unseemly gusto. It would draw England and France to act in the closest harmony, with the Queen and her husband as protectors of the Huguenots, who would be loyal to Henri III, while the Guise would have to end intriguing in England and Scotland. These elements and more did not sit well with men like Sir Walter Mildmay, who felt affronted by the whole conceit.

Walsingham had been out of the country and had perhaps been reluctant to accept that this was not some piece of royal flim-flam. He held that Anjou was using her as a screen to hide his low intentions in the Low Countries, while she was bluffing, and when he returned to England in October 1578 he found to his chagrin that the negotiations would go forward. A year later and the Privy Council debated the matter. During that time the scorn and disgust most Englishmen felt for the French had breeched the decorum of the day. For months sermons had been preached against the marriage, and the Queen shrilled about having the preachers whipped. Public criticism found other voices, such as lampoons fixed on the door of the Lord Mayor denouncing the marriage of an English queen to a Catholic foreigner and absolutist prince. They had had this foisted on them some twenty-five years in the past; to contemplate it again was unthinkable, and the wave of indignation culminated in the greatest opposition publication of the reign: *The Discoverie of a Gaping Gulf* (1579), by John Stubbs. It came just after a *Letter to Queen Elizabeth touching her marriage with Monsieur* by Philip Sidney, acting as the spokesman for the Leicester–Walsingham circle, when Leicester's own clandestine marriage to the former Countess of Essex had not long before been revealed to the Queen, who loathed her, by Simier.

Sidney's patrician prose became the eloquent, tough, highly charged closing argument of the lawyer Stubbs to the jury of the English public. With learning, biblical and secular, and complete frankness he demolished the giddy superfluity of the arguments for the marriage. 'The *Gaping Gulf* remains in effect a commentary on St Bartholomew and its infamous perpetrators.'[8] When the arguments made by Stubbs, the brother-in-law of the Presbyterian leader Thomas Cartwright, in his incendiary piece were repeated in council, Elizabeth suspected collaboration between Stubbs, and a member of the anti-Anjou faction, and at length she banished the ailing Walsingham from the court. Rumours of his input into the book and help with its publication certainly reached France, and so one of the great men of her government got bruised. The unfortunate Stubbs, who knew all these men and was by marriage himself a kinsman of Lord Willoughby, fared far worse, with a vicious punishment specified by a vindictive monarch. There was a royal proclamation against his book, denouncing it as odious and seditious, and after it had been suppressed Stubbs, his distributor William Page, a gentleman servant of the Earl of Bedford, and his printer Hugh Singleton, a radical puritan propagandist, were brought to trial. The guilty verdict was certain, although the judicial means was challenged by two brave law men. The punishment was atrocious; Stubbs and Page both had their right hands severed with a butcher's cleaver before a silent multitude in the marketplace at Westminster – not the City of London, where sympathy would have been even greater for the victims of state mutilation. One month after this Singleton having by a whisker avoided the same – someone at court having secured a pardon for a returned Marian exile on the outer fringes of the Leicester–Walsingham group – set about printing Edmund Spenser's *Shepheardes Calender*, a sequence of pastorals and also propaganda for the anti-Anjou cluster, published anonymously. In January 1580 Elizabeth wrote to Anjou that the marriage was not to be.

Both Leicester and Walsingham had to meet with Elizabeth to be berated by her, spitting through her decaying teeth as abuse poured out of her mouth. Leicester may have offered to go into exile, playing a defiantly risky hand.[9] As we know, Walsingham withdrew from the court, perhaps not entirely dismayed if he was indeed ill, to be free to breathe country air in the season when imported Russian furs were donned. The country house that he had been given after his knighthood in 1577 was a former dairy estate forfeited to the crown in 1554 by one of the Wyatt rebels. He returned to court at the end of the year, but had no prompt meetings with the Queen. The retreat at Barn Elms (Barnes) was not an immediately obvious choice for Walsingham, who may have felt inhibited by royal generosity about exchanging it for another or even selling it. However, it is possible that he grew to cherish it and the garden, because the riverboat journey to it recalled for him the boat rides along the Brenta from Padua to Venice – in effect he had now a riverside villa, and it would be wonderful to discover something more of the configuration and decoration. Meanwhile, Stubbs was back in prison, and remarkably did not die of a wound infection combined with shock. He continued to enjoy close and cordial relations with the triumvirate after his release in 1581, and when he did die it was in Normandy serving in Lord Willoughby's ill-fated expedition to assist the French Huguenots. By then his magnificent polemic and wrecking of Elizabeth's nuptial plan had thrust her into the role of royal vestal virgin.

Philip Sidney's retreat from the court was lengthy. He was fortunate to have a comfortable refuge with his sister, Mary, Countess of Pembroke, whose writing, like her reading was unusually public for a Renaissance woman.[10] Could he have doubted when he wrote it that his letter – a text which circulated in 1579–80 – would stir yet more anti-Sidney feelings in the vengeful Tudor who had effectively ruined his father, Sir Henry? It was circulated widely and a copy reached Languet; a challenging piece of writing that also took on the dominant poetic form at court championed by the young Earl of Oxford, a 'new lyricism' with the French influence strongly highlighted. Oxford was a conceited and mercurial young man of literary promise, and because of his ancient lineage indulged by Elizabeth. For a brief time he became the idol of her court. Swooping on the proposed marriage to Anjou, he became too an enthusiastic advocate, so it caused a friction with Philip Sidney that burst into public antagonism. On the famous venue of the royal tennis court at Whitehall insults were exchanged, and Sidney for honour proposed a duel. But the man lower on the social scale than Oxford was forbidden to fight by Elizabeth, and worse, had to apologise to his enemy. Enough to make any man squirm, especially a stiff-necked individual who took great pride in being a Dudley-Sidney; so hankering for a supportive environment Philip quit the court for the country. Oxford behaved just like a loopy second villain in a Jacobean tragedy (yet to be written), making outraged plans to have Sidney assassinated by dreaming up a supposedly foolproof mode of murder, which he did give up – albeit not for some time and even then reluctantly.[11]

Chapter 6

FIGHTING TALK

A journalist wrote recently, 'Politics is impersonal; it has to do with domination and survival.' If Walsingham had stalled over the first part of the claim, the second would have won his enthusiastic endorsement as a reader of Machiavelli. Yet at the time he became Principal Secretary, the politics of North Sea Europe depended very much on special people, most notably the Prince of Orange and his dealings with the German Protestant princes, Elizabeth I and the court of France. During his time as ambassador there Walsingham had received Count Louis of Nassau at the embassy on the quai des Bernardins, and reporting this to Leicester he made clear his own conviction that the only way to curb French ambition and Spanish tyranny in the Low Countries was for England to send troops there. The cause of the Dutch found a strong advocate in him, but had not received a very encouraging response from Elizabeth, who was only pricked to activity when the French showed stronger signs of interest, and after the Massacre as they withdrew she followed suit. Just when Drake was terrifying the Spanish in the Caribbean, to lend the Dutch real aid would aggravate Spain, with possibly devastating results. The détente with France was heavily bruised and distressed, and to come to terms with Spain was eminently desirable. So in March 1573 the Convention of Nymwegen re-established commerce between England and the Spanish Netherlands. There the new Spanish governor was to be from late in the year Don Luis de Requesens, who sent envoys to England for talks in December, and within eight months another Convention (this time of Bristol) was signed, after the Queen had warmly greeted the arrival of Ambassador de Mendoza in July 1574 on a temporary mission. Requesens was told Spanish ships would be allowed to victual in English harbours, and when Mendoza arrived in London it was to a courteous reception. Walsingham's chilly politeness masked antipathy: 'men of judgement think that the chief end of his coming is to entertain us with

Spanish compliments to lull us asleep for a time until their secret practices be grown to their due and full ripeness'. Ambassadorial active was set against regal passive, with ministerial resistance to both. Behind all other causes of friction we see that the matter of religion headed Walsingham's list of preoccupations. But he had not been long enough in office to risk even modest hints of his desire to control English foreign policy, and for the time being he held office jointly with the deferential Sir Thomas Smith. Walsingham by his own admission was a stout-hearted, even choleric man, and he anticipated that at length England would be engaged in an armed struggle against Roman tyranny, personified by its strongest supporter, Philip II of Spain.

Elizabeth shrank from war as from a courtier with halitosis. She hated its wasteful futility and was afraid of the men she had to appoint to take her place in battle. Moreover, she had an undisguised dislike of the martial air about the Salvationist Protestantism espoused by Walsingham. He could charm foreign heads of state, including Catholics, but he eschewed the dandified self-promotion of the courtier, and surely despised their sophistication and archness; he preferred plain dress and plain speech, eventually shading into curtness. Elizabeth preened in nonchalant flattery, even to saturation point. The tough resistance of Walsingham to doling this out to her could set off tantrums, and when she lost her temper she became a fallible judge of policy, then lapsing into a coarseness of tongue as she snapped some pre-Reformation oath at her imperturbable Secretary. She was frightened by the awful necessity of making up her mind, especially when early in 1576 it seemed that war would swamp her either way. Favouring Orange might lead to a war with Spain, with every expectation of defeat; decide against him and there could be a conflict with France – even Burghley thought so, and he had the task of dealing with the Spanish and Dutch envoys in England. It also fell to him to calculate (in so far as he could) the financial and military requirements of supporting William of Orange, and the tactics of an expeditionary force. In council the situation was talked to a standstill; Walsingham's opinion was careful, ordered and somewhat lengthy. He hesitated to give his voice for war because wars are rippled with the unexpected and their outcome is uncertain. Nevertheless he took the view being expressed by the Foreign Secretary in early 2003, that oftentimes it was more dangerous to avoid war than to seek it.[1] Sir Thomas Smith complained that the irresolution shown by Elizabeth 'doth weary and kill her ministers,

destroy her actions and overcome all good designs and counsels – no letters
touching Ireland, although read and allowed by Her Majesty, yet can I get
signed. I wait whilst I neither have eyes to see or legs to stand upon.' There
was a melancholy truth in this – Smith had cancer of the throat and in April
had to retire, as he notified Burghley. By 29 April Walsingham had taken over
from him the overseeing of the Privy Seal, and at the beginning of May Smith
left the court for his Essex home after writing a clutch of farewell letters to
his friends. His absence 'marked the real beginning of Walsingham's escape
from Burghley's tutelage'.[2]

In the Low Countries, Alva had gone; Requesens was dead in March 1576,
and his successor was the ambitious half-brother of Philip II, Don John of
Austria, who raised hopes of a sustained period of mollifying the Dutch and even
the English. One gesture sure to win the approval of Walsingham and those of
similar opinion was the expulsion of the English College by Requesens in 1575
from Douai in Flanders; young Englishmen had trained as seminary priests
under the supervision of Dr (later Cardinal) Allen, while the town was Catholic
controlled. The death of Requesens came just days before an English envoy went
to the Low Countries in an attempt to broker a deal between the rebels and
Philip II – rather like an American under-secretary trying to bring the Israeli
government and Yasser Arafat to negotiations. The English envoy was William
Davison, a Salvationist or 'forward' Protestant and close friend of Walsingham.
He was to demand a cessation of fighting by both sides, and to threaten both in
turn that Elizabeth would join forces with the other if one refused. The Council of
State that ruled before the appointment of a new governor said they would have
to consult Philip II, and as Walsingham had realistically expected, Davison's
mission was effectively skewered. He wrote to him on 23 April to return home,
as the matter of English trade and shipping with the Low Countries deteriorated
and Elizabeth and Orange organised tit-for-tat seizures of incoming vessels; the
latter had the Merchant Adventurers' fleet bound for Antwerp detained in
Flushing. Elizabeth was incensed, and Walsingham's brother-in-law was sent to
Orange to require their immediate release.

Robert Beale went over to the Low Countries in April carrying a letter of
protest from the Privy Council that had Walsingham's signature, and he told
Beale bluntly that any more Dutch meddling with honest English trade would
prompt Elizabeth to join with Spain against them. 'This you may assure the
Prince from me, will fall out to be true.'[3] Despite this tone from an ally, the
Prince of Orange declined to give way, and there was marked exasperation on

the English side. Beale had evidently failed with threats, so perhaps William Winter could loosen the Dutch hold on English shipping with a more emollient tone. He left England on 22 June and by July ships and cargoes had been released; Winter and Beale returned to England together within a week, with an apparent diplomatic success to present to their government. But what came out shortly was that the Merchant Adventurers had been privately negotiating with Orange, agreeing a loan of 253,000 florins if he released their ships. Money spoke sweetly, and he heard. What Elizabeth simultaneously heard was an insulting reproof to her, which would cost Orange dear. Walsingham wrote candidly and at length to Orange, almost as if he was in service to the Prince (a situation he might have preferred), setting out advice on how to deal with an angry Queen and council. A leak of this to his enemies at court made for a difficult situation, and by the autumn of 1576 he was clearly in need of new allies, not just the Earl of Leicester. The courtier chosen, who became a secure friend for at least a decade, was another Gray's Inn lawyer and member of the Gentlemen Pensioners, Christopher Hatton.

This personal alliance is something of a curiosity because of Hatton's suspected papist leanings and pro-Spanish line. The explanation may be another mutual friend of both men, Sir Thomas Heneage, who succeeded Hatton as Vice-Chamberlain in 1587. Elizabeth had flirted with Heneage, a married man, in the mid-1560s, and when the dalliance lost its piquancy Heneage, like Hatton, was able to achieve cordial relations with Leicester. In the current situation Walsingham was working more and more closely with the Earl in matters of foreign policy, but he was still an unpredictable ally, and the triangular friendship gave each strength. The same was true in the Low Countries, where by October 1576 had assembled a Congress with representatives of Holland and Zeeland, plus those of the Estates General – held at Ghent. They fumbled their early exchanges and achieved nothing; any project for union appeared doomed. Yet the reverse proved true, because late in October the news of the sacking of Maastricht by Spanish mutineers reached the Congress, and by 17 November, a week after the signing of the Pacification of Ghent, they had also heard of the barbarity of the sack of Antwerp. The key item for which they signed was that all the contracting parties would do everything to remove Spanish soldiers from their soil. In a very few months the forces of anti-colonialism had convened in a remarkable way, forming a league 'which looked strong enough to dictate terms to Philip'.[4]

But almost immediately there came a rift. Don John of Austria had arrived in Luxemburg and Orange wanted him treated as an enemy, but in direct opposition was the Estates General, strongly opposed to such a policy. Indeed, they proved this by opening talks with him, and despite a hiatus made an agreement the following February. To some extent the Estates General benefited from the attentions of Elizabeth, who sent Edward Horsey to Don John, threatening to provide the Dutch with men and money if Spain refused to sign up to the so-called 'Perpetual Edict'. Ironically, William of Orange refused to sign it. The benefit even extended to actual funds, the Estates envoy Sweveghem arriving at the English court on 15 December 1576 and *miraculo dictu* departing on 30 December with a hefty £20,000 and the promise of more. Was Sweveghem gifted in diplomacy beyond the example of his peers? No – Elizabeth was betraying her nerves over France, and then Anjou (formerly Alençon) was very seriously scrutinising the possibility of going to the aid of the Dutch. As for Walsingham, it comes as no surprise that he supported William in opposing the treaty-making of the Estates General, and surely distrusted Don John even now, since he was becoming very cosy with English Catholics in exile in the Low Countries. Happily for the Principal Secretary and his princely ally there, William of Orange was himself in a much stronger position, with three more northern provinces on his side, and in February 1577 the capitulation of the Spanish governor in Utrecht. Moreover, he had won a strong popular faction among the Southern Provinces, and even in the Estates General itself. Unhappily for Walsingham, in the spring of 1577 he was seriously ill again and housebound for nigh on three months, so that John Somers, one of his secretaries, had to take on his duties.

The Spanish representative in London, de Mendoza, would charge that Walsingham had been bribed by William of Orange. Why, when the Prince evidently already had his support? Even when sick Walsingham maintained his links with the Prince, offering advice from time to time and finding it acted upon in a way he had never achieved with his own monarch. One suggestion may have been that Don John should be arrested, and Orange certainly thought about it. In panic at the rumour Don John seized Namur in July 1577, having fled early in June from Brussels, capital of the Spanish Netherlands, to Mechlin, as his strength decayed. The effect of this was to collapse any vestigial support he might have had in the Estates General, and to push Elizabeth to the side of the Dutch and her most senior ministers –

Burghley, Leicester and Walsingham. Their representative (an unusual instance of the collective) was again William Davison, a man without heraldic credits and a servant of Walsingham since the latter's political apprenticeship.[5] If Davison could, as briefed, get to communicate with Don John, he was to offer Elizabeth's services as a mediator; else his main effort was with the Estates, supporting and cajoling. If they wanted the aid of the Queen, from her lips came the promise; and for Orange an offer of troops.

No wonder then that the Estates General sent an embassy in September of the Marquis of Havrech and Alphonse de Meetkerke, who explained the break with Don John. When they were given the opportunity to ask for aid, their numbers became strikingly inflated: an eight-month loan of £100,000; 5,000 foot soldiers and 1,000 cavalry under the Earl of Leicester. The following day Elizabeth left for Windsor and Walsingham remained in London to hold talks with the envoys, offering a caution on the request for troops and the suggestion that Leicester's name for commander be suppressed. Given his friend's huge anxiety to go in just such a position of leadership, Walsingham must have been voicing the Queen's thoughts. Nor did the Queen's generous offer, when it came within a few days, lead the Protestant cause forward; she soon became anxious about giving Spain a *causus belli*, and the answer of the Estates to her offer (when it came) was tepid indeed; something very surprising to their own envoys and to Walsingham, who seems to have become very indignant, and required Davison to make this plain to the Estates General. 'I may not forget to let you understand how greatly the States refusal of our men is misliked here by honest and well-affected gentlemen. . . .'[6]

Don John, it will be recalled, had scampered out of Brussels, where on 23 September William of Orange was received with plaudits and popular acclaim. Two weeks later the belittled governor was told by the Estates General that he was no longer to be accepted in that post. A way was being opened up for Orange, but there was a hindrance in the cluster of southern Catholic nobles who found him unacceptable and had been treating with Archduke Matthias, the younger brother of the Emperor Rudolf II. The Duke of Aerschot, his brother the Marquis of Havrech, and the Counts of Bossu, Egmont and Lalaing hardly had to make the case to the Archduke before he fled Vienna in secret. Within days Aerschot and his clique urged the Estates to recognise Matthias as their governor. His alacrity in responding suggests a youthful exuberance, and Matthias protested his good intentions in letters to Rudolf, who pressed him in a brotherly fashion 'not to endanger the prestige of the house or the Catholic religion'.[7] Davison heard about this unexpected development and promptly informed Elizabeth. For a clearer understanding of what had been mooted, Walsingham was told by her to interview de Meetkerke, and the two men met on 18 October. The case put by the Principal Secretary was concern that this impressionable young prince (who would much later succeed his brother as Emperor) at this time might be a puppet of his uncle Philip II. The envoy sought to refute this and other concerns, saying that Havrech had consulted Orange about Matthias before leaving the Low Countries and had gained his assent. He might have added that it was lukewarm as assents go. Walsingham was still yoked to Orange as a supporter, and in one of his late October letters to Davison he noted 'that no favour is to be had here without the mediation and furtherance of the Prince of Orange, to the end, that if through envy they cannot be drawn to honour him for his virtues, they may at least be moved to make much of him for necessity's sake'.[8]

When asked about Elizabeth's promise to lend the Estates General funds, William advised her to stick to what she had said. But Elizabeth was afraid of internal dissensions in the Low Countries arising out of the Archduke question; Aerschot and many about him were seized in Ghent, and this increased her fears. Moreover, the Estates General were strangely torpid and reluctant to respond to her offers, which likely stemmed from their jealousy of Prince William; Havrech continually urged them to send their answer, but apparently they had no wish to augment his forces by an English alliance. It took them until November 1577 to respond, by which time their affirmative was insufficient for her. They wanted money and troops – she now wanted answers to questions such as what did the Estates mean to do about the Archduke? Why had Orange left Brussels? What were their prospects of success if she did aid them? And as she hesitated Don John's man arrived in London to defend his master's actions in an interview with the Queen on 1 December. In the immediate aftermath of this her current appetite for bold involvement petered out, and she fell back onto the pitiful stale notion of mediation. This came at the end of the campaigning season, and at the English court it gave the opponents of Leicester a chance; early in 1578 the struggle in the Privy Council between interventionists and non-interventionist was renewed, and during the season of winter diplomacy she sent envoys to the active participants. Thomas Wilkes was sent to Philip II to seek the recall of Don John, the appointment of a governor of royal blood and more agreeable to the Estates, and the ratification of the Pacification of Ghent. Thomas Leighton went to Don John and the Estates to push for peace, while Daniel Rogers was sent to the Protestants of Germany. Don John now offered peace as a path between tall hedges: on one side the maintenance of Catholicism, and on the other due obedience to Philip II; until the Estates took this path he would press on with the war as his service to Philip bound him to do. Leighton did not return to England until early February 1578, by which time the Estates were hankering for men and money, and all Walsingham could do was stall as the Queen waited for Leighton. In fact Walsingham, of course, would have preferred that she send what the Estates General wanted at once, but being sick in his head and stomach he could not urge his argument in person. His conciliar opponents had her ear at this time and persuaded her to dawdle, although we may doubt she needed much to mark time.

It was now that events conspired against her. Not only did Leighton return with Don John's refusal to quit fighting, but also on the same night – 5 February 1578 – came the news that he had defeated the army of the Estates. The Privy Council hastily met. The discussion rumbled its way to agreement that Walsingham's policy was now to be followed: there would have to be an outflow to the Low Countries of men and money. Leighton would return to the Estates for talks that would finalise what needed to be done. But a late development suddenly presented itself to Elizabeth – Daniel Rogers arrived back at court with the favourite councillor of Duke John Casimir of the Palatinate, Dr Bentrich. Speaking for the Duke, Rogers outlined what the German prince was offering: the desire to serve Elizabeth and the Protestant cause in any way he could. Substitute Casimir for Leicester; give him money to fight; avoid making an open declaration of war on Spain. It was a diplomatic swerve that none could have foreseen, and on 14 February Walsingham had the bumpy task of telling the agent of the Estates General, ahead of course of the final decision, made almost one month later. While Elizabeth dithered (again) Davison reported that Anjou was aware of her shift, and had taken advantage of it to offer his assistance to the Estates, in which the pro-French cluster had gained in strength. This in conjunction with other things led her to settle for the apparently bold John Casimir, asking him to enlist 6,000 Swiss infantry and 5,000 cavalry to defend the Low Countries, who heard her policy shift from Rogers. John Casimir would be paid £20,000 immediately, and at the time of muster another tranche of £20,000. The

terms in all were frankly displeasing to the Estates; but for their defeat at
Gembloux they might have looked elsewhere, but their options had shrivelled
and Rogers got their assent before riding on to the Palatinate. Meanwhile
Havrech, with Privy Council support, squeezed a £5,000 loan from Elizabeth,
and permission to export a large quantity of arms. He might have got more
but for the arrival of an envoy from Spain: Don Bernardino de Mendoza.

Unlike the achingly clumsy de Spes, the new Spanish ambassador was a
tenacious and bold operator, whose appointment demonstrated the concern of
Philip II for the direction of English policy. So, when Havrech returned to the
Low Countries in April with pockets full of air rather than specie, he very likely
had Mendoza to blame for Elizabeth rowing back on her former declarations.
Just the policy shift guaranteed to enrage the Estates and send them looking
for French aid. When that country was divided by civil wars that flared and
died and flared again, their hope of anything was merely that. But in
September 1577 the treaty of Bergerac* began the process of establishing a
civil peace, although this barely extended to Henri III and his irksome little
brother Anjou, whom the King placed under guard early in February 1578
while imprisoning a clutch of his brother's favoured friends. Within days
Anjou fled from the Louvre – an escape assisted by his sister Marguerite,
Queen of Navarre, who had visited the Low Countries some months before
this, ostensibly for her health. Anjou fetched up in Angers, the chief city of his
land holdings, and once again civil war seemed to be threatening, so Catherine
de Medici hurried after him and got assurances that he did not mean to
trouble the realm. He had, he said, another project of a much more serious
nature; his intention now was to aid the rebellious Netherlanders, having been
approached by the Catholics of Artois and Hainault. Marguerite's visit to Spa
to take the waters had actually stirred them.

* The treaty also halted the advance into France of the army under John
Casimir.

Chapter 7

THE MEN OF BUTTER

Although through 1577 Walsingham could not yoke Elizabeth to his view of what needed to be done in the Low Countries, the temporary eclipse of Burghley – beset with the misery of his daughter (unhappily married to the Earl of Oxford), the distress of his wife and physical ailments – had allowed the initiative to pass to Leicester, and above all Walsingham himself. It was this 'above all' that a more buoyant Burghley intended to diminish after Walsingham had got his long awaited knighthood in December, simultaneously with Heneage and Hatton. Mendoza thought Burghley had become jealous of Walsingham 'as the younger man confirmed his control over the day to day business of policy formation'.[1] Life for Walsingham was so freighted with business that Dr Thomas Wilson was put in to assist him, being firmly of the Leicester grouping. This was the more unified cluster in Privy Council dealings; their conservative colleagues – Bacon, Burghley, Sussex, Hunsdon and other minor figures – made a less coherent cluster, differing, for example, on religion.* Burghley's resilience would be tested in 1578, as would the cohesion of those who had sought to trim his power. Leicester was bemused and distressed that his longed-for intervention with an expeditionary force had not happened. Walsingham was more sanguine, although by May 1578 there was evidence in bundles that John Casimir of the Palatinate 'was not an adequate counterweight to the Duke of Anjou'. But maybe the election of Matthias as governor in December 1577 was – certainly it interposed a superior block to the swelling ambitions of the French prince. And although he tried, he failed to prevent it. Even so, he continued with his efforts, and dealt separately with the Count Lalaing

---

* A few years later Ralegh called these two camps the 'men of war' and the 'scribes'.

and other nobles in Hainault, a move that made the Estates General nervous. They did not want Anjou's aid but were afraid to reject him, fearing that it might nudge him to the enemy, or else the annexation of Artois and Hainault. Having delayed until April, what they proposed – a campaign by him limited to Burgundy and Luxemburg and the regions beyond the river Meuse – would keep him out of the Low Countries proper. The sweetener was an annual pension of 200,000 francs.

But none of this was nearly enough for Anjou. He wanted to be their protector; he wanted two strong towns to secure the good intentions of the Estates, and if they renounced their allegiance to Philip II, he wanted to be their governor. An alert Davison reported these exchanges to London after the Estates had told him of their dilemma, and as the pace of the negotiations accelerated, the undesirable presence of Anjou in the Low Countries seemed increasingly likely. The Privy Council in London met to try to work out a policy to prevent this, although Sir Nicholas Bacon opined that the Estates General only needed to be careful about their terms with Anjou for little harm to be done. Otherwise a unified force of Anjou and Don John might do great harm. Burghley disagreed with his brother-in-law, wanting to send ambassadors to the Estates General, and Walsingham approved of this without any inkling, as it seems, that he might be one of them. The lobbying of Leicester to go was cordially ignored by Elizabeth, who in the remarkably short time of a week had paired Walsingham with Lord Cobham, Lord Warden of the Cinque Ports – two Kentish men in tandem, balancing on either side of the religious divide. 'It was rare for Tudor politicians to be seen to embrace diplomatic service; there are few parallels for this keenness.'[2]

Believing that he could make intervention government policy, Walsingham was more or less unfettered, but absence from court meant exposure to attack, and for defence and blocking he had Hatton and Leicester. Would this centre hold?

Possibly not, if the preliminary eddies about William Davison were anything to go by. He had been sent to the Low Countries because he was Walsingham's protégé and a voice to holler from abroad for intervention. This made him a target of whispers at home for not being impartial, and for twisting language to serve his own ends. The scrutiny that Walsingham gave Davison's reports seems to suggest that the charges were not dismissed as frivolous, and that the envoy had shifted too far towards the Dutch: 'although things be ordered much against your mind, yet you must submit yourself to the same'.[3] In a letter to the Principal Secretary on 16 May Davison snapped his derision and pointed boldly at Sir Thomas Leighton as his enemy of late. Confirmation of this came in a letter to Davison from Thomas Wilkes, and he added that he had tried to calm Walsingham, but he indicated too that Davison had said too much in front of his own entourage. Since Leighton was a clear follower of Leicester, it makes the godly party seem rather hollow, especially since Walsingham followed the line of least resistance with the Earl. Perhaps Leicester was simply nervous about his courtship and intended marriage to Lettice Knollys – the former Countess of Essex, a court beauty of renown and rarely there because of Elizabeth's towering jealousy – becoming public knowledge. Leicester had already seen his prestige diminished by diplomacy in the Low Countries, and he may well have feared more. The slide of his faction may also have been signalled by the Queen sending Sir Edward Stafford to France, to the King and Anjou, just before the time he married the cast-off mistress/wife (?) of Leicester – Lady Douglas Sheffield. Stafford's task was to winkle out the attitude of Henri III to his brother's purposes, and get him to prevent Anjou from entering the Low Countries. If the ancient bait of marriage could do this then Elizabeth was prepared for a late matinée of this old comedy. Except that it was not funny and Catherine de Medici was supposedly delighted at the prospect of someone taking on her erratic son, who developed an attention deficiency when thwarted.

Walsingham and his junior partner in the embassy, Cobham, had their instructions drawn up on 12 June, and the key component was that they should do everything to bring about peace between Don John and the Estates. The cooperation he gave or denied would serve to mark the future policy, which could be peace, but might be war if the Low Countries' suffering continued. If John Casimir, Anjou and the Estates could not muster the force to defeat Don John, then Elizabeth would send other forces out of England for their relief. After all the minor functionaries who had crossed to the Low Countries, Elizabeth chose a political and diplomatic heavyweight with something of a Francophile reputation. Before their departure from court on 15 June, Walsingham and Cobham visited Bernardino de Mendoza to assure him that they went as peacemakers, bearers of olive branches, and while he accepted this graciously, his private view was that they went to cause mischief, a view shared by the Venetian ambassador in Paris. Mendoza also spotted the seniority of Walsingham who, despite a month of preparation, made his personal defences of his position literally on the hoof. On 16 June

he wrote to Hatton from Gravesend, and again the following day from
Cobham Hall.[4] The enormous party of nearly 200 was itself no small
problem, but they finally took ship at Dover on the evening of 20 June,
arriving at Dunkirk the next day.

Back in England Walsingham had at least two men of business –
facilitators – working for his advantage and protection. One was Francis
Mylles, a senior secretary in Walsingham's London office, and his task was to
follow the court when the Queen went on progress – this year principally in
East Anglia. While she was staying at Long Melford in Suffolk with her
Master of the Rolls, he had actually to absent himself, for Sir William Cordell
was Catholic, and she received two envoys from Anjou who were royally
treated, partly at Cordell's expense. Any letters for Walsingham delivered to
the court were scooped up by Mylles, who also gathered court gossip and
exchanges passed by the other man of business – Edmund Tremayne, courtier
and Clerk of the Privy Council. Close to the Earl of Bedford and Walsingham,
his principal efforts for him were secret, but it's known that one of them was
to keep Hatton alert and up to the mark. This was necessary because Hatton,
although dancing attendance daily on the Queen, lacked intellectual weight
and *gravitas*. Could he hold up if the Queen tested him with one of her
aberrant patches? When she took a particular dislike to the starting point of
Walsingham's negotiations, Tremayne and Hatton conferred before Hatton
talked to Elizabeth about specifics, yet he emerged confused and it fell to
Tremayne to try to gauge the seriousness of the exchange. He then wrote it
down and showed it to Hatton, who gave it the nod, and so it was forwarded
to Walsingham. As the embassy went on, Walsingham could relax a little
over how he was being represented to Elizabeth by a man who clearly
thought of him as a role model. Hatton did his best, and Walsingham
continued to use him for his most piquant comments to the Queen. Having a
court career was always a strain on the nerves because it involved
considerable dependence on the cooperation of other people. 'At the heart of
courtly writing was uncertainty about its sincerity.'[5] The importance of
trusted, alert secretaries was very great, and almost as important were
messengers, the ideal being someone close to the writer – a friend or servant
with many years of service. The safe transmission of a letter from abroad on
a personal matter was, of course, always desirable; but for diplomatic letters it
was essential, hence the growth in the use of ciphers. Letters written by
Walsingham to Hatton and Leicester might be read aloud in the presence of

Elizabeth and others, so they could not simply be flung together in ink on bifolia – that is, folded folio sheets, which in the absence of envelopes were folded once or twice more before fixing with the letter-writer's seal. Tremayne developed a good opinion of Hatton; but for all that, the latter's inexperience sometimes led him into error in interpreting the full intentions of Walsingham. The letters from Walsingham indicated to Hatton that he was valued, which boosted his self-esteem and caused him to write a letter of friendly assurance to Dame Ursula Walsingham.

Even so, compared with Leicester, the proud and dangerous politician with 'something of the night' about him, Hatton was a dormouse under the flight of the hawk, the very bird of prey friends and supplicants most often sent to Walsingham for his hunting pleasure. Whenever Leicester spoke all manner of men and women listened; he had an alert brain and the ability to argue a case for a policy with a vehemence matching that of his colleague. His involvement in the matters that ruined Norfolk may have been shifty, but he remained sturdily consistent in his dealings with Walsingham for years to come, until a financial crisis set off by his difficulties in the Low Countries. Being passed over for the embassy was a blow to Leicester's self-esteem, and while Walsingham and Cobham were meeting with the Estates in Antwerp, the Earl was with Elizabeth on progress, leading the godly party in minor but successful skirmishes with Suffolk's Catholic gentry. Back in London Leicester had to put his weight behind an effort to protect Walsingham from an Elizabeth growing increasingly testy, and to reinforce the picture of solid good will he too wrote to Ursula Walsingham. She was gratified to have this evidence of a 'most assured friend', and told Thomas Randolph this so that he in turn reported this to Leicester. Among the godly activists Randolph was important, directing the circulation of social energy: as Mitchell Leimon relates, during the summer of 1578 Randolph had practically besieged Burghley for the advancement of another godly Kentish man, Roger Manwood. If he had time to reflect on their efforts and those of others, Walsingham had every reason to be relieved that he was so well backed, a situation that in part stemmed from his affability and amenability to all at court.

The embassy that travelled with Walsingham and Cobham was remarkable for its great size, and when numbers failed to engage attention, rich presents helped. Among those who travelled over was a group of captains who might be called upon to master fighting men in the event of an intervention, so it is not straining things to call this embassy Leicester's reconnaissance party.

Information gathering was becoming a Walsingham obsession, so sending out three parties of agents led by friends and clients, according to his instructions from Elizabeth, chimed neatly with his inclination to ferret. Unfortunately, like weapons inspectors for the UN in Iraq in 2003, they had too little time and too many places to visit; and language problems in the southern Netherlands did not help the Englishmen. In Antwerp the ambassadors were greeted with unfeigned cordiality, as Pruneaux, one of Anjou's agents, noted dyspeptically: 'They spend a lot of money and give fine presents.' Even so, when the talks began, with the representatives of the Estates led by Prince William, the terms for peace they set out were too exacting: Don John and his army would have to leave the country, handing over to the Estates all towns and command posts; Archduke Matthias was to be recognised as governor; and the whole question of religion should fall within their remit.

Walsingham and Cobham tried to modify what was on offer, but to no avail. In such circumstances there was no real hope of peace, and Walsingham was clear about this when he wrote to Leicester on 14 July: 'they are determined not to enter into any treaty until he (Don John) be retired with his forces and such holds delivered up into their hands as he presently possesseth.'[6] As for Anjou – he had them puzzled, for although they were charged to meet his representatives, only one turned up to say the Duke's deputies would assemble in Antwerp soon; but by mid-July the embassy was still waiting, and everyone, including the Estates, was confused. Even so, the invisible Valois remained a player because, after months of being held off by the Estates, and in spite of his brother, Henri III, he was rapidly assembling an army of sorts on the frontier. Add to that his cosy dealings with the provinces of Artois and Hainault, and it was obvious that a shift was imminent. For the English ambassadors this meant prompt help for the Estates, and more money through moneylenders.

The weeks passed and Walsingham and Cobham had achieved nothing. The delay in meeting William of Orange seemed to upset Walsingham, who recorded his irritation in a letter to Leicester, but later modified it as Orange became more open. 'The more I deal with him, the more sufficient I find him.'[7] The two strands of their instructions were followed in sequence and to no purpose, so really all they could now do was to wait for further commands from Elizabeth. The swoop of Anjou and a few men on Mons served only to confuse matters; to check him required nerve and money provided by Elizabeth to the Estates. But put this to her and she frowned her royal displeasure, so that Walsingham felt more and more listless and estranged. A letter to Hatton expressed this in the language of high rhetoric: 'It is an intolerable grief to me to receive so hard measure at Her Majesty's hands, as if I were some notorious offender.' To Randolph (his second cousin by marriage) he wrote, less dolefully and with a marked wry humour that given whispers of the ambassadors being hanged when back in England, it was his hope to have a jury trial in Middlesex. Courageously, when they saw how pointless it was to press the Estates for debt repayments to Elizabeth when they borrowed at 25 per cent interest, Cobham and Walsingham borrowed £5,000 on their own private bonds to lend to the Estates, hoping that she would reimburse them once the advisability of such an action was grasped. But would Elizabeth ever get to this point?

As ever she was in two minds. One of them looked to a revival of the Anjou marriage proposal, and an adroit Duke determined to push the mechanics of this to their limits, as he did in negotiating with the Estates. Elizabeth had required Walsingham to talk to Anjou, and in August he went to Mons for a conference that bolstered the Duke's confidence. Walsingham was not personally implacably hostile to the Queen's marriage to Anjou, but he was aggrieved that in his absence those commissioned to make a ducal-Estates pact had made great progress and signed a significant deal. For a substantial army (10,000 foot, 2,000 cavalry for three months) provided at his expense and neutrally – Anjou was not to meddle in the government of the Low Countries – he was named 'Defender of Belgic liberty against the Spanish tyrant', and a very short time was deemed appropriate for making terms with Don John. This was signed just days before the English ambassadors, who saw the logic of what had been achieved, received from Elizabeth a letter dated 9 August in which she returned to the old notion of money and men being offered to the Estates to prevent what had just happened.

The treaty did not come into effect until 1 September, so after some teeth grinding, Walsingham and Cobham approached Orange asking what measure of aid the Estates now expected from England. His reply was a bump: more money, more troops at her expense, and two minor towns as security – Sluys had gone from the reckoning. This hike in requirements was then put to Elizabeth, and while they waited, no doubt with some trepidation, they tried to nudge Don John into making terms with the Estates. In this matter they had the support of Rudolf II's ambassador Count Swartzenberg, and to a lesser degree that of the envoy of Henry III, still wanting to curb his brother.

Before meeting with Don John, Swartzenberg was in conference for hours with the English ambassadors and took from them a letter, which emphasised Elizabeth's desire for peace, and their readiness to meet with him to this end. Don John's reply was in turn courteous, but not exactly full of hope: Swartzenberg was more optimistic – perhaps too much so, for it was his assessment, in conjunction with the letter from Don John, which allowed Walsingham to nurse a cautious optimism recorded in a letter to Heneage. With the willing nod from the Estates (not yet locked into an agreement with Anjou) Walsingham and Cobham sought a face-to-face meeting with Don John, who provided for their security with safe conducts. They were en route even before his reply, and heard from him in Malines, before proceeding to Louvain. From there they had to pass through the plague-infested town of Jodoigne and on to the village of Perwez. The following day, Sunday, two gentlemen arrived to conduct the ambassadors to Don John, who was approached across a flat plain, seated under a spreading oak.

Walsingham and Don John; here was a meeting of opposites where civility ruled despite the rumour that Walsingham had employed the disaffected half-brother of the Earl of Sussex, Egremont Radcliffe, in conjunction with the composer Alfonso Ferrabosco (I), to murder Don John. Born in 1543, Ferrabosco first left Italy in the late 1550s to join the musicians about Charles de Guise, Cardinal of Lorraine. By the time of his further removal to England, Ferrabosco had many contacts in diplomatic circles. Walsingham naturally rejected the charge when he heard about it, and did so with passion; Radcliffe did have a connection with the Principal Secretary, having but recently been released by him from the Tower of London, and although he seems to have escaped torture there, he was tortured by the aides of Don John. Moreover, though Walsingham recorded his admiration for the latter, his politics polluted the situation in the Low Countries. Don John seemed more conciliatory towards his subjects and Elizabeth than any predecessor, or so Walsingham likely thought until he got to read a packet of letters written by the soldier. Written by Don John, intercepted by Walsingham's Huguenot acquaintance, the soldier and author François de la Noue, sent to William of Orange, then passed to one of Walsingham's agents, possibly Wilson when he was in the Netherlands, they revealed a plot to poison Elizabeth and have Mary, Queen of Scots marry Don John. The decrypting was done by Philip van Marnix St Aldegonde, long a friend of William of Orange, and the contents were soon disseminated to towns and cities throughout Europe in the résumé produced in seven languages by the gleeful Estates. Don John was making friendly professions to mask a deeper belief that if Holland and Zeeland could be forced to submit to him, the conquest of England and all that would flow from it must follow. But then he was himself destabilised by the decision to reduce the numbers of Spanish troops in the Low Countries, and he was not able to make peace with the Dutch. His negative response was delivered at 8.00 a.m. on 31 August, just hours before the treaty between the Estates and Anjou became effective.

By this time Walsingham was feeling jaded and even stoically nervous at the plague threat, for one of Cobham's men had gone down with it and as he, Walsingham, remarked, he had no privilege in this matter above the rest. Indeed, the pattern of his ill-health so far suggested quite the opposite. The following days saw nothing achieved as each side protested its poverty and need. On 15 September Elizabeth wrote to the ambassadors to return home if they could see no mechanism for improving the situation. Burghley had wanted Walsingham to prepare for a meeting with Anjou in case the Duke sent for him, but this unpleasant prospect was avoided and the ambassadors left Antwerp on 27 September for Dunkirk and the Dover crossing. They arrived at court on 7 October 1578 to report their total failure according to their instructions, yet while Elizabeth had no reason to applaud, 'the stalemate was preferable to the options she had been presented with over the summer'.[8] The possible stalemate was himself still in the Low Countries leading a large army; but very soon Don John was dead. The rumour of his death reached the English camp on 1 October, and was confirmed a few days later. Some sources said it was the plague transmitted from his pregnant mistress. Others, including Walsingham, thought syphilis the primary cause, and an autopsy apparently confirmed their view.

Chapter 8

THE PAINS AND PLEASURES OF PATRONAGE

Several years before Walsingham and Cobham escaped unscathed from the plague in the Low Countries, there had been a terrible outbreak in Milan which killed around 18 per cent of the population.[1] When the ambassadors returned with their slightly reduced party, the government was fearful of a major outbreak in England. Plague orders were then drawn up that may have had Milanese proclamations as their source. London, with its hectic daily round of population movement, was the city most at risk and in the autumn of 1578 a number of Privy Council instructions culminated in the banning of Lord Mayor's Day. By November the increase of sickness and ignorance of accurate mortality figures led the Council to order the Lord Mayor to send the Recorder and two aldermen (living furthest from the infection) to confer with the Council in order to create plague controls for the city. Happily, Walsingham escaped the sickness, and despite the battles that could rage in his immune system his doctors (including Lopez) and an attentive wife kept him active and working. Among those who took his gold for physic was the famous pioneer chemist and entomologist Dr Moffet, and then Geoffrey le Brumen, the Huguenot family doctor to the French ambassador's household. According to Mauvissière's successor, Châteauneuf, there was a suspicion that le Brumen was a double agent in the papal service.[2] Since Walsingham put his life in his hands for various ailments, the whisper may have been set off by professional pique. The illness that periodically tortured him was perhaps the stone; men have this ancient affliction more than women, and the pain can be monstrous. Symptoms also include nausea and vomiting, haematuria (blood in the urine) and perhaps fever.

Apart from the muff-carrying men in black who attended him, Walsingham had a second wife who surely took very seriously the duty of caring for her workaholic, frequently sick husband. The wives of noblemen were sometimes even more skilful than middle-class wives in making salves and ointments, and in brewing herbs for tisanes and cooling drinks. Some of these could be made from herbs and drugs purchased at the apothecary's shop if homegrown medicinal plants were not available in quantities. Garden snails were pounded into poultices by the wife who needed them in the sick room; if Walsingham had had ague, Ursula Walsingham might have offered him ravens' eggs, and if they failed, a spider to be swallowed whole in treacle.[3] Other comforts for domesticity she brought with her, having inherited quantities of goods from her first husband – beds, sheets, blankets, coverlets, cushions, quilts, canopies, curtains and tapestries – so their first London residence together was well set up. This was part of a former Catholic hospital or almshouse known as a 'Papey' and the size of the rooms may have made it desirable. These 'Papey' almshouses for aged clerics were common in Pre-Reformation London and the country. Later the Walsinghams moved to Seething Lane, near the Tower, a property willed to his wife and then his daughter Frances. Her second marriage to the Earl of Essex was in March 1590, and their son Robert was born that year in Seething Lane. It probably became No 33, which remained a St Barbe dwelling or business address into the early nineteenth century.

The great men of Elizabethan England, and even those of the second division, loved to build houses symbolic of power and wealth. Walsingham, however, recoiled from this, although there may have been some refurbishment of his country house at Barn Elms (a royal gift of a dairy farm and house), and later the Savoy chambers that came with the office of Chancellor of the Duchy of Lancaster; he preferred to spend his income on other things, increasingly his agents and spies. Even so, by choosing not to build a 'prodigy' house and by his second marriage, he did not need to live austerely. The house at Barn Elms was demolished late in the seventeenth century, but a 1649 survey noted then a large, rambling timber and brick building, with perhaps thirty rooms. Quite a contrast to the stone grandeur of Apethorpe Hall, near Oundle, home of his sister Mary and brother-in-law Sir Walter Mildmay.

Until Elizabeth's reign most novelties and fashions in interior design came from Continental Protestant countries. This was particularly true of furniture, the joinery wood of Flanders taking the place of the old rude and clumsy seats. The joined open-base chair *c.* 1540, now in the Burrell Collection (Scotland) does not look enticingly comfortable, but heavy layers of clothing (especially in winter), padded skirts and breeches improved matters, as did a generous supply of cushions. The household could also afford chairs and stools with fixed upholstery – items found in the wealthiest. Curtains and hangings on walls and beds made for greater warmth and comfort, as did rush matting on the floor. To gather unto them fleas and noxious odours Elizabethans thought dogs extremely useful, and the older Marcus Gheeraerts produced a famous small painting of the Queen with an olive branch in her right hand, her forearm resting on a high-backed wooden chair covered with red material, a sword at her feet, and close to the sword and the hem of her dress, a little dog of the bichon type.

To some rather unimaginative historians, the portraits of Walsingham (of which more later) conventionally dressed in black have tended to confirm for them that he was an austere Protestant politician with a tenacious and murky hold over a pan-European spy network. For them theatre and music had no part in his life, and the notion of him as an art collector cannot be; allow these things into his life and he has to be reassessed. Such a process is necessary because compelling evidence exists to support the general impression held in his time that, far from being indifferent to such things he was in fact a great patron – a Maecenas of the arts in the often used reference of the time. This classical accolade would accord him a position close to that of Leicester, employer of versifiers and poets, builders and decorative scene makers, musicians and so on. He was also an art collector who had accumulated pictures to make one of the most spectacular art collections in England before those of Charles I and the Duke of Buckingham. Leicester's patronage was used to highlight and advantage Protestant politics and culture, and apart from personal delight Walsingham sought the same. Didactic drama had a key place in this effort and the festivities at Kenilworth (1575) show Leicester at his most ebullient and open-handed. He was alert to just how useful a tool drama could 'be as a means of influencing public opinion and of maintaining links political and cultural between the patron at court and local society . . .'.[4] In their private exchanges in quiet moments he could lightly tutor Walsingham, since of the two he had the greater experience and was just the man to sharpen the other's understanding of theatre and its use to them.

No doubt Leicester, who travelled more about England than did Walsingham, laid emphasis on the peripatetic aspect of theatre companies. Even so, not every company conformed to this, so while the Earl of Derby's Men toured widely, apparently Sussex's Men did not, and these were the companies favoured by the Master of the Revels, Edmund Tilney, from February 1578. Before him the great patrons of touring companies were Leicester, his older brother Warwick and the Duchess of Suffolk. These three were highly active in Protestant propaganda, and since the players knew the emphatic views of their patrons they could also create didactic acted pieces that echoed these views for household entertainments held at Easter and Christmas. However, with Tilney at the Revels, supervised by the Lord Chamberlain, the Earl of Sussex, his kinsman, these companies lost their advantage, and having dominated the court calendar were nudged aside by the 'Tilney cluster' – Sussex's Men, Derby's Men and Lord Strange's Men. These companies swamped the performances by adult companies between winter 1578 and spring 1583, an uneasy situation that would not have been lost on Leicester and Walsingham. Their patronage had been given to acting groups of not more than about thirteen or fourteen men and boys: perhaps six leading adult actors, three or four hired men for the minor parts and three or four boys to play women and children. It seems possible that they could augment the numbers by using enthusiastic locals for non-speaking parts that might people the stage.

By 1583 the Earl of Sussex was ailing. Taking the waters at Buxton did nothing, and so he staged a deathbed scene at his home in Bermondsey, famously warning those gathered around him to beware of Leicester and his wiles. By then he was a little late, for Leicester and Walsingham had already taken up the matter of theatre and theatre companies, a moment seized because Sussex's deputy since late 1582 was Lord Hunsdon, and the Vice Chamberlain was Sir Christopher Hatton. Moreover, 1583 was the year Sir Philip Sidney married Frances Walsingham, and Sidney was godfather to Richard Tarlton's son.[5] We join the ends of the loop by noting that Tarlton, the comedy actor, wrote a death-bed note to Walsingham, after the formation of the Queen's Men, which he joined from Sussex's Men. Of course, London was alive with theatrical activity before 1583, when Tilney got his instructions to form the Queen's Men from the new impresario Walsingham. The Principal Secretary probably had no time or inclination to go to performances even before receiving the dedication of Stephen Gosson's anti-theatrical tract *Players Confuted* (1582), but as has recently been pointed out 'he was aware of the cultural influence drama could have', and a culture cannot be isolated from politics.[6] This was well within the period when the forward Protestants had been pushed and pummelled and punished by a Tudor counter-attack over the failure of the final Anjou marriage negotiations. The creation of the Queen's Men might allow a veiled thrust back at the court enemies, for a hidden tussle over the naming of the next Lord Chamberlain was under way simultaneously, and their formation gave the edge in the new starry company to Leicester's threesome – William Johnson, John Lanham and Robert Wilson – over the duo from Sussex's Men, Tarlton and John Adams. In a sense the entire country was made up of queen's men with an interest in cultural homogeneity that rolled like a juggernaut over dissent and Catholics. Walsingham had returned from his Low Countries embassy after the proclamation of the Cologne peace conference, which ended the 1578 negotiations, determined that this should be the government's policy – recusancy would be prized out by legislation (which proved faulty when the time came to uphold it) and oppression, increasingly costly when Walsingham resented spending money on the enemy. But he was now employing growing numbers of intelligencers and spies, and the formation of the Queen's Men chimed with this surge in growth of the secret network.

This is not to say that the Queen's Men were spies, but like all licensed travellers they moved about to give the impression of overarching government control – 'an extensive court influence within which the actual size and constitution of the spy system could not be detected'.[7] Some of the prestige of the Queen's Men was in their name, and they seem to have had the privilege of access to the court, and although their principal task was performing on a stage, their very presence in a country town tugged the emotional drawstring between the royal court and places that never saw a progress. The actors may not have been telling the court anything (at least anything not already known), but no doubt the Jesuit missionaries, when they scrambled in after 1580, kept away from the Queen's Men, with their richly suggestive company title. For Leicester and Walsingham, the new company must have seemed a means for bringing the theatre back into the service of Protestant ideology at just the time when extreme Puritans were attacking it as party to gross behaviour and unseemly representation. Yet from the extremely well-read Walsingham and the Barn Elms literary circle, which included Philip Sidney, came the thought that English history might be a wonderful resource for playwrights in the future, and unsurprisingly we find that 'the Queen's Men established the English history play in the popular theatre before other companies took it up', combining broad anti-Catholicism with a transparent Protestant style.

In his quietly unobtrusive way Walsingham was an inspiration to a younger generation of writers and intellectuals, and clearly regarded by such as Christopher Hoddesdon, husband of Alice Carleill, who sent his own son Francis for a period in the Secretary's home. Fulke Greville thought so highly of him as a mentor that in 1578 he slipped riskily over the Channel to the Low Countries to accompany the ambassadorial party of Cobham and the Principal Secretary. This was interpreted by Elizabeth as a defiant gesture, and on his return Greville was banned from the court for many months. Greville developed a remarkable contact list crammed with the names of men of importance and quality in the intellectual life of his time. Philip Sidney was more to him than any of them; it was devotion untainted by any hint of jealousy or criticism. Add Edward Dyer, the diplomat and neo-Latin poet Daniel Rogers, and Edmund Spenser, and there is the literary core of the Barn Elms group gathered under the benign presence of Sir Francis and his retiring but sweet-natured wife Ursula, who avoided contact as far as possible with the acrimonious life of the court. Spenser's literary milieu may have taken in the London residence of Lord Lumley at Tower Hill, another gathering place for men of letters, where he could have talked at length to men who had known Lumley's late brother-in-law, Humphrey Llwyd, the Oxford-educated writer with antiquarian and chorographical interests, who when he lived in the Arundel household at Nonsuch was a few miles' ride from John Dee. He was deeply struck by Llwyd's manuscript called *Cronica Walliae*, in which is told the story of Madoc, ancient explorer and discoverer (some think) of America – a notion that so seized Dee it became the basis of his vision of a British Empire, and he felt it was Elizabeth's sacred duty to build it. A manuscript copy also went to Abraham Ortelius in Antwerp, who hankered after a complete history of Roman Britain, with the hope after Llwyd's death in 1568 that Daniel Rogers (his own nephew) would take up the challenge. Rogers never did, but he was a pivotal figure in the diplomatic relations between England and the Netherlands. Like so many others he thought of Walsingham as his 'especial friend and patron', and he was also a close friend of Hugh Singleton, whose mutilation as the printer of Stubbs's *Gaping Gulfe* was averted. Sidney's other mentor, Languet, took great pleasure from his conversations with Rogers and Robert Beale, Walsingham's brother-in-law and secretary.[8]

In public and private Walsingham was a sturdy part of an intense literary culture. The writer Gervase Markham acknowledged that his own family were 'ever immortalie obliged' to the great statesman, after Robert Markham (his father) had allied his fortunes to Walsingham. It seems likely that his library was divided between the house in Seething Lane and Barn Elms, though in numbers of manuscripts and books it probably did not rival either the library of Lord Lumley, which in 1609 had 2,800 printed books, or that of John Dee who, in the 1583 inventory, had amassed some 2,500. But Walsingham was a bibliophile, and although deeply read in theology and the recipient of many pamphlets of varying tedium from Puritan evangelists, his interests ranged beyond Calvinist divinity, as his friendship with Dee underlines. One presentation copy was Bizari's *Historia Rerum Persicarum*, which Walsingham acknowledged by letter in July 1583. As Principal Secretary and a lawyer he surely had law books and, given his health problems, others on medicine and remedies. The Folger Library now holds his presentation copy of Dr Walter Bayley's *A Brief Discourse on the Baths at Newnham Regis* (1587). As a well-travelled man from his youth onwards through life, he must have owned books on geography, natural sciences and possibly art and architecture. Until rivalled by Leicester's art collection Nonsuch had the finest collection of paintings in Elizabethan England, and in the *Faerie Queene* (Book III, Canto XI, stanzas 29–46) Spenser reveals an acquaintance with the pictures and tapestries hung at Lumley's Tower Hill house; we know from the Worsley inventory that Ursula Walsingham inherited both sorts of decoration from her first husband, although the picture of Cleopatra was valued at only 3*s* 4*d*.

As for music, once again it was Lumley who had the largest library in a private house in Elizabethan England, but the notion that the Walsinghams, their family and friends were without music in Seething Lane or Barn Elms seems perverse given that the Walsingham Consort books are manuscripts copied for use in his household, and there are pieces in it named for him and Dame Ursula, and their daughter. The books are an incomplete set of part-book copies containing portions of some thirty-two works for 'English Consort' with the lute, pandora and cittern as the plucked instruments alongside the viol (bass), flute and treble viol (violin). Traditionally these pieces were written in a three-part dance form, with lute divisions on each sectional repeat. In the Walsingham books the consort lessons also have written divisions for the flute and violin, with particularly fine examples of this special treatment found in the consorts by Richard Allison, whose technique and style are thought by some to be more accomplished and individual than those of Daniel Bacheler. Julia Craig-McFeely has countered the view that Bacheler's harmonies were awkward or clumsy, and a good deal of what he wrote derivative, by stating with strong authority that he was an exceptional musician.[9] One possible reason for his neglect until recently has been the difficulty for lutenists of his ornamental style with arpeggios, trills and tremolos.

The son of a yeoman farmer, he went at seven years to his maternal uncle, Thomas Cardell, a court lutenist and dancing master, for training. Seven years on this apprenticeship was assigned to Walsingham, a rearrangement advantageous to all three. Within two years young Daniel was composing music for consort. Indentured until 1595, by then he was part of the household of the Essexes; the medley of popular tunes known as *The Lady Frances Sidneys Felicitye* was certainly his effort. No doubt, too, some of his music was played by the glamorous sister-in-law of Lady Frances, for this was Lady Penelope Rich, an accomplished lutenist. Whereas Burghley was immune to the delights of music, Leicester, Walsingham and the Sidney-Devereux circle were among devotees of the new-style consort music. This had fast matured in the hands of a few lute composers: John Dowland, Richard Reade, John Johnson – probably the lutenist loaned by Sir Thomas Kytson to Leicester for the Kenilworth festivities (1575) – Richard Allison and Bacheler, amongst others from other European musical traditions.

Kytson was a rich wool merchant resident at Hengrave Hall in Suffolk, with his London home in Austin Friars, and John Johnson was his 'Master of the Musicke'. In the mid-1570s the Kytsons had hired John Cosyn as a resident teacher of the rudiments of the virginals to their children; employment lasting from Christmas to Easter. The Kytsons were Catholic-leaning and certainly friendly with the Duke of Norfolk, which aroused the sharp suspicion of Elizabeth who had Sir Thomas gaoled. Lady Kytson's brother William Cornwallis was a wealthy Catholic courtier, who was brother-in-law to the Earl of Northumberland and Sir Thomas Cecil, with an influential cluster of court connections among the Catholics and yet also including men like Burghley and Pallavicino, and according to the French ambassador Mauvissière, with Walsingham too. Philip Sidney was a friend of Sir Thomas Cornwallis, father of Lady Kytson, and through the young man she made an appeal to Walsingham to intercede for her incarcerated husband. This he did, and with Kytson's own personal plea to the Queen it was sufficient to obtain his release. Several years later Elizabeth made the East Anglian progress already referred to and stayed with the Kytsons – the visit when he got his knighthood.[10] As for Sidney, he always regretted not being able to make music himself, but he surely heard more than ever when he moved in with his in-laws, and there may have been friendly competition in music-making between the Walsinghams and Kytsons – even an exchange of musical resources. In the matter of dealing with, and even befriending Catholics, Sidney's ease has falsely suggested a leaning by him to their side.

Hiring in musicians for an evening, a grand dinner or a wedding feast was not especially cheap, although it was certainly less expensive than having them on the payroll. It was certainly known for lutenists to engage themselves as grooms or serving men, rather than as instrumentalists. Perhaps this was the status in the Walsingham household since *c.* 1581 of the poet-translator Thomas Watson, who took such an interest in the Italian madrigal. He seems to have been born into a Catholic family and raised in the faith, before being schooled at Catholic-leaning Winchester. A brief period was spent at Oxford before he exiled himself to Europe, studying law in Padua, in Douai seminary, and then in 1577 he returned to England. His first book was a Latin version of *Antigone* (1581) which declared his versatility to a narrow audience, and he followed it, while employed as a diplomatic messenger by Walsingham, carrying letter packets between Sir Henry Cobham and James Beaton, spokesman for Mary, Queen of Scots, with the innovative sequence of 100 eighteen-line poems he called sonnets, *The Hekatompathia* (a publication of 1582). This struck sparks among the young writers, and by the 1590s the true sonnet sequence was a fashionable coterie exercise. As for the Italian madrigal, it had long been a transfer in the baggage of Italian musicians settling in England, and was primarily heard in the houses of noblemen and specialist musical groupings such as that about the London lawyer and gentleman, Nicholas Yonge.[11] In 1588 Yonge edited *Musica Transalpina*, fifty-seven Italian madrigals with English words, fourteen of them by Alfonso Ferrabosco I who had left his family in England in 1578 virtually as royal hostages, but never returned; and two by the privileged Catholic composer of genius, William Byrd, who went on to write the first two English madrigals.

Thomas Watson was a letter carrier in tandem with Thomas Walsingham, the Kent-born cousin of the Principal Secretary, both chosen because they could be trusted with this important task.[12] Another who undertook the sometimes risky task of letter-carrying was John de Critz, of a family originally from Antwerp, the painter who in about 1585 produced one of the most alert and recognizable portraits of the Principal Secretary in his usual dark clothes against a dark background, his neck encircled by a fine linen ruff, and just above waist height a jewel on a gold chain. Through the 1580s the most fashionable portrait painter in Elizabethan England was George Gower (1540–96) whose 1573 portrait of Sir Thomas Kytson is now in Tate Britain. In 1581 Gower became Serjeant Painter to the Queen, and this accolade may have made a commission from Walsingham too difficult. He employed de Critz on the Paris run every year from

1582–8, save for 1584; perhaps it was simply familiarity with the artist that got him the portrait commission; or possibly he was cheaper than Gower, who had doubtless hiked his fee since painting Sir Francis Willoughby and his wife, Lady Elizabeth, for 10s and 20s: 30s for the two, which today might be £750. For message-carrying the payments made by the Treasurer of the Chamber show quite generous amounts ranging from £10 to £15, with £26 for two missions involving a wait in Paris. It was, even then, an expensive place.

Walsingham was a cultivated man with great energy of the mind, who had lived at different times in France and Italy, and it is possible his taste in art was permanently ahead of that of his contemporaries. Did he banish to a dark corner the old parlour portrait of Henry VIII inherited by his wife? He had been in northern Italy as Titian's career surged to its extraordinary peak, and given the local as well as international fame of the artist, it seems unlikely that Walsingham could have been in Venice without learning of the elderly resident genius. Alas, he Walsingham had neither the fame nor the handy fortune to allow him to seek sittings. Less than twenty years later his future son-in-law, Philip Sidney, was also in the city, and he found a portrait painter to produce a likeness for his mentor Hubert Languet. The sitter had a grand option: Tintoretto or Veronese – the former boasting he could equal or outdo the latter for half the commission price. Sidney, growing into his role of English *milord*, chose Veronese, and the sittings for preparatory sketches took three or four days. In the same period the artist did a detailed drawing of Sidney, whose youthful face had been ravaged by childhood illnesses. Five or six months later, two of Sidney's friends delivered the portrait to Languet, who was rather taken aback by the youth he saw. Later, after more time in company with the young man himself, he got to like the painting more, but then wished it broadly hinted at Sidney's good humour with a smile.

When Languet died in the house of Philippe du Plessis-Mornay, the picture went to him and hung in his great gallery at least until 1619. Subsequently, as Roger Kuin has documented, the painting was in an auction in Normandy in 1697. Then it vanished. Or did it? Is the Boston Museum of Fine Arts *Portrait of a Young Man* certainly by Tintoretto, or is it a mis-attribution of a later date, and actually by Veronese? If by the latter, could the subject be Philip Sidney?

A pity then that Mornay (who so admired Walsingham and Sidney) did not have a copy prepared as a present for the older man, who had done so much for the Protestant cause in which they all believed so fervently. It would have been a pleasing addition to the Walsingham collection, which may have got its first large panel oil painting as a gift from Elizabeth. The picture is now called *Allegory of the Tudor Succession*, and is attributed to the learned exiled poet and painter Lucas de Heere (1534–84) who is known to have taught the young John de Critz (*c.* 1551/2–1642), a Walsingham courier, thrice married and the father of sixteen children. His sister Magdalen de Critz married Marcus Gheeraerts the Younger in May 1590, and Sir Roy Strong has recently suggested that the sitter for *Unknown Lady*, *c.* 1600, showing a pregnant (?) woman in a deliciously embroidered robe and elaborate headdress may be Frances Walsingham, at that time wife of the disgraced Earl of Essex, whose family crest included a stag.

When it is remarked of Cassius in Shakespeare's *Julius Caesar* that 'he hath a lean and hungry look' it is partly a reflection on a man eaten up by ambition and partly an amused parallel hint that the great men of Elizabethan England generally put on weight as they grew older. Given the calorific value of their diet this is not surprising, and even a former athlete and horseman like Leicester, who would leave the court for fresh air and exercise, grew in girth in his last years as state banquets settled into flesh. But Walsingham, not apparently given to formal exercise, remained a lean and lame man, with a liking for hawking and gardening. But not riding, for he passed on to Robert Markham a fine Arab horse that he had been given.

At Barn Elms he had a garden that he could take pleasure in improving, and when he had a visit from Burghley he got free firewood, since the only exercise the Lord Treasurer engaged in was chopping down trees. Since Walsingham planted hawthorns and to chop them down is bad luck, Burghley may have taken his axe to scrub oaks on the estate lands of some 463 acres. Only a small part of this would have been formal gardens, which were possibly the result of Walsingham's employment of a Dutch gardener, who was buried with two of his children in the churchyard of St Mary, Barnes, as was Walsingham's daughter, Mary.[13] The more decorative planting may also have been influenced by the herbalist and botanist John Gerard, who maintained the Cecil gardens in the Strand. He could also have given advice on the growing of herbs for medicinal and culinary use to Dame Ursula, the very epitome of the reticent good wife so admired by puritan writers. We know that there were two cooks among the household staff – Henry Calthropp and John Cordell – perhaps one for town and one for country. In her will Dame Ursula bequeathed them £3 per annum, while Nurse Horde, who surely helped mother and daughter through pregnancies, got £10.

Chapter 9

BEATING BOUNDARIES

When Walsingham came back to England in October 1578 his energies were given to seeking out and punishing recusants – inspiring, directing and controlling, so that one day he could seal the ruin of Mary, Queen of Scots. Every mention of her elicited a groan or a growl in the Privy Council. In 1569 a correspondent of William Cecil (soon to become Lord Burghley) warned him that this tall lady had 'an alluring grace, a pretty Scottish accent, and a searching wit'. To George Buchanan, the great Scottish Calvinist classicist and polemicist, sometime tutor to her son James VI, she was alarming, a woman of 'unbridled licentiousness' – a whore of Rome 'raging without measure or modesty'. Her protective title was Scottish, but she was as much French, having been educated with French royal children and been intimate with her aggressive Guise relatives. Her choice of England as a route for her flight to France was a calamitous mistake, and the French were deeply aggrieved when news that she had been arrested reached them. The French ambassador in London was required to make an official protest to Elizabeth. By then the text by Buchanan, *Detection of the Doings of Mary, Queen of Scots*, had done its intended work and left her reputation as black as her clothes. Walsingham got his copy in the Latin original late in 1571, and at the end of the year Henry Killigrew reported giving the same text to the Venetian ambassador. To the English government she was like a whirlpool drawing into herself exiles from Scotland, admiring Catholics in England and papists abroad. So when the match with Don John was put gently into the shallows like a trout for a pike, Walsingham was soon apprised of it.

Similarly, he was early on told about Thomas Stukeley's enterprise, which had a broad appeal to some exiles when Ireland seemed to be edging towards becoming England's close approximation of the Low Countries. Pope Gregory XIII, the successor to Pius V, tried his best to set off a war of religion in the Queen's domains. He gave his blessing to a piratical, quixotic Devonian adventurer, Stukeley, to invade Ireland with papal forces. Walsingham's spies were becoming greater in numbers and efficiency and tracked Stukely around Europe. His papal armada actually turned out to be one leaky galleon with four small cannon. This ramshackle effort collapsed and James FitzMaurice picked up the remnants, who under his command were shipped into Dingle in Kerry. The coast was guarded (at least it was thought so in London) by Sir Humphrey Gilbert, who never had much luck with the sea, winds and tides. FitzMaurice got into Smerwick, but found no large support, for the Earl of Desmond, who had returned home in 1573, was not inclined to leap to his defence. Fitzmaurice made the key element of his rising clear in a proclamation: 'This war is undertaken for the defence of the Catholic religion against the heretics.' Ironically FitzMaurice was killed in a clash with local Burkes, but Sir John of Desmond picked up the dropped sword to continue the rising, which in itself is very suggestive about the lamentable quality of government troops. In 1583 Sir John was killed as the rising spluttered out, and a dismal year for the Desmonds reached its bloody climax in November when the Earl was chopped down by an O'Moriarty in revenge for ill treatment of the family by the Earl's followers.[1]

Scotland and Ireland were like kissing cousins, with the Scottish and Irish Gaelic-speaking areas linked into a single cultural area. Certainly the administration in Dublin was very suspicious, and with reason, about the extent of the Scottish connection in the north of Ireland. In 1580 Sir Nicholas Malby warned Walsingham that Lady Agnes Campbell, her daughter and Sorley Boy Macdonnell were between them threatening to turn Ulster into a replica of Scotland. At this time the hope of English Catholics had focused on Scotland, where an improbable courtship was going on since the arrival there in September 1579 of Esmé Stuart, cousin to James VI and holder of a French title, seigneur d'Aubigny. His eruption into Scottish politics to secure the Lennox inheritance may have been at the invitation of the Scottish Privy Council, hoping to mentor their juvenile ruler. Or he may have made the journey as an emissary of the Guises, and whoever made the link saw it grow into a beauty of a passion, the emotionally frail young King lavishing gifts and titles on his sophisticated cousin. This Catholic interloper had to be restrained, and in April 1580, after an examination of his faith, d'Aubigny agreed to be instructed by ministers in Edinburgh, and by the summer he claimed to be a Protestant – a change viewed by many with suspicion, and by his wife with distress. Others still thought James VI vulnerable to Catholicism, and the general purpose became to mount an *impresa* – an armed assault on England from Scotland, led by the Duke de Guise. The first to voice this thought may have been Mendoza, the Spanish ambassador with many English Catholic contacts at all levels of society. Court Catholics in England at this time included the Earl of Oxford, Lord Henry Howard, Charles Arundell (whose mother was a sister of Henry VIII's fifth wife, Catherine Howard), Francis Southwell, Thomas, Lord Paget, Lord Compton and others.

With Anjou's marriage to Elizabeth again brought out of the political rummage-box, and the Queen displaying an extravagant attachment to the idea if not the man, even Mendoza thought Catholicism was advancing and the match apparently inevitable. Certain English Jesuits, like Fr Robert Persons, were desperate to break the boundaries of their island with a groundbreaking first mission. Earlier proposals to the General of the Society, Everard Mercurian, had failed to convince him, but now his hesitations were overcome by Oliver Mannaerts, Assistant for Germany, and Claudio Aquaviva, Provincial of Rome. Three Jesuits were selected in early December, one of whom – Christopher Perkins – made a striking response to the idea. He would go gladly if while in England he could attend Protestant church services and take the Elizabethan oath of allegiance. Not quite what his superiors in the Jesuits were looking for. No surprise then that he left, returned to England and joined the established church. The other two, Robert Persons and Edmund Campion, together with Mannaerts, had an audience with Gregory XIII on 14 April 1580, and they asked for and were granted a special understanding of the 1570 papal bull against Elizabeth. This meant they could not be accused of *directly* seeking to overthrow her government by seeking converts, since for the time being adherents would not be obliged to rebel. Neither Burghley nor Walsingham would regard this benignly, since it seemed to prepare for the time when the bull could be enforced. The Jesuits were directly preparing a fifth column.[2]

On 18 April 1580, Campion, Persons and Emerson, three priests from the English College in Rome, three elderly Marian clergy, two laymen and the Bishop of St Asaph travelled from Rome via Bologna, Milan and Geneva, apparently unconcerned that the proportions of the group might alert spies. The prospect of the Anjou marriage charged them with optimism, and Persons later asked Theodore Beza (not universally regarded with adoring optimism by the European Calvinist affinity) how he could declare that he and Elizabeth were of the same religion 'seeing that you do defend the religion of the Puritans which she so much abhorreth and persecuteth'.[3]

Travelling hopefully they reached Rheims, where English seminarists pushed
out of Douai had found a bolt-hole, partly financed by the papacy and given
the protection of Henri, Duke of Guise. Henri III regarded the Duke with
intense disapproval and denied him any royal preference at his court, which
meant loss of access to the royal treasury.[4] Guise was so desperate for money
that an approach from the Spanish ambassador to France was not ignored.
Juan de Vargas Mexia met the Duke on 7 April 1578 for a long conversation
that, had Walsingham been able to hear it, would have had him shaking with
rage – the choleric in him. Guise was now as hot for an attack on England
and the freeing of his cousin Mary, Queen of Scots.

Of course Walsingham knew a good deal about Rheims and the Jesuit
threat. On his prompting, the searchers in southern England's ports all looked
for Persons and Campion, who arrived separately on 16 and 26 June
disguised as a captain and a jewel merchant, but failed to pick them up. In
the world of Anglo-French macro-politics options were worked up and then
dropped; in England's micro-politics Campion began his efforts in the
Marshalsea prison in the cell of the secret Jesuit Thomas Pounde, where he
met Edward Brooksby, who led him to the charismatic George Gilbert, whom
Persons had reconciled to Rome in 1579. It was he who now took him on his
first missionary tour through Northampton, Derby, Worcester, Gloucester and
Hereford. As for Campion, he was taken to a 'safe house' in Chancery Lane by
Catholic gentlemen, and his arrival publicised by a sermon on the text *Tu es
Petrus* given on 29 June, the feast of St Peter and St Paul. Such risk-taking
was soon known by the Privy Council, who sent out spies to listen for more
sermons; an effort that had crypto-Catholics warn Campion to be more
discreet, as they fretted out the political implications of the Jesuit mission.
Campion did try to settle this queasiness with his analgesic *Brag and
Challenge*, saying the intention of the mission was spiritual rather than
political. For him perhaps, if not for Persons, and even the *Brag* seemed to
hint at contradicting its own author, for this broadside challenge to the
authorities hinted at what might come if Anjou married Elizabeth: the
creeping disintegration of the religious settlement of twenty years' standing.
Campion challenged the divines of the Church of England to a rhetorical
combat, confident he could utterly overthrow them. The response was that
the hunt in England for Campion and Persons was stepped up, but oppression
was costly and Walsingham deeply averse to spending money on the enemy.
So they had to be made to pay for their own persecution. How could this be

done when hitherto the only revenues forcibly taken from English Catholics were the confiscations of the property of those who for whatever legal reason had incurred the penalties of high treason, provisors and praemunire, or felony, the fines of 100 marks or upwards on those who actively depraved divine service, or the one shilling fine for every unexcused Sunday absence from it? These aspects of anti-recusant law did not yield enough to support a new campaign of extirpation. The obvious way to increase the take from absentees was a hike in the fine.

Discussions on this began in 1580, and by December there were proposals for a statute to this end, so that when Parliament met in January 1581 it was the Chancellor of the Exchequer, Sir Walter Mildmay, Walsingham's brother-in-law, who eloquently put the case, and the desired bill passed on 18 March – *An Acte to retaine the Queenes Majesties Subjectes in their due Obedience'*. It was the fourth section that imposed the notorious fine of £20 per month on absentees from Sunday worship. Mendoza recorded the absolute horror of English Catholics as the bill was swiftly advanced, and their failed attempt to demolish it with a royal veto by a bribe to Elizabeth of 150,000 crowns. Despite all the lawyers in the House what the bill omitted was crucial: it said nothing about any provision for seizure and confiscation of lands and goods when the first fine remained unpaid. The inability to pay the sum required became at once an excuse for paying nothing, and until 1585, perhaps even later, the law as it remained was effectively neutered – which suited Elizabeth but not her Secretary of State.

In the midst of this comfortless situation news from Scotland, which Robert Persons had come to believe was the key to the total conversion of Britain, gave a flicker of hope to English Catholics: Sir James Douglas, Earl of Morton, and Protestant regent to James VI, was arrested and sentenced to death. There was turmoil too (albeit less sacrificial) at the English court over the period of the Christmas festivities of 1580/1, when Leicester put pressure on the errant Earl of Oxford (now a Catholic). The married seducer of one of the Queen's maids of honour, Ann Vavasour, the equine-faced niece of Lord Henry Howard, now reported to Elizabeth the names of court Catholics with whom he had been associating, declaring their involvement with the French ambassador, Mauvissière. Howard and Francis Southwell were accused of working to restore Catholicism, and in a quaint move Oxford tried to bribe Charles Arundell to confirm the allegations. When he refused to do so and all three heard of a Privy Council arrest warrant they scurried to Mendoza, who

hid them until the threat of the Tower abated, and they passed to house arrest
in the residences of Hatton and Walsingham. Ann Vavasour fared less well,
having inconveniently given birth to a son in the chamber allocated to the
maids of honour; Elizabeth was incensed and Ann was hauled off to the Tower
in March. Oxford tried to smooth over the birth with a gift of £2,000 to the
mother and property for the baby. Before rumours that he might then flee
abroad could become fact the Earl was arrested and found himself alongside his
former lover. Even after his release he was beset with problems, for Ann had
another protector in Thomas Knyvet of the Privy Chamber, and a dangerous
feud developed. As for the pro-Anjou marriage cluster, they were effective no
more and an enquiry about the Queen's hand came from an unexpected source
– Czar Ivan IV, represented by ambassador Pissemsky, sent to conclude a treaty.

Campion's *Brag* did not usher in a Catholic revival, although it gave
inspiration twenty-five years later to Robert Catesby and other Gunpowder
Plot conspirators. For the time being the text merely served as a prompt for
the more severe legislation we have already noted. When Edmund Campion
left St John's College, Oxford with a travelling fellowship in 1570, he went to
Ireland seemingly to avoid going to Louvain or Douai, where there was a
recently established 'Oxford house'; forty-one Fellows left Oxford (1566–75)
for these two Catholic enclaves. One of the Douai-trained priests was John
Hart, whose doctoral examination in law in Padua in June 1574 had been
witnessed by Philip Sidney, arrested on his return to Dover and sent to Oxford
to have his papistry trashed by the Puritan academic John Rainolds.[5] The idea
of this route to recanting was Walsingham's, but Hart proved obdurate so the
Tower beckoned. It was typical of the Principal Secretary that such an effort
should be privately done, for he wanted to deprive Catholicism of the oxygen
of publicity. It has recently been suggested that the *Brag* was put out for
circulation as a challenge to disputation. It was followed by *Decem Rationes*,
printed clandestinely and distributed (400 copies) in Oxford's St Mary's
church on 27 June 1581, in time for the graduation ceremony again
challenging for a debate and giving ten reasons for a Catholic triumph. When
Campion was captured, lurking about in Oxford, manifestly courting
martyrdom he too fetched up in the Tower, and after torture he got the
debate he wanted – only it was rigged. Because Elizabeth had once thought
highly of him, Campion was tried under the old Treasons Act, and John Hart
was to be executed with him on 1 December 1581. But Hart was so appalled
by his fate that he switched sides and confirmed it to Walsingham in a letter.

Later he recanted again, and back in the Tower kept a unique Latin diary. Released in January 1585 with twenty-one others and forcibly exported to France, he died in Rome in July 1586.

Much more of a political activist than Campion, Persons was seeking to impose first a Catholic government and then the whole confessional panoply. Persons' 'Scottish' strategy was to convert James and then make him King of England (with the aid of the Guise faction and Spain if necessary). The failure of James to comply was a blow that led Persons from the possible to the improbable – a new candidate in the Infanta of Spain. The sympathetic courtiers were in prison, and Campion was a few months away from his martyrdom, when Persons was forced to flee back to France in August 1581. He stayed for the time being in Rouen, writing books, laying stress in the first on Catholic loyalty to Elizabeth and the disobedience characteristic of Protestants. The missionaries who followed Campion (their *beau idéal*) and Persons were young men whom Walsingham sharply stigmatised as the spawn of the seminaries, and to do those in Rheims or Rome as much damage as possible Walsingham began covert operations. Having dealt with the body of Campion, the Privy Council did their best to see off the body of his written work by confiscation and destruction. Even the Queen's godson, Sir John Harington, was questioned in December 1583 and again in 1584 about the distributing of Campion items through an employee formerly in Rheims, James Baker, 'a very rebellious papist and seditious person'.[6]

Together in this, Burghley and Walsingham looked balefully on the publishers and distributors in England of Catholic texts printed by clandestine presses. These could be in England or abroad, and the French embassy was one opening for the distribution of this material by the ambassador's butler and cook, Girault de la Chassaigne and René Leduc.[7] According to the spy known as 'Henry Fagot' writing from inside the embassy in May 1583, the carrier was a Pierre Pithou and the seller an Englishman. One of their import stations was the Half Moon tavern in Southwark, whose landlord got a hefty payment for storing a new consignment. Also bribed were searchers on the south coast at places like Rye, because of the fear that government agents would pounce to prevent the spread and sale of the texts.

A distributor with a spotty record, William Parry was a former servant to the Earl of Pembroke, had married money and so squandered it that he was imprisoned for debt. An obscure family link to Burghley may have been exploited usefully to get his release to spy abroad on exiled English Catholics, though from 1577–9 he was back in England. It was very likely during further intelligence gathering trips that he joined the enemy as a convert. Yet he got a seat in the 1584 Parliament, and there it was he betrayed himself by vehemently criticizing new anti-Catholic legislation. Allowing that Parry might know more or have ripe contacts delayed his beckoning trip to the Tower, where Walsingham conducted one of his rare interrogations. Evidently Parry had exhausted his usefulness, had plotted to assassinate Elizabeth, and he was executed in March 1585.

Campion and Persons, who had mounted a highly charged intellectual and moral assault on English Protestantism, had a following. Perhaps the nation would have benefited if the spiritual Campion had lived on and the political Persons who approved of George Gifford's plan to assassinate Elizabeth had been executed as we may think he deserved. If he had been, the lives of English Catholics would have been less blighted by persecution, and Robert Catesby might have lived comfortably at his beloved Chasleton.

When the Jesuits first came to England other priests regarded them with frank suspicion and unease. One who followed the route from Rome was Jasper Heywood, whose childhood had been privileged by the upper-class milieu in which he grew up. Before his time at Oxford his study group had included Princess Elizabeth – he was now a mature man, not a seminary juvenile. He disembarked with another Jesuit, William Holt, and Tynemouth in the summer of 1581, and travelled to a somewhat frosty meeting with Persons, then in hiding at the home of the Bellamy family, Uxendon Hall, Harrow.[8] Frictions developed between the aristocracy-leaning Heywood, whose journey south had been aided by Percy family adherents, and the disciplined, tough-minded yeoman's son. Heywood was in London at the time of Campion's capture, and very likely had his own first meeting with his nephew, John Donne, the future metaphysical poet and Anglican. Then it was north again, and in three months he reconciled 300 to Catholicism. This spiritual volatility was deeply shocking to the triumvirate guiding the Privy Council, as Burghley revealed in a pamphlet written after Campion's execution. Yet despite the morbid fear and apprehension of many, Heywood continued his mission by visits to Oxford and Cambridge, intending the universities to be conduits to the seminaries abroad. This surge of recruits happened, but after some months faltered. Heywood thought this was due to one of the Rouen pamphlets written by Persons and distributed in the two university towns; it enraged the Privy Council, which ordered heads of colleges to force the Oath of Supremacy from selected students, many of whom, being barely teenagers, gave in.

Heywood, as noted, entered England through the domain of the Earl of Northumberland, a man much put upon by a suspicious Privy Council. Disregarding a warning from Burghley, the Earl's son, Lord Henry Percy was allowed to meet secretly with Charles Paget, the brother of Lord Thomas Paget, exiled to France in 1581 and a staunch Marian. According to Northumberland his son was seeing Paget to absorb the arts of conversation and study – an attempt to cure his stutter? The Earl could have gone further and admitted that French officials were arranging for Henry Percy to meet Anjou and other courtiers, and if in a confessional mood he might even have declared his correspondence with Henri de Lorraine, Duke of Guise. No wonder the well-informed Elizabeth had Northumberland marked for her 'greatest enemy'. In exchanges between Persons and William Pullen, captain of Tynemouth Castle, the future arrest of the Earl was anticipated, and they thought to put a protective shield about one so vulnerable: the idea was to lever the Percy brothers out of Paris for Rome and an education by the Holy office.[9] By their slippery reasoning the Privy Council would be stymied, and to get the Earl's agreement Pullen returned to England. But the Earl now knew too that his son's meeting with Paget had been revealed to Sir Henry Cobham, the English ambassador in Paris, who had written of it immediately to Walsingham – the youth was consorting with a fugitive. Fear seized the exiles, and Paget even tried to bribe Walsingham, who on 4 May 1582 wrote coldly to spurn the offer because, of all the tough-minded men in Elizabeth's government, he was implacable: 'you love the Pope and I do not hate his person but his calling'.

We can be sure that a few of the men employed in lowly positions by Walsingham might well have been tempted by a bribe, but the cadre was as well paid and resourced as he could manage out of thin state funding, now beginning to grow, and his private income from offices, land investments and trade – most notably in Russia. When he got letters from minor operatives like Maliverny Catlin he tried to help by payment, but sometimes he would recommend someone for employment. So, for example, when the pro-English old soldier Masino del Bene retired to Germany after the Massacre of St Bartholomew's, with its anti-Italian undercurrent, Walsingham wrote to Leicester putting up del Bene for royal employment. Another favoured Italian with a sometimes bumpy career path was Tomasso di Vicenzo Sassetti, a

Florentine mercenary related to the Valori and Strozzi families. Formerly prominent and wealthy merchants, the Sassetti had fallen on hard times, and Tomasso became a wandering bravo. He was one of the comparatively small cluster of Italians based in London in the late 1560s, a mere eighty-four, with many of them court musicians. Sassetti was plucked from the gallows having been found guilty of murdering a yeoman called Richard Foden.[10] His saviour was Leicester, who gave him a pension of £50 to act as his body-guard after soldiering in Ireland.

From 1570 to *c.* 1585 Sassetti was used as a diplomatic courier and intelligencer by both Leicester and Walsingham. He made frequent trips to Paris, and new arrivals there might find him sliding onto a bench beside them as he called for a pot of wine, always a welcome gesture in this bruisingly expensive city. Herein he might learn anything – that Savoy was levying troops to mount an attack on Montferrat; that Spain in the Bay of Biscay was building fifty heavy ships. Or his assignment might be more personal as when in January 1573 he accepted a commission from Walsingham to find a postal messenger from among his Italian chums to serve under Leicester. Even so, Walsingham, who regarded Sassetti as very well informed on the politics of the Low Countries, did not choose to invest his complete trust in him.[11] Unlike his employer, Sassetti was not in Paris to hear or see the bloody tumult of the Massacre, for he was making the bone-jarring journey to Lyons in company with the wealthy and influential banker at the French court, Ludovico da Diaceto. Back in Paris on 9 September he worked frantically to prepare a narrative of the events, and within days had completed the *Brieve Raccontamento*, which fetched up in the papers of Giacomo Castelvetro, an immigrant to England in the 1570s who had dealings with John Wolfe, the London printer and promoter of foreign texts.[12]

During the winter of 1583/4 the invasion plan, which had briefly stirred so many, advanced not one jot. Privy Council surveillance of young fugitives and travellers had been pushed to the level where virtually any packet of letters meant for cross-Channel delivery was scrutinised. Even Nicholas Faunt, who had served Walsingham scrupulously, was nervous about this, and his letters to Anthony Bacon, who was still on his extended jaunt, became an index of unease. Faunt reasoned that Bacon, now in Lyons, now in Montpellier, could not venture into increasingly anti-English Italy, and he was disinclined to write of what he knew was going on in the highest echelons of power. But by hinting of these things invisible to Bacon he hoped to win his return, failing in this respect because Bacon was disinclined to travel north. This found itself an echo of Walsingham's own wish to stay put in London early in August 1583, when Elizabeth elected to send him to Scotland – a decision he hated as much as the country, especially when he feared the Queen and Principal Secretary might inadvertently wreck his clandestine efforts, notably in Paris, where the would-be invaders of England met in conference. Out of these deliberations came the decision that Guise would personally lead some 5,000 soldiers to land near Arundel in Sussex. The larger force of 20,000 Spanish troops would be directed to Lancashire to raise the recusant north of England, still smarting, it was believed, from the defeat of the northern earls.

Much would depend on the attitude of Northumberland, and Charles Paget risked a visit to Petworth to talk to him early in September. The project did not have unanimous support in Spain in the person of Philip, or in England, where Francis Throckmorton told Mendoza of his scepticism. By mid-October Walsingham was home, waiting for something heftier on Throckmorton whose brother Thomas had left the country with the aid of the Countess of Arundel. The Catholics who met at the Fleet Street house of Lord Paget were in a state of high anticipation. The ailing Walsingham waited. The pain of his kidney stone enforced the pause. Simultaneously Robert Persons and Dr Allen continued to seek advantage from contacts with Philip II, assuring him through ambassador Tassis that Englishmen wanted no other patron than he, and that some of the English ports should be directly in Spanish hands. Yet the invasion plan was becalmed; Walsingham had seen off all enemies so far, and information acquired late in 1583 moved the Privy Council to take action against the plotting of Northumberland. Round-the-clock surveillance of the French and Spanish embassies led to the arrest at his house at Paul's Wharf, on the night of 5 or 6 November 1583, of one of Mendoza's London contacts, Francis Throckmorton, letter-bearer for Mary Stuart – as 'Henry Fagot', Walsingham's spy in the French embassy, had already indicated. Fagot also emptied his quiver of barbed arrows into Lord Henry Howard, the slippery courtier whom Elizabeth would favour from time to time. As for Henry's nephew, Philip Howard, Earl of Arundel, the spy alleged that he was dealing with Catholic exiles and giving sanctuary to the head of the Jesuit mission, Jasper Heywood.

Early in December 1583 Heywood made his way to Rye to cross the Channel under orders from his superiors.[13] Just as the boat was bobbing into Dieppe, the sails were suddenly filled by an errant gale that flung the vessel at last back on the English coast, looking at Queensborough on the Isle of Sheppey. Alert port officers arrested Heywood and sent him to the Privy Council for questioning. From what they knew already, it was likely that his attempted exit was linked broadly to others of the *impresa*. He was interrogated, but gave up only what Mendoza had said about Philip II and the Pope dividing the costs, before going to the Clink. This was a less harsh environment than some, and one of the great men of the Privy Council surprisingly took an interest in Heywood's welfare: Leicester's brother, Ambrose, Earl of Warwick, an altogether less flamboyant character than Robert Dudley. Heywood was frequently questioned, but revealed little and said nothing about Northumberland, whom the Council wanted to shunt back into the Tower. He was, of course, already familiar with it, since for his involvement in the Ridolfi plot he had already spent almost two years confined there, before paying a fine of 5,000 marks (£3,333.33) and gaining his freedom in May 1573. Arrested again in mid-December 1583 he was by January in the Bloody Tower, before dying mysteriously in June 1585.

Chapter 10

'MURDERS MOST HORRIBLE'

The predicament of Jasper Heywood worsened some weeks later when he was indicted for treason. The following day, when he was present in court with fourteen similarly accused priests, he was bustled out to be confined in the Gatehouse. There the attempts to squeeze information from him continued with threats and then blandishments. When he turned down the offer of a bishopric, he went back to the Tower close in proximity to Lord Henry Howard and the Earl of Northumberland. Walsingham evidently suspected that Heywood knew more of the invasion plot, and he was shown the Tower rack before a barrage of questions from Thomas Norton. Lawyer, MP and remembrancer to the Lord Mayor of London, he was a highly placed clerk and secretary who became an intermediary between the City and the Privy Council. Walsingham and Hatton each drew him into their circle, and he had a status separate from his public employment.[1] Norton had spoken and materially assisted Mildmay against recusants in the passage of the anti-recusant and sedition acts. Along with his other work it is no surprise that he alienated the Queen, although in February 1584, a few weeks before his death, she acknowledged his worth with personal thanks. Before his demise Norton had charge of the Tower rack, and Heywood resigned himself to being a candidate for 'immoderate stretching'. By March he had been tortured but he remained compellingly silent, and on trial in May at Westminster for some reason no judgement was ever delivered. The trial began and ended *sine die*. In a legal limbo, he went back to the Tower and the expectation of a future execution.

Despite the vigilance of Walsingham and his cadre against all the ongoing asymmetrical efforts directed against Elizabeth and England, he could not seal off the country from continental Catholicism. Show trials and public executions did not defeat the spirit of resistance, the zealots aflame for martyrdom provided by an obliging government, but now increasingly minded to try a new tactic put up by Burghley. He wanted summary deportations of priests and new laws to make it illegal for them ever to return. Even in the Tower Heywood had sought outside help to resist this, and Lord William Vaux headed those who prepared a petition to Elizabeth appealing for toleration. Persons had already sent William Weston over to replace the incarcerated Heywood, and he wanted to meet his predecessor face to face, because as Persons reviewed it the petition might compromise the whole political design of the mission. Weston was a memoirist who wrote years later, but the visit to the Tower, in a bogus family group that was actually partly made up by Heywood's sister and his nephew, took place at Christmas 1584.

Another Jesuit who saw all boundaries as porous was Henri Samier (variously de Samerie, de Samrez, Samerius), who thought nothing of crossing the Channel to visit Mary Stuart in the guise of a physician; Elizabeth had banned her from having a priest. Sometimes the physician was Monsieur la Rue, and at other times he was the fast-moving Hieronymo Martelli. In the summer of 1584 he visited Mary, saw Mauvissière in London on her behalf, and then returned to Paris, from whence he wrote the uplifting sentence: 'The affairs of your majesty are the affairs of God.'[2] Being a majestic solipsist, albeit one in despair, she probably read this again and again, each time through tears of self-pity.

It had been a year for the lachrymose even before this. Early in June the Duke of Anjou died at Château-Thierry, north-east of Paris, of a tubercular condition probably dating from childhood. Any tears shed were surely of relief. Whereas in July, when William of Orange was shot down in Delft by an assassin, any tears were surely for the victim, and the tragic sense that this could have been Elizabeth. If it had been, how would Burghley and Walsingham have dealt with the Stuart line? Could there have been a timely assassination of Mary to open the way for James – young, single, male, Protestant and free to claim the English throne, so vastly more desirable than the Scottish? Fortunately for Walsingham, those English Catholics who plotted Elizabeth's murder only once found the moment when it was indeed possible – and the would-be killer lost his nerve under the Queen's atramentous scrutiny. To reduce the possibility of such a moment, Walsingham and Burghley were driven to invent a mechanism intended to deal with her extreme injury or death when the law would be suspended, a national device called the Bond of Association. This was a pledge of allegiance to Elizabeth, and a threat to the succession of anyone on whose behalf an act of harm to her might be carried out – whether unsuccessful or successful. It threatened retribution on Mary and even her son; it was a covenant of the Protestants and also 'a quasi-republican statement'.[3]

As news of the murder of Prince William reached a horrified and shocked London, Francis Throckmorton was dragged to Tyburn and executed on 10 July 1584. To drive their point home, the government published a pamphlet about the dead's manipulation of the truth, a post-mortem rebuttal of his open court testimony that what he had said under torture was *not* true. Both Protestants and Catholics in London were deeply afraid of the future – the former for their Queen, while the latter were haunted by the notion of thunderous knocking at their door by Walsingham's subordinates. The city was swarming to the darkest corners with informers who saw menace and possible profit in the simplest things. The exiled Catholics in Paris were much better placed to produce texts to counter government propaganda, men like the former courtiers Charles Arundell and Thomas Throckmorton, whose sister Muriel married Sir Thomas Tresham, and whose sister Anne married Sir William Catesby and gave birth to the gunpowder conspirator-in-chief, Robert Catesby. With some input from other exiles and a little editorial assistance from Persons, they produced a richly detailed, insolent satire on the life and times of Leicester who, since his marriage to the former Countess of Essex had blighted his court career, had been struggling to restore it. Now, all the pain and distress he had caused Catholics over some twenty-five years was regurgitated by them in a mocking, even lewd satire, *The Copie of a Leter, wryten by a Master of Arte of Cambridge*, which quickly became *Leicester's Commonwealth*, the implication being that he had supplanted the Queen. The book artfully speaks well of her, Burghley and Walsingham, an aspect of concentrating their broadside that must have had the authors collectively grinding their teeth.

The first indication of the existence of this scurrilous book came in August 1584 from Sir Edward Stafford, the somewhat wayward ambassador who had casually rejected Walsingham's good offices and settled solely for the approval of Burghley. It was the Lord Treasurer who secured him the rather rare knighthood just before Stafford went over, but the brusque turning aside from Walsingham, who had come to regard ambassadors as subordinates to him, was not at all diplomatic. Not only were ambassadors under his patronage, but also their staff might be picked out by him, so that embassy reporting was multi-voiced.[4] A laconic ambassador might cause grumbles in London, but Stafford was loquacious beyond all merit in letters, and Walsingham tried to reduce their bulk as Elizabeth complained about letter postal costs. Barely six months after his arrival in France, Stafford's private correspondence was breached and read, when Walsingham's searchers in Rye seized a packet of letters and opened them all.[5] The post of searcher, as Michael Questier has pointed out, was important for the gathering of intelligence. So, for example, Anthony Atkinson operating in Hull from 1587, reported on Catholics as much as customs fraud, since priests travelling from the Low Countries arrived on the east coast, especially at Hull and Newcastle. A friend of Atkinson, Henry Sanderson, did much the same work in Newcastle, and both men had friendly dealings with Richard Topcliffe, the admiralty court judge who travelled north frequently on Crown business. For the driven, brutal Topcliffe, 'the influx of seminarists into the North was simply a continuation of the northern rising by other means'.

To soothe Stafford's indignation about the interference with his mail – the rape of the letters – Walsingham drolly suggested the ambassador should direct all his private mail to him, and he would oversee all post to Stafford. This helpful notion Stafford managed to swerve around by an appeal to Burghley's good instincts, but Walsingham still held the cost-cutting line, which Stafford thought niggardly since the packets were most often given to Walsingham's messengers like John de Critz. Stafford was also ruffled by the activities of Henry Unton, relative of Leicester, the hated former partner (if not actual husband) of Stafford's wife, Lady Douglas, and associate of the Principal Secretary.

With hundreds of copies of *Leicester's Commonwealth* coming off the presses, Persons was keen for the Jesuit brother Ralph Emerson, who had worked with Campion, to start using the smuggling routes he had recently set up for both priests and prose. On his next assignment Emerson did porter over a consignment of *Commonwealths*, but in London a suspicious landlord of an inn got him arrested. After questioning he was placed in the Counter in Poultry Street, and seeing the potential for harm of the whole text the government began to probe for its provenance. The Lord Mayor sent a copy to Walsingham, who immediately assigned it to Thomas Morgan as the anonymous author. He in turn sent it on to Leicester, who was angry beyond all measure. As his messenger to Stafford the earl picked out Richard Hakluyt, the embassy chaplain, who was to demand that the ambassador should trace the line of production. Hakluyt's principal preoccupation was stacking up information about overseas trade, but the book trade was beyond his remit. Nor was Stafford interested in following up the little domestic flap (as he saw it), since it trashed the reputation of a man he loathed, and he reported late in October that it had likely been printed in England – not Paris or Rouen. He did make the not altogether stupid recommendation that the business be shunted aside – but he had not been libelled and lampooned. The bright hostility of the book found it many cheerful subscribers, and even a proclamation from Elizabeth failed to prevent its secret distribution. A rumour in Paris had Leicester hiring an assassin to seek out and murder Arundell. Paranoid nonsense? Perhaps, but it did chime neatly with the contents of the libel. And then just to pinch Leicester's self-esteem one more time, Stafford reported in March 1585 to Walsingham, a French translation with an especially odious additional charge.

Not a few members of the Privy Council disliked the Earl with all the warmth mustered by the exiles, but any hint of glee at his embarrassment was not enough to split their unity. There was relief for him in this, but his anger was not dissipated at a time when the larger political milieu commanded attention and the push-and-pull policy against Spain and France was evidently decaying. Following the murder of Prince William, the resistance in the Low Countries began to falter, while in France, risen again in a new form, the League, once a mechanism for resisting heresy, was now aiming to exclude Henri of Navarre from succeeding Henri III, and was likely therefore to re-ignite civil war.

The seventh war of religion that had begun and ended in 1580 was fought mostly in southern France, where the Huguenot forces were massed. For Paris this was a time of relative calm, as institutions crucial to both religious renewal and the fierce Catholicism of the League emerged in the city. The League of 1585–94 (often called the Holy League or *La Sainte Union*) was unified in its desire to restore Catholicism in the whole of France and wipe out heresy. On 31 December 1584 the Guisards met representatives of Spain at Joinville, where they and a good many Jesuits agreed to support Charles de Bourbon after the death of Henri III. To fund this effort they got an agreement for Spanish subsidies, and what this signalled was the decline of France as a power counter-balance to Spain – confirmed for many in May 1585 when Philip II ordered the seizure of all English ships in Spanish ports. If the Guisards prevailed France itself – or at the very least those parts closest to England – could fall to Philip. A Spanish victory in the Netherlands could not then be far off, so that England would be isolated and virtually helpless before the towering strength of its greatest enemy.

It was a prospect to make all but the most optimistic buckle, yet they did not do so, even when the Parry plot came along to add a further layer of gloom. This chimed with Walsingham's increasing alarm at the scope of Mary's correspondence and the desire to hem her in by stricter guardianship under Sir Ralph Sadler and Sir Henry Neville. The anti-recusancy legislation of 1581 was practically inoperative, and Walsingham complained bitterly of the corruption of the court as a cause of recusancy growth.[6] This was a veiled rebuke for the studied indifference of Elizabeth who, as Leicester noted, was 'slow to believe that the great increase of Papists is of danger to the realm'. It may too have been a poke at Burghley, protector of Stafford in Paris, and William Parry, former lawyer, debtor, traveller and intelligencer.[7] Obscurely related to Burghley, and possibly to the other Parrys about Elizabeth – Dr Henry Parry, a chaplain; Blanche Parry, her confidante – William Parry (also called Dr Parry, again mysteriously) took a seat in the House of Commons in 1584, and not only began distributing seditious books but also used his place to harangue anyone willing to listen on the circumstances of English Catholicism. His vehemence got him locked up by the sergeant-at-arms, but released within twenty-four hours by Elizabeth. Such an unguarded mind and mouth may have been exploited by her as Parry wrestled with his debts and devised a double-dealing remedy for himself and his fellow Catholics. He put it to the young Catholic gentleman Edmund Neville, already under suspicion of treason, that they should assassinate Elizabeth.

Neville might have been the choicest assassin so far. Leaving England in 1575 to serve in the Spanish armies in the Low Countries, he missed his father becoming at an advanced age Baron Latimer.[8] There was a family fortune that the government hoped would lure Neville back, and maybe this too caught the glittering eye of Parry. Under pressure Neville consulted other exiles, including his kinsman Westmoreland, before deciding to return to England – an upset for the Spanish, who nullified his commission and pension. No sooner had he returned than Neville found he had still powerful enemies on the Privy Council, and the promised advance to title and wealth was stalled. How he fell in with Parry is not clear, but the approach came from the convert to Rome who had taken a vow while in the city to kill Elizabeth – the site for this was to be the Palace Gardens, Westminster at a date unknown. Although he let on to a courtier that a plot was going forward that he greatly misliked, Neville was arrested along with Parry, and both went to the Tower. Walsingham strode from Seething Lane to do the interrogation of Parry, who hastily assigned the whole plot to Thomas Morgan. After confessing under torture, Parry was convicted on 15 February and executed on 2 March 1585, thus becoming the first victim of the Bond of Association. Neville's future was undecided and he was tested with an offer of service under Drake, which he turned down – boldly but unpardonably – because it meant attacking his former lord, Philip II. Within a short time he was back in the Tower for having plotted to deliver Flushing to Parma just when it was about to become the redoubt of Sir Philip Sidney – new son-in-law of Walsingham. He remained a prisoner for the next thirteen years, and for the rest of his life Neville was deprived of his title and inheritance, even after his father died in 1590.

Neville would not have seen Jasper Heywood in the Tower, but he might have been momentarily elated when the Jesuit and twenty other priests were forcibly embarked on a ship bound for France in January 1585. The day before this export of papist prayer and piety, Henry Stanley, 4th Earl of Derby was sent as ambassador extraordinary to Henri III to invest the King with the Order of the Garter. His suite was sizeable, some forty-five, including a boy called John Donne, the nephew of Heywood, for whom Oxford study had ended prematurely. Stafford greeted the posse, and on 23 February they entered Paris to be welcomed by *le beau monde* before retiring to the Hotel de Longueville. Five days later Henri took the Garter oath, and afterwards Vespers was sung in the neighbouring church of Augustin Friars, so that the English did not walk out of a mass. Heywood's reception by Mendoza, now ambassador to France having been forced out of England the previous year, was effusive, and simultaneously about Derby there were many who wanted a secret meeting with Thomas Morgan, who in correspondence to Mary noted Stafford's apparent eagerness to help her cause.[9] Stafford may have made this slide in her direction out of conviction that truly Mary was the legitimate heir to the throne, or because he had some inkling that Burghley favoured her and this might allow him to trump Walsingham. Not that Elizabeth was thrilled, for all his claim that it got him close to those with treacherous intent; he was ordered to stop. Meanwhile the Privy Council had noted Derby's liberality in organizing his embassy so that many anti-Elizabethans had been able to withdraw. Among those who sought out Derby in Paris was his long exiled sister – Lady Morley. Walsingham no doubt stored away the knowledge that among them too was a Burghley nephew, Anthony Cooke, fleeing his creditors. Cooke, with William Stanley, second son of Derby, and others, had earlier been travelling in Europe under the supervision of Richard Lloyd, acting as eyes and ears for Walsingham, and he was in Paris with the Derby embassy until he returned to England to serve with Leicester. He became a secretary and went with him to the Netherlands late in 1585.

The question of an armed intervention in the Netherlands after the August 1585 fall of Antwerp to Parma's siege train led to heated and ill-tempered exchanges among the Privy Councillors, among whom Leicester and Walsingham were feeling particularly bruised, for it was Philip Marnix St Aldegonde, former adviser to Prince William and governor of the city, who signed a treaty allowing for payment of a fine of 400,000 guilders. For their part, the Spanish released all prisoners and granted a general amnesty. The wrangling continued unchecked when the Dutch delegation arrived. As Paulus Buys who had resigned as Advocate of Holland in October 1584 observed, it was Burghley representing the Queen who controlled the purse strings, while Leicester and Walsingham, being strongly pro-Dutch, had to be cultivated, so the wily Dutch envoy gave a dinner for the Earl during which the broad outlines of Anglo-Dutch cooperation were set out. Early in August 1585 the main Treaty of Nonsuch was signed with a later ampliation pact. Although Leicester's name did not appear in the treaty designated as governor-general of the United Provinces, few can have doubted the place would be his. He seems to have assumed this too, for he quit the palace in Surrey the next day for his annual holiday at Kenilworth. And Walsingham was going to join him, but called it off because of atrocious weather. This may have been convenient, since to be so much in Leicester's company while he rambled on in rage at the great libel must have been a strain that Walsingham could do without.

In his view its European circulation made it a component of the endless international Catholic conspiracy. For others it was a squib, and the exiles who had compiled it with such evident relish were actually less dangerous than one man – Thomas Morgan.[10] He had met with one of Sir Edward Stafford's personal servants, William Lyly, in the autumn of 1583; now, two years on, Walsingham had Lyly detained, on the grounds that he had read *Leicester's Commonwealth*, a 'Marian' tract read by a Marian pensioner. It was an error of judgement by Lyly that got him sent for examination to the Earl himself in the United Provinces. Leicester sent him back to England for further questioning by a committee for the Privy Council. They had likely been briefed by Walsingham, but Lyly nimbly avoided any traps and disguised the full extent of his dealings with the engaged exiles. The net result was that lack of evidence prevented any case being brought against him, and as Stafford went on moaning about Lyly's absence Walsingham reluctantly allowed him to return to Paris in January 1586.

The two men were at odds for years – Walsingham the master of diplomacy, Stafford a wriggling, defiant junior quite unlike the men who after 1573 succeeded Walsingham in the embassy, and were close allies of Leicester. Stafford's efforts to expand his own remit – for example, the connection he made with Charles Arundell – could have been the signal for Walsingham's shift from seeking to control Stafford to an attempt to wreck his career, because, as has been shown, Arundell was a key figure in exiled circles in Paris, a city pullulating with spies and counterspies.[11] To some in London Arundell was equalled in importance by Thomas Morgan, whom Henri III had locked up in the Bastille at the urgent request of Elizabeth. Yet neither Morgan there nor the Earl of Northumberland in the Tower had been sealed away, and both bought access to the greater world. The Queen wanted Morgan on English soil for questioning in a room close to Northumberland, so she sent over William Waad, one of Walsingham's close associates, to get him. To his chagrin Waad failed.

Meanwhile Hatton reopened the interrogation of the Earl: Northumberland's warders were changed and replaced by a servant of Hatton, Thomas Bailiffe, who within a few hours had to report the death of the Earl by shooting. The surgeon who did the autopsy, supervised by Lord Hunsdon, retrieved three musket balls from the wound. Suicide, said the government, of a man tainted with suspicions of treason. Bailiffe gave no evidence to the enquiry held in Star Chamber; instead Hatton heaped opprobrium on the stubborn, alienated Earl. The Percy family had been tragically unlucky over a half century: Sir Thomas Percy was executed for his part in the Pilgrimage of Grace; the 7th Earl, also Thomas, was executed after taking a leading role in the Northern revolt of 1569; and now Henry was dead in bizarre circumstances that strongly suggested a government murder. The new Earl of Northumberland was Lord Henry Percy who, as we noted, had become linked while travelling in Europe with Catholic exiles; on returning to England to take up his grand inheritance, the Lord Henry became a marked man who already had the attention of Walsingham. Being by some calculations seventh in line to the throne also gave him a sparkle with Catholics.

Chapter 11

REELING IN SCOTLAND

Whatever the dangers and difficulties tumbling out of Europe to threaten England in the period after the Massacre of St Bartholomew's, the general expectation in government circles in London was that the ecstatic Guises had won supremacy in France, and would act energetically in Scotland on behalf of Queen Mary Stuart. It was Walsingham's friend Henry Killigrew whom Elizabeth sent as an envoy to Scotland, bidding the Scots who had driven the Stuart out to be on their guard, while in private it was hoped to deliver her back into the hands of the Regent and others for prompt execution, but in such a manner that no blame attached to Elizabeth. Not very surprising that the King's party baulked at this, making stiff conditions, and before adjustments could be negotiated the Regent died, so for the time being the project was abandoned. Certainly dynastic and geo-political considerations gave Scotland real significance in the eyes of Walsingham and some of his contemporaries. He wanted peace there because, as he expounded at length to Leicester: 'If that footing place were taken away from our foreign enemies, our danger would be the less.'[1] Walsingham's fear of French intervention in Scotland became so acute that bribing the Scots seemed too slow, and he urged that they be coerced. As he had previously noted in the Leicester letter: 'Violent diseases must have violent remedies . . .', and so it proved in May 1573, when Edinburgh Castle fell to English forces, effectively ending Elizabeth's long struggle, open and covert, against Mary Stuart in Scotland, which had been underway for thirteen years. For the five years after the taking of the Castle Anglo-Scottish relations were strikingly mild; Regent Morton worked hard to stabilise the country and the economy, and in great measure succeeded to the surprise of many.

This period of retrenchment began to slip away when Morton was forced from office, only to force his way back, and by the autumn of 1579 the false sense of security that had overcome Elizabeth as she picked up the threads of the Anjou marriage was dissipated by a glamorous Frenchman arriving not in England but

Scotland. It was Esmé Stuart, Seigneur d'Aubigny, who had been escorted to his ship at Dieppe by the Duke of Guise. D'Aubigny was nearly forty, educated, cultivated and *un bel homme* whom Mary, Queen of Scots, being herself a schemer and so able to recognise one, distrusted very promptly, although later it was d'Aubigny (then Earl of Lennox) who got James writing again to his mother. As early as 1580 Robert Bowes, the English ambassador to Scotland, received instructions to begin a counter-offensive against Lennox, whose career curve even unnerved Beza in Geneva – enough to warrant sending a spy-musician to serve at the Scottish court. Bowes was supposed to warn the young king of the Frenchman's ambition usurping his gratifying affection, but James had no inclination to listen to such sententiousness. Sir Henry Widdrington wrote to Walsingham that the lad could hardly bear to be apart from Lennox; 'often he will clasp him about the neck with his arms and kiss him'. Bowes concluded that Elizabeth had to be more generous, and no one argued that case more strenuously than Walsingham, who found her loss of focus on Scotland very troubling. The drift away from Morton eventually left him exposed to his enemies, and on 31 December 1580 he was imprisoned in Edinburgh castle. D'Aubigny had planned this, and James Stewart (later Earl of Arran) acted for him. In June Morton was brought to trial, and his sentence of death was just what everyone expected. Anglo-Scottish relations were almost completely severed for a year, until May 1582 when decayed rumours came strangely back to life.

One was that James was going to be kidnapped and shipped to France, where according to a shocking scenario of Walsingham's he might be married off like his mother. It would have been a stunning blow, making void all that had gone before in twenty years, and the English party in Scotland wanted urgent countervailing activity by Elizabeth to secure a marriage with a Danish princess; Frederick II of Denmark had two daughters of approximately the right age. As for James, he could not afford to make a marriage that would alienate Elizabeth; it might be dynastically necessary, but it was not urgent. For certain Scottish lords – in particular Gowrie, Mar and Lindsay – yanking James away from Lennox and Arran in the Ruthven raid was the key; he was a captive for ten months. This enforced separation actually had the desired effect: Lennox failed to rescue the adoring youth, whose ardour now cooled. According to Mendoza (then in London) the conspirators were heavily outnumbered by their enemies, who held off for fear that the Ruthven raiders might actually kill James. Henri III decided to send an ambassador envoy to Scotland, and by the time La Mothe Fénélon reached there Lennox had himself quit the country late in December. Within five months he was dead. With his inventive mind engaged by the arrival of Fénélon Walsingham did mull over the notion that the envoy was there to arrange a marriage between James and a princess of Lorraine. Mary now hoped (absurdly) that James would marry a Spanish infanta; the Spanish ambassador Mendoza picked up a rumour that Walsingham and Leicester had said to James that if he married Dorothy Devereux, sister of the Earl of Essex and Leicester's step-daughter, assuring them that he would not change his religion, they would get a declaration in English law that he was to succeed Elizabeth. There were other, crazier marriage fantasies, but when Elizabeth herself heard this last she hurled insults like cannonballs at Dorothy's mother, Lettice Knollys, formerly Countess of Essex and now Leicester's wife. The likelihood of Walsingham being involved seems remote given his discretion and his sweeping grasp of the possible; probably Fénélon retiring to France floated the story to embarrass Leicester.

Useful to be reminded here of one marriage that Walsingham did grow into favouring – that of his daughter, the attractively vivacious and dark-haired Frances courted by Sir Philip Sidney. The two men, though separated by age, got on strikingly well, and there was no barrier to the union save Sidney's continual shortage of money, amounting to poverty. He had been appointed royal cupbearer around 1576, and the annual fee payable within the Queen's Chamber of £30 probably stems from this office. But he still had tax debts, according to the collector of the 1576 subsidy, Nicholas Rutland, and though Sidney contested this, the Exchequer did not accept his argumentative stance against payment. However, since the granting of his American patent in 1582 he had something of value to put up for bidding, and now he was as keen to sell as Walsingham was to assist. A year on – in July 1583 – Sir George Peckham became the purchaser, with grand plans for a Catholic emigration scheme, and Sidney was liberated from his financial shackles for a wedding in September. By then the loving father of the bride was in Scotland, a situation he had resisted with every ounce of his strength, given the state of Scottish politics, where the pro-English clique was dismissed from the court.

Elizabeth as usual walked on her own dainty heels. Despite the advice of intelligencers and Privy Councillors that she grant pensions to James and his captors, thus yoking them to England, she sat on her purse and made some pointless overtures to Mary which Walsingham at least initially regarded as hopelessly unsatisfactory. Even the visits of two separate French envoys, Fénélon and Mainville, did not alter Elizabeth's stance, though it was very likely the latter,

Mainville, who laid the foundations of a court revolution; the King, with the aid of the Earl of March and the Archbishop of St Andrews, escaped from the clutches of his Ruthven trap-setters. He was joined by James Stewart, Earl of Arran, close associate of Lennox, and before the end of August Arran was in a prime position. Walsingham was quite unambiguous when writing to ambassador Robert Bowes that every effort should be made to diminish the power of Arran, just so long as nothing wayward could be assigned to Elizabeth: do 'not omit any occasion that might tend to the abatement of his credit . . .'.[2] She was considering sending an envoy, a Privy Councillor as Walsingham thought, who admitted in a late July letter to Bowes that his own name had been pitched in with Hunsdon, Hatton, Edward Wotton and even Philip Sidney. In a brief pause for reflection Elizabeth did finally decide to send Walsingham, who let out a mighty yelp of resistance; Mendoza may only have exaggerated a little when he claimed that the Principal Secretary refused to go to Scotland even on pain of death. Walsingham anticipated a horrible journey in a coach put at his disposal because of his poor health, and at the end nothing to show for all the effort. He left for Scotland on 17 August with a large train of some eighty people; one wonders who had the pleasure of riding in the coach with him until Newcastle was reached on 26 August – nine days of road bumps and colic. Was Marlowe – on university vacation – in the entourage? Walsingham was certainly accompanied by Arthur Throckmorton, travelling via Huntingdon and Apethorpe, home of his sister and brother-in-law.

Two days later the envoy and his entourage arrived in Berwick-upon-Tweed. Through Robert Bowes he received the King's safe-conduct, and luckily took the trouble to read it. Was it a joke or a crafty insult? It restricted the party accompanying him to sixty, and it was extended to him as long as he (and they) behaved properly. The Principal Secretary returned the document to Bowes and told him to get it revised, or find out what was meant by the bizarre contents. In a letter to Robert Beale, who was doing his job in London as stand-in, Walsingham explained that the King was so surrounded by England's enemies that a safe-conduct seemed essential. Such a thing might restrain them in a country where all forms of justice had been 'quite banished'.[3] Bowes went at once to James, who blamed 'the oversight of the clerk', and with the new passport Walsingham went forward into the detested country where both his escort leaders were supporters of Mary. James chose not to see him immediately on request, so Walsingham began information-gathering for himself and concluded that Arran and Colonel Stewart were the progenitors of the current situation; James was unpopular with his nobility, and the whole slant of the government was progressively anti-English. As for the government, it was a feeble, lack-lustre thing of very little account, likely to fall soon. By being brusque with them he could do best for Elizabeth, and at Edinburgh he ignored the muted attentions of Arran and Stewart. His oral comment to his letter-carrier to Elizabeth was that Bowes should be recalled, the borders strengthened and Mary watched hawkishly.

On 6 September James Melville, acting for James, arrived to greet Walsingham and to apologise for the delay in meeting him – it was a meeting of friends, for Melville had often been a guest at the Secretary's home during a period of exile. Now they travelled together north to Perth for the meeting with the King on 9 September. Walsingham and Bowes were received in tandem, and James was soon red-eared at their list of his failings and errors. He tried to defend himself by huffing about being an absolute monarch, at which they scoffed and added that if he did not listen to Elizabeth she would leave him to his own devices. The interview ended with Walsingham making plain English contempt for Scotland, saying that incursions across the border must cease or be punished. It seems clear that James felt humiliated, and the following day appointed four of his councillors to meet again with Walsingham, but he declined to have any dealings with them. Arran and Stewart sought an exchange and again he refused a meeting, saying his remit allowed him only to deal with James. And for his own part he was a fastidious diplomat, whose lofty tone must have maddened the Scots. Nor was he sure he would escape censure, so he tried to ensure Burghley would provide 'friendly and careful defence'. Arran seems to have squashed his own rage at this high-handed treatment, but he did contrive to snap at the mighty Secretary's heels by barring many Englishmen from the King's chamber and by hiring Kate the witch, a common scold paid six pounds and some material to sit outside the palace screeching insults at Walsingham and his gentlemen; very likely he found her utterly incomprehensible, worse than the King. Arran's final revenge was to seize a royal diamond ring presented to Walsingham as he departed, only passing it on when the diamond had been forced from its setting and a rock crystal put in its place.[4]

The second interview of Walsingham with James took place two days after the first, and seems to have been a tutorial for the King in statecraft, with some of its political theorizing on loan from Plessis-Mornay's *Vindiciae Contra Tyrannos*.

When James spoke after the stream of exposition (how much did he understand when it was delivered in an unfamiliar southern English accent?)

he declared as usual his intention to follow Elizabeth's prescriptions. The other declarations were noted by Walsingham, who sent a copy of his notes to the King for confirmation. When they came back from James they had been meddled with by Arran, and Walsingham wrote a note to James declaring how unsatisfactory these official offers would now be to Elizabeth and the future of Scotland. He left for Berwick after the rapid putting together of a little stratagem as his parting gift, that would in theory leave James 'bridled and forced, whether he will or not, to depend upon your Majesty's favour and goodness'. Nothing came of it because Elizabeth would not support it. The reason? She was taken with the idea that Arran himself could be sucked into the English affinity, very likely a notion put up by Lord Hunsdon. Walsingham's opposition to this was unyielding because he thought Arran a slippery knave, and that his wife, even more greedy, was trying to ingratiate herself with Mary. Hunsdon was also thinking of the marriage of James to either his niece or his daughter. Both sides in England became more than a little irritated with the other.

From June to September 1584 William Davison was temporary ambassador to Scotland, and like so many of England's representatives he was deeply prejudiced against Arran, who was anti-Presbyterian, but not a Catholic. Elizabeth took an altogether less censorious line, promising he should 'taste of the fruits of her favour'.[5] Arran had come through an effort in late April to oust him, having had weeks to prepare for the poorly kept secret effort of Mar, Angus and Gowrie, which John Colville told Walsingham might well succeed. Not in Elizabeth's view, for she refused to aid the conspirators.

We can be sure that Walsingham hoped it would, and perhaps did something to assist, yet Gowrie was seized at Dundee and the others scrambled into Stirling castle, where James put his courage to the sticking-point and prized them out for execution or diaspora across the border into England. This collapse of treason dealt a heavy blow to the intelligence sources constantly sought out hitherto by Bowes, who panicked about the disgrace about to tumble on him and Walsingham. Arran had triumphed; Hunsdon thought his policy of cozying up to him vindicated; Walsingham was temporarily bruised and buffeted; Elizabeth did nothing much for the exiles. Her advances to Mary for a plan of action contemplated the previous autumn found the Scottish queen in a stubborn, resistant mood, and Walsingham wrote to Davison that she was 'refusing to mediate the restitution of the distressed noblemen (Angus, Mar and Glamis) unless Her

Majesty will grant her liberty'. But by June, when Arran became Chancellor of Scotland and Hunsdon was appointed to deal directly with him, Mary had modified her position, and Walsingham then wrote to Davison, now in Scotland to stir up trouble, that she might employ her credit for the relief of Angus, Mar and Glamis. He was also mistakenly of the opinion that at this time Mary could command her son; but then Bowes thought this too, and he was better informed on Scottish affairs than virtually any other Englishman.

Hunsdon did eventually meet Arran in mid-August, and the latter set about making the King's case against his disruptive courtiers. He asked too for a passport for Patrick, Master of Gray, who would acquaint Elizabeth with the full measure of James's thinking. Walsingham allowed this, although his letter to Hunsdon regarding Arran is stiff and unforgiving. With Davison called home late in August, the next arrival in England would be Gray, but weeks passed and Hunsdon's reminder to Arran in mid-September that Gray was now expected did not secure his presence. Another month, another brisk reminder and Gray got moving, meeting Hunsdon first at Berwick where they attended church together and sang the psalms. According to a satisfied Hunsdon, James was explicit that Walsingham should be chopped from the loop: 'I know him to be my great enemy.'[6] Davison was deeply distrustful of Gray, as were others writing from the borders and France, and this may have suggested to an alert Walsingham that the new man was for 'turning'. Gray wanted power and influence, and Arran was marked for ejection; moreover, Gray was immune to the famous charm of Mary, whose secretary, Claude Nau, was to be received at court in London in order to speak for her release from custody. She had confidently expected Nau and Gray to work together, but had her hopes dashed by the handsome, lordly Scot, who was taken up by the Leicester grouping in London. Even when he proved less loquacious on state matters, like the plotting of the Guises in Scotland, than had been hoped, it scarcely mattered for a providential gust of wind had saved the captured Father Creighton's papers for perusal during a Channel crossing. Besides, Gray seemed promising and the demand from the King that Mar *et al.* should be removed from the border was agreed; to separate them from their followers Oxford was designated as their retreat, which occasioned an amused sneer from Gray about them being back in school. They complained, so Elizabeth allowed a few hundred pounds to relieve their expenses.

As for Mary, she was effectively shunted aside by Gray. To Elizabeth came the realization that her hopes and fears of Mary's supposed power in Scotland were equally worthless. There followed a stagnant period in Anglo-Scottish relations, with diplomats and intelligencers finding nothing but surface froth. The attention of Privy Councillors was re-engaged by tangential events in France, where the Guisards now headed the Holy League and re-ignited the war in March 1585 with the seizure of Châlons. Grabbing the league idea, Elizabeth hoped cooperation with Gray could ruin Arran, and her envoy to Scotland in May 1585 was a cousin of Walsingham, Edward Wotton (b. 1548), who reached Edinburgh at the end of the month. Arthur Throckmorton had approached his friend and patron Walsingham for a place in this embassy too, but cousin Francis Throckmorton's execution for treason made this impossible. Part of his task was to deliver a gift of some fine horses to the hunter King, and to fund him with £4,000 *pourboire*, although Walsingham warned it was not enough. He also warned against Wotton getting too close to conspirators hoping by violence to bring down Arran. After a conference with Leicester he wrote that 'we cannot think that God will prosper any such bloody attempts, whereunto that nation is overmuch bent'. Wotton, too, was in favour of any possible moderate course, and thought the putting aside of Arran had better be left until after he, Wotton, had left Scotland. By early July he had put the Queen's league proposals to James, who approved, but as ever wanted supplementaries, such as being made Duke of Cornwall, and an agreement that Elizabeth would do nothing to exclude him from claiming her throne. Without hesitation Walsingham buried these notions, and suggested Wotton should discourage them.

In an update to Wotton on what was obsessing London, Walsingham had to admit it was not Scotland: 'the cause of the Low Countries at this time wholly entertains them' – mainly because Leicester's leadership of forces to aid the Dutch had not been settled. Elizabeth had no time to give over to Scottish matters, and then suddenly the opportunity to remove Arran dropped into her bejewelled lap. In late July at a meeting of the border wardens of England and Scotland, Lord Russell, son of the Earl of Bedford, was killed in a shooting, which the English Warden, Sir John Forster, decided was an accident. Wotton made no claim either that it was actually a murder dreamt up by James, but it did give London leverage on Arran, who was placed under a very mild regime of house arrest, and the Scots were forced to negotiate a league that gave them much less favourable terms than had seemed possible. It is at this point we can see the outline of duality in English policy, with Walsingham hiving off from Elizabeth's in order to take matters forward to advantage. While she gave Hunsdon a secret commission to continue negotiations with Arran,

Walsingham regarded all Scots as light-minded derelicts: 'I see so great treachery in that nation as I have no desire at all to have any extraordinary dealing with them.'[7] Low in his esteem at this time was the greedy Master of Gray, whose proposal was that the exiled lords (Mar, Angus and Glamis), chafing under English protection, should be allowed to slip back to Scotland 'to sink or swim', in the phrase used by Francis Milles writing to Wotton.

With Elizabeth dithering about her promise to James in the matter of the lords, Walsingham needed to devise a scheme that satisfied her, that did not alienate James, and that got the lords home and pitched Arran out. He needed also to protect Wotton and did so, writing on 28 September: 'there is now resolution taken in the causes concerning Scotland such as will not dislike you . . .'.[8] The outlined project was simple: Glamis (evidently considered the smartest of the three lords) would go to the borders 'to confer with his friends', with Angus and Mar waiting until it was seen what support they had. Milles would deliver 600 angels* to Gray to further the cause. Some days later Wotton was instructed to withdraw to Berwick, which he did, and on 17 October Angus and Mar arrived in Sterling. Within two weeks James was the obedient puppet of the returned ones, who had Arran proclaimed a traitor, and his effects and lands confiscated by the King. A parliament was summoned that reinstated the former exiles and cleared them of any so-called crimes. From London came William Knollys to declare the Queen free of any taint of plotting with them – probably technically true – and a blithe James declared his satisfaction and his desire to conclude the projected league. It was this that Henri III tried to thwart by a late intervention, but Walsingham had a trump card in Thomas Randolph who could more than hold his own ground against French intrigues. What Walsingham needed was something to force open the Queen's coffers and a restraint for her late impulses to hinder the promoters of the league. But Randolph, had already won the King over; he signed the articles and Milles, who was attending him, came back to London with the document. Even now Elizabeth proved obstinate over money, and for weeks Walsingham was walking on eggs, but Randolph, assisted by Gray and Archibald Douglas of the English affinity, smoothed away the difficulties, and in early July, after English and Scottish commissioners had met at Berwick, it was done – the league existed and James was a pensioner of Elizabeth. He would eschew dealings with her enemies and put up troops in the event of an attack on England.

* 1 angel = 10*s*

Chapter 12

THE INS AND OUTS OF CONFINEMENT

We left Thomas Morgan, depressed and angry, in the Bastille. The Catholic gentleman from south Wales who had taken over the establishment and annual income from the French on behalf of the exiled Mary, Queen of Scots, had been arrested on 9 March 1585. His attitude towards the Duke de Guise and the slothful James Beaton, Archbishop of Glasgow, who sat on their bejewelled hands and did nothing to get him released, was one of fury, while his attitude to Elizabeth was modified by exchanges with an imprisoned Huguenot, the Comte de la Magnane.[1] Among the English Catholic exiles, two Morgan camps formed: those for him and those who suspected the erosion of his loyalty. Walsingham and Stafford sought to exploit this with contact through Christopher Blount, whose life Morgan had once saved. A Catholic with a Poley mother, Blount had been tutored privately in Louvain by Dr Allen, but now he was following his father, Thomas Blount (d. 1568) by serving in the household staff of Leicester. The younger Blount's mail carrier was Robert Poley, and one of the most spry agents to enter the service of Walsingham. Blount needed to consolidate his dealings with Morgan so that he could whisper of a channel of communication to Mary in Tutbury castle (Staffs) being available. The knowledge of this would surely stimulate the flow of letters, allowing the government to gobble up details. So, in June 1585 Robert Poley was sent to Paris to deliver the Blount letter to the prisoner in the Bastille.

Through an exiled English intermediary Morgan got to hear of Poley's arrival in late June. To know more of his mission a receiver was nominated, Thomas Throckmorton, one of Morgan's closest allies.[2] But Poley declined to talk to him or anyone else until he had met with the prisoner himself. Morgan and the loyal group outside of the prison felt some trepidation about such an encounter, wondering if Poley might enter with a concealed weapon to kill him; an assassin directed from London was not utterly impossible, since Parry's confession that his plot against Elizabeth had been 'fathered' by Morgan. The answer was to maintain a barrier between the two men, and so it was they talked through Morgan's cell window. As the conversation progressed Morgan relaxed, and through 'Barasino' (Throckmorton) he got the Poley letters, having been tranquilised by the tone and demeanour of their carrier. This success meant Blount had hooked Morgan and handed over a cipher key for use by both ends of the correspondence. Poley also benefited by a payment of thirty pistolets given to him by Charles Paget, who told Mendoza of the new communications channel.

By the autumn of 1585 Poley was a busy man, moving in and out of the French embassy in London, where mild-mannered Mauvissière had been replaced by Châteauneuf, a staunch Marian. The Queen of Scots was ailing and the cause (beyond her age) was Tutbury, essentially a dank heap where many were unwell, leading her to complain constantly – pleading for healthier surroundings in a year of appalling weather. The year had seen long falls of rain and eventually floods, 'which have done great hurt in these parts'. So wrote Sir Amias Paulet, Privy Councillor, ally of Walsingham and now gaoler of Mary. A Somerset man, he had done dutiful service on Jersey and greatly helped the wave of Huguenot refugees before his appointment as English ambassador in Paris.[3] It came as a relief to him when his term ended in November 1579, and he was able to return to govern Jersey following the death of his father. The island must have seemed something of a Paulet fiefdom, for brother George became the island Bailiff, and son Anthony the lieutenant governor. This Jersey interlude was years before any mention that Sir Amias might find himself a royal gaoler. It came about through a linked series of adjustments and changes about Mary when her custodian of years, the Earl of Shrewbury, at last wriggled free. Sir Ralph Sadler took over for a year, and then in January 1585 Burghley wrote to Walsingham to say that Lord St John of Bletso had absolutely refused the task, to the exasperation of Elizabeth. On her command Burghley then assigned Sir Amias, who was spending the Christmas holidays at Rycote, near Thame in Oxfordshire, the home of Lord Norreys, whose daughter was the wife of Anthony Paulet.

Since Paulet Snr was not in the best of health and not wealthy, the royal choice raised many eyebrows: why 'pick out a Paulet', whom John Somers, assistant to Sadler thought for some time was merely to assist Lord St John. Actually, the royal choice may simply have followed Walsingham's selection of

1. Sir Francis Walsingham (1530–90), Statesman and spymaster; attributed to John de Critz *c.* 1585. (*National Portrait Gallery*)

2. Francis Russell, 2nd Earl of Bedford (1527?–85), Protestant patron of Walsingham for Parliamentary seats; by an unknown artist. (*Woburn Abbey*)

3. Sir Ralph Sadler (1507–87), diplomat and later gaoler of Mary Queen of Scots; by Hans Holbein or his studio? (*Metropolitan Museum of Art, New York*)

4. Sir John Hawkins (1532–95), naval administrator and slavery freebooter; by an unknown artist. (*National Maritime Museum*)

5. Mary Queen of Scots (1542–87); engraving by Thomas de Ley (1579).

L'obiect de ce portraict, fera veoir au Lecteur
du visage les traicts bien formez de L'auteur
mais son esprit diuin cogneu en son histoire
Luy fera beaucoup plus estimer sa memoire

Jaspar Isac *Fecit*

6. Michel de Castelnau, Seigneur de Mauvissière, French ambassador to England, 1575–85; engraving by Jasper Isac in *Les Memoires de Messire de Castenau*, Paris, 1621.

7. Robert Dudley, Earl of Leicester
(1532–88); miniature by
Nicholas Hilliard (1576).
(*National Portrait Gallery*)

8. Captain Christopher Carleill (*c.* 1551–93). The step-son of Walsingham was courageous, affable and partially sighted, as Robert Boissard's engraving shows.

9. Queen Elizabeth I (1533–1603); late (possibly posthumous) portrait by an unknown artist. (*Weiss Gallery, London*)

10. The young Robert Cecil (1564–1612), later Earl of Salisbury, after a portrait by Marcus Gheeraerts. (*Courtauld Institute of Art*)

11. Hubert Languet, Protestant diplomat and mentor to Sir Philip Sidney.

12. Philippe du Plessis-Mornay (1549–1623), Protestant diplomat and published controversialist author. (*Engraving by L. Gaultier*)

13. 'Godly zeal pluck'd out of his pulpit'. The preacher in this 1569 allegorical print stands for Gospel truth, the intruder (a friar?) for its foes and the congregation for the indifferent.

14. Domestic items such as might have been found in Walsingham's town house in Seething Lane near the Tower of London, or his country residence along the Thames at Barn Elms, gifted to him by the Queen. Its position meant he could avoid horseback journeys to and from London.

15. A letter from Walsingham to Thomas Phelippes, cryptanalyst extraordinary and a key secret service operative, 3 August 1586, referring to the postscript to Mary Queen of Scots' letter to Anthony Babington: BL Cotton Mss. App. L, f. 44.

16. The funeral cortège of Sir Philip Sidney, arranged on a vast scale by his father-in-law Walsingham to trump any possible public mourning for the recently executed Mary Queen of Scots.

17. A preacher at old St Paul's Cross, a place sometimes used by the government to disseminate propaganda. Walsingham's night funeral service was held in the old Gothic cathedral.

a man thinking much as he did and speaking very good French, important for dealing with Mary. Paulet accepted the post and was due to take up his duties on 1 March, but did not arrive at Tutbury until nearly two months later. In the interval he enquired about the liberty allowed his royal charge, who bridled at having one so lowborn lord it over her. He ranked far below a Talbot earl, and while in France had shown himself to be her enemy. In reply Elizabeth briskly reiterated Paulet's qualities, and at length he arrived at Tutbury with his pregnant wife, his son George, some forty servants and thirty soldiers.[4] His secretary was Edward Reynoldes, a Fellow of All Souls, Oxford, who would later enter Essex's service – probably with an approving nod from Walsingham. On hand was Sadler to make the formal introductions to Mary and her household. From now on her confinement would be strict, because this late assignment was, to Paulet's truly Salvationist imagination, a literally heaven-sent opportunity. The tone of the future ordering of the household was hinted at when Paulet's first action was to remove the cloth of Estate that hitherto had hung in the Hall. Sadler had allowed this status symbol, but Paulet had it removed to demonstrate a stern attitude from the beginning. Every concession was but a preliminary to another: 'whatsoever liberty or anything else is once granted unto them cannot be drawn back again without great exclamations'. No doubt this brought a nod of recognition from Walsingham reading the comment. And so Paulet gradually eroded all the little freedoms Mary had snatched or wheedled into being, and he tried to cut costs when the whole establishment liked luxuries that suggested it was not a prison.

But it was a prison, albeit one with velvet cushions. The castle guard was bulked up and strangers were forbidden to enter the building. Mary's own staff could not leave without a soldier escort, and she was forbidden to continue giving alms to the neighbourhood poor. The reason? Paulet's twitchy view that such people might give way to an impulse to carry messages, or be more open to bribes. Everything coming in or going out was scrutinised so that secret correspondence halted, and this was much less to Walsingham's liking or intent, so that he and Phelippes (who could do an impression of Morgan 'to the life') had to come up with a scheme approved by Paulet and accepted by a suspicious Mary. To him the women who did her laundry were a particular worry, since he suspected them of smuggling messages in and out within the bundles, and his suspicions only increased when he found out that two of the washerwomen were related to Mary's coachman. His privileges were curtailed, including the established former dining rights with the guard servants. Paulet's quotidian frame of mind was not improved by passages of gout, and acknowledging his bouts of ill health London sent him Richard Bagot to assist. With so much evidence of illness and general debilitation among captives and captors, and the French pressing for the provision of more salubrious quarters for their cousin, the hunt was on for a new place of restraint. Various large properties in the area were assessed, including Tixall, the home of Sir Walter Aston. Paulet realised this would infuriate Aston, one of the few (as he thought) loyal-to-Elizabeth landowners in 'this infected shire'. So Chartley Hall, owned by Essex, was chosen, and his resistance put aside. Paulet was pleased to have a country house still with a large moat. As he wrote to Walsingham: 'The water which environeth this house is of such depth as may stand instead of a strong wall.' Even better was the solution to the laundry problem; an abundance of water meant the washing could easily be done in-house, because, as he ruefully admitted, his trawl of Somerset had failed to find anyone ready to make the move.

At this time Essex was preparing to accompany his stepfather to the Netherlands and spending freely on a train of followers, so that his Knollys grandfather, Sir Francis, rebuked him for the 'wasteful prodigality'. To lose Chartley (even temporarily) may have seemed too much, and no doubt Walsingham the diplomat was called upon to soothe away the grievance felt at an important point in the young man's public career. So the move to Chartley was made on Christmas Eve 1585, and on her arrival Mary straightaway collapsed. This proclaimed her distress, and even Paulet was moved for her sake to forward her complaints about her bed, which she found 'stained and ill-favoured'. She wanted a down bed, and he supported her in this, but generally his stiff efforts were aimed at reducing the hefty household expenditure. Moreover, on a rather cruelly practical note, while she was ill and her legs were infirm he could be certain that there would be no escape attempts.

At this time Mary was the complete prisoner. The task for Walsingham (and less forcefully Burghley), the task they set themselves, was to deprive the captive of life by flexibly legal means. This could be done only if sturdy proof was obtained that Mary was directly involved in an effort to murder Elizabeth – the violent notion that scarcely ever ebbed among the Catholic exiles half-maddened by her toughness, and hating the piercing ingenuity of Walsingham, notably the Bond of Association. There were, as he very well knew, men seething at home and abroad at the curbing of the tragedy queen; the confederacy of knaves was working, and what he had to do was act as midwife to the monstrosity that was about to be carried to term. When it was born, fully out in the open, he and his agents could seize the whole matter and crush it, dealing with Mary in the aftermath. One of his most loyal and thorough agents as organiser for Iberian espionage was Dr Hector Nuñes (b. *c.* 1520 in Evora, Portugal), a long-term crypto-Jewish resident of London with a secret clinic in his home in Marke Lane. Like Dr Lopez later in the reign, Nuñes provided Walsingham and Burghley with up-to-date information about Spanish activities in the Low Countries and Iberia, and later reported on his countryman and fellow exile, Dom Antonio, Pretender to the Portuguese throne. Nuñes also maintained contacts with Spain through letters (even writing to Philip II and his officials), even though it seems to have been Don Guerau de Spes who did most harm to his efforts in commerce.

Walsingham was compelled to intervene to protect Nuñes in July 1573: letters were written to the Lord Mayor and the Master of the Rolls, Sir William Cordell. But the immigrant was under pressure from such as Philip Corsini, the member of the great Florentine mercantile family who moved to London in 1559 and who within ten years was the largest importer of European goods into England. By 1584 his brother Bartolomeo had joined him and was also trading successfully – so well, in fact, that he occupied a large merchant's house in Gratious Street. Yet this was the time of the trade embargo of Philip II that intensified the problems of Nuñes, who found himself in the Admiralty court declaring a loss of £1,452 of goods and cash. Lean times for him and unease for the Pallavicino brothers, the famous merchant bankers and moneylenders. Horatio Pallavicino wrote a letter – moderate in tone – to Walsingham, that they would be willing to wait for repayment if good security could be mustered. Their anxiety was that Nuñes, now in his mid-sixties, would die and his property would be scattered. Pallavicino wrote again to Walsingham on 5 August, but there is no documentary confirmation that he ever got his lands back.[5] For twenty and more years commerce was the feed-pipe for getting intelligence matters in merchant cipher put before both Burghley and, more importantly, Walsingham. This may have prompted the letter probably penned by John Somers but signed by Walsingham to nine named Italian merchants in the City of London. It recommended the bearer, a qualified river pilot by the name of John Raynolds, as a safe pair of hands to bring any argosy from the lately repaired harbour at Dover to the Gore channel in the river estuary; any ship without local knowledge of navigating the Goodwin Sands was liable to be wrecked.

The letter is of particular interest because Agostino Grafigna was one of the nine named Italians, and early in 1584, perhaps nudged by Burghley, he had begun reporting directly to Elizabeth about his conferences with Parma, who was angling for terms with England and was even minded to send commissioners across the Channel to sketch out a framework for negotiations. Sir James Croft, a Catholic, was one of the Privy Councillors keen for this to develop, and Cobham and Mildmay joined for differing reasons. By discrediting the Italian Grafigna with Elizabeth, Walsingham created a gap to be filled by his own men, Hector Nuñes and his Lisbon kinsman Geronimo Pardo. One of the tasks assigned to the former was to correspond on Walsingham's behalf with Antonio Castilho, former Portuguese ambassador to London, and now a highly placed official in the Spanish government. Writing to Walsingham on 23 March 1586, Nuñes made mention of a letter he had written to Castilho saying forcefully that Elizabeth certainly did not want to annex the Low Countries, but did want security for England. He added that Castilho wanted a letter from Walsingham 'declaring her Majesty to be inclined to peace'. This would help Castilho get a peace agreement. Further he wanted Pardo to become an active agent for peace, no longer simply a messenger. So, would these matters advance through diplomats or designated commissioners? Would subsequent meetings be held in a French port? When he had answers Pardo, with a safe-conduct, should travel to them aboard an English ship. On 30 September 1586, some two weeks into the Babington show trial, Nuñes again wrote to Walsingham with regard to obstacles in the peace process: the Acts of Toleration in Religion for the Low Countries had not been sent to Philip II. Castilho held back on exposing them, convinced they were 'the occasion of a new war'.[6] Nuñes envisaged Walsingham writing to Castilho that he should come to London to converse privately with Elizabeth, getting Philip's permission for such contact. The emphasis was to be on Castilho as the King's mouthpiece, and it should be done soon because of the 'great preparation of men and ships in Lisbon'.

Walsingham was convinced he knew its destination. Usefully he had available for employment a Spanish-speaking messenger, Charles Chester, once imprisoned on the Canary Islands for heresy, who in January 1586 had carried two letters to London, one from Stafford and one from Mauvissière. Despite the

tone of what Stafford noted about Chester (or perhaps because of it),
Walsingham placed the latter as the English minder to a remarkable Spanish
hidalgo, Don Pedro Sarmiento de Gamboa, one of the outstanding figures in
their efforts to colonise South America. In August he had been captured at sea,
then brought to London and Windsor. Gamboa had long Latin conversations
with Elizabeth, and as a soft prisoner was specially housed by Ralegh, whose
own dreams of El Dorado were disastrously increased by long talks with the
Spaniard.[7] He also got to talk with Burghley and Howard, so it is reasonable to
suppose that they saw him as a possible agent for improving relations with
Spain. Walsingham either held off from meeting Don Pedro, or perhaps they
were deliberately kept apart given the Principal Secretary's known feelings
about Spain and war. Which is why the designation of Chester to accompany
the Spaniard when he was freed late in October to go to Paris is so interesting.
Ralegh had become a sort of sponsor to Don Pedro, even giving him a
departing gift of 1,000 escudos to pack in his pouch. When Richard Hakluyt
wrote to Ralegh on 30 December these coins were probably in a French
Huguenot's pocket, for the Spaniard proved doubly unfortunate in his travels,
being taken again while travelling through France to Spain.

Hakluyt, like Stafford, regarded Chester with some suspicion, and his
mention of him to Ralegh was not a rousing fanfare. As it was, when Chester
came back to London in January, Walsingham authorised payment to him of
£13 6s 0d, supposedly for the letter-carrying, but also it seems for spying on
Anthony Poyntz, engaged by Walsingham to spy in Spain.[8] A son of Sir
Nicholas Poyntz (strongly connected to Leicester), a former student of Inner
Temple, the scoundrelly Anthony had done nothing to enhance the ancient
family's reputation. In December 1586 he was actually staying with
Mendoza, before seeking out Parma. For a spymaster like Walsingham, a
rogue like Poyntz was useful if not caught pillaging for secrets. If he failed in
his mission or turned traitor or double agent, he was simply expendable, for
he never got close to English state secrets; someone like Stafford was much
more destructive. During the time Leicester had been trying in every way to
assist the Dutch insurgents, Poyntz was supposed to be spying, but the Earl
made the classic error of paying out too much too soon: £100 before the ex-
felon had done anything behind enemy lines. Walsingham and Leicester also
got into a tangle about sending Poyntz to Spain, and as a destination that had
to be delayed as Poyntz carried letters to Elizabeth, who was aghast at her
representative's behaviour, including the profligate distribution of war funds.

It seems that Poyntz elected to sell his services (such as they were) to both sides, achieving this through Mendoza, for when he did eventually reach Spain he had the ambassador's approval. Writing to Walsingham, Stafford reported a meeting between Poyntz and Sir Francis Englefield, the senior Englishman in the service of Philip II. To anchor Englefield's attention, Poyntz declared that for 4,000 crowns he or associates of his sister Anne (wife of Sir Thomas Heneage) could assassinate Elizabeth. This the Spanish let swing in the air; it was both treacherous and stale. Both London and Madrid regarded Poyntz with suspicion, and both seem to have waited on the possibility that he would betray other agents. Bernal Luis, who was the brother-in-law of Hector Nuñes, escaped the attention of Poyntz, and working in tandem with Geronimo Pardo they reported to Nuñes. Pardo himself actually took ship to London in June 1587 with a cargo of salt and two packets of letters in cipher which gave a full account of warlike preparations in Spain. Pardo translated them for Walsingham, and within two months was on his way back to Lisbon, from whence he sent three more ships loaded with cargoes and information.

The papers that poured into the office of the Principal Secretary had to be dealt with systematically and stored in a way that made retrieval and reference possible. I envisage rooms set aside for storing heavy iron-clad chests, as well as bundles of linen, canvas and leather bags, wicker cases, boxes, chests and hutches for correspondence, maps and drafts of letters. For a simultaneous like effort we can look to the records of the Duchy of Lancaster, which were concentrated in London in the sixteenth century and came under the control of Walsingham late in his career, when he held the office of Chancellor of the Duchy. To facilitate searches among duchy documents there were written indexes, but the memories of duchy officers about the whereabouts of specified items were equally important. Clerk of the Council, Matthew Bacon, spent thirty years compiling a directory, and this has a good selection of periphrastic expressions: 'in a white canvas bag in the broad flat trunk in the study'; or, 'in a great box behind my seat in the ground'. How fortunate for Walsingham that he retained his eyesight and rarely forgot an item of significance. No wonder either that his secretariat grew – a point of correction for some observers of his working methods. Yet this filter reading by trusted men long in his service was essential for the Principal Secretary if his control of information was to be maintained.

Chapter 13

THE PRAYERFUL PURITAN

Walsingham was born as the preliminaries to the great contested drama of the English Reformation were beginning to exercise minds and moral imaginations. Queen Anne Boleyn's patronage of evangelicals such as Hugh Latimer and Nicholas Shaxton gave the reformers a niche at court as early as 1530. Preaching became a central element in the striving for change, and in a well-placed and prosperous household the young Walsingham would have had to be very inventive to avoid the torrent of words. The turbulence of the times spurred by Henry VIII's decision to divorce Queen Catherine provoked 'a passion for preaching and sermon-going probably not equalled in England since the heyday of the 14th century friar-preachers'.[1] In London's parish churches, the frequency of preaching increased quite startlingly, and this was bound to have a measure of influence in the surrounding sees, where until the Reformation the weekly Sunday sermon was a rarity. The ecclesiological high point of the year was Lent – a medieval tradition that had strength within the royal court lasting beyond the Tudors and Stuarts. Walsingham as a small boy was raised within a family where the father had suddenly left them without a guiding hand and the mother rapidly remarried for the sake of stability and a nurturing presence – a family clinging to the notion that God's presence in the everyday world was absolutely predictable, and too the presence of demonic forces. Fundamental concerns such as salvation and damnation were expounded at home and in the classroom, and a clever boy like Francis was very soon reading the Bible and its exegetes. In Protestant and Catholic Europe the Reformation brought with it a massive campaign of education in Christian doctrine.

The essential pessimism that originated in Judaism was shared by mainstream Protestantism and its sinewy offspring Puritanism. They derived it from early Christianity, with its clangorous affirmation by St Paul, St Augustine, John Wycliffe (the Oxford theologian and translator of the Bible into English in the fourteenth century who is now represented by a bearded robot in the most improbable amusement park in Florida – the Scriptorium), Luther, Calvin, Bucer[2] and Peter Martyr Vermigli. As a reformed minister he and Bernardino Ochino fled to Strasbourg via Basle in the 1540s, before coming to England on the invitation of Archbishop Cranmer. In 1560 a preacher of huge reputation a decade before, Thomas Sampson, wrote to Peter Martyr in an almost hysterical tone requiring to know how at this time he could serve in the English church when a crucifix and a candle adorned Elizabeth's chapel and there was scarcely a sermon heard. The Queen seems to have taken little from them; the picky, authoritarian daughter of a terrifying, vicious father wanted deference to her before all else. Those who by choice or accident neglected to give it to her suffered directly or indirectly. She nurtured pulpit grudges and did not hesitate to eject from the religious life of the court those who pinched her conscience or aggravated her. She wondered if preaching had any efficacy in court or country, and her stiff disregard for pulpit evangelism meant that the English Deborah, sent by God to restore the true faith, was not just deaf to good advice but, as brave, unfortunate John Stubbs was to find out, actively hostile.

This is not to suggest that in her capricious way she rejected sermons totally. In fact she did have her favourite preachers, like Richard Fletcher, who was rewarded and promoted until he shocked the vinegary old Queen by a rich marriage, and so was banished from court in 1595.[3] Long before that she had also registered her dislike for 'prophesyings', 'those training sessions' for the ministers (in market towns mostly) whose education had been cut short by lack of funds or indifference. After Archbishop Grindal's refusal to cull 'prophesyings' in 1576, Elizabeth intervened to suppress her archbishop and the preaching gatherings. These were often conducted before a lay audience, many of whom sat with their Geneva Bibles on their laps to follow the scriptural references of the preacher. This mass-produced and unlovely version of the Bible, produced by Protestant exiles in the city in the last years of Mary's burnt-out reign, is very possibly 'the most influential English book ever'. Through its dissemination the English learned to read – half a million copies were printed and sold in a country with a population of about three million – and to discuss and challenge after a prophesying session of two or three sermons that might be settled on the same text. Later the ministers would talk over supper, reviewing the sermons and refining ideas over which they had stumbled. By 1574 Colchester in Essex had just such a prophesying, probably held under the auspices of the town preacher, Nicholas Challoner. Before him there had been a trio of learned men, and two of them, John Pullen and William Cole, had a hand in the translation of the Geneva Bible. The latter had been a Marian exile and had remained in Antwerp until 1564 preaching to the Merchant Adventurers.

In the two years from 1576 to 1578 the town recorder was the Puritan William Cardinal, chief legal counsel for the town, and replaced by Walsingham, who had no Essex or Colchester connections but who continued to serve as recorder until he died. He did this office in conjunction with other recorderships, earning modest but useful fees, and it did mean that he could put his law training to use. The choice of Walsingham may well have been occasioned by an outbreak of strife between Puritan authorities in the town and church papists. In late October 1578 the town bailiffs reported 'men very obstinate in the Popish profession and religion, who refused to attend sermons'.[4] The following year, in May, the bailiffs sought Walsingham's assistance when John Christmas was ordered to appear before the Privy Council (for libelling one of the well known recusant family of the Southwells?). When these parochial matters had been sorted through and the town settled back into its routines, Leicester and Walsingham both received letters of thanks, and the Principal Secretary gently replied that the Queen could very quickly be alienated by rapid and shrill claims to rights and privileges. He sketched the benefit of being thankful that 'God's word [is] sincerely preached and the sacraments truly administered'.[5]

Walsingham was alert to the damage that could be done by the leading townsmen becoming choleric and inflexible. In this attitude he was supported by the town clerk, James Morice, who held the office from 1576–97, while remaining in London. A reformer who was also an intellectual, he had Latin, Greek and French texts in his library, and was well known to Walsingham. It was on the nomination of the Principal Secretary that Morice and Francis Harvey represented Colchester in Parliament in October 1586 (a seat taken by Arthur Throckmorton three years later), and Morice quickly scandalised the Queen by a proposed Bill of Inquiry into the abuses of the Court of High Commission, used by Archbishop Whitgift to strike at the growing strength of Puritanism, with nearly fifty ministers deprived or silenced in Essex alone. The protests of Walsingham and others at the deprivation of good men and the intrusion of unfit persons into their livings had not altered church policy, which had secured the support of the Queen, or at any rate was known to be in conformity to the royal wishes. Elizabeth demanded that Morice's bill be given up to her, and he was arrested by the sergeant-at-arms, put in prison and deprived of his means of earning a living. He proved something of a terrier in such matters, being detained in prison again in early 1593 on the orders of the Queen; this time he remained locked up for two months.

Protestants of every leaning lived and felt their faith, with the Fall from Grace as the defining moment in man's relationship with God, and its attendant consequence the doctrine of justification by faith alone. Man was sorely wounded by sin, and for many Adam's fall had come close to excising every faculty for good in his spiritual nature; for Puritans that task had been completed. Notwithstanding this absolute spiritual deficiency (so evident in Marlowe's character John Faustus), the fall of Man had not swamped a natural ability to reason. Within an earthly arena man could choose the good – but this was not in itself redemptive. In their spiritual bindings mainstream Protestants had a hint of elasticity, but the ropes of the Puritans were utterly inelastic. William Perkins, the outstanding systematic Puritan theologian of his time, described the Fall as 'a revolting of the reasonable creature from obedience to sin'. Like Calvin he believed in man's total corruption; and it was Calvin's Geneva, which gradually came to represent the New Jerusalem for the Reformed movement, while Rome was demonised. Calvin's Academy (founded in 1559), which was intended to provide a centre for the education of Reformed ministers, proved highly successful; by the following year it had attracted 300 students from all over Europe. Being a politician with deep religious convictions, but without the time or means to follow the example of Calvin, Walsingham took years to do the next best thing – he established at Oxford a divinity lectureship to which he wanted the Puritan John Rainolds appointed. A prominent divine and a leading controversialist against papistry, Rainolds was a man of the widest learning, familiar with Greek and Hebrew language and literature. From 1572 to 1578 he was reader in Greek at Corpus Christi College, and he was among the few in Oxford who was favourable to Ramus, but had real reservations about laying siege to Aristotle.[6] Puritanism did not scorn knowledge as such, or even regard it as irrelevant to God, but it was wholly irrelevant to salvation. The Word, spoken, read and commented upon, was everything.

Even so, when it came to finding a replacement for Nicholas Challoner as town preacher in Colchester, the town's worthies were quick to offer the post to Challoner's choice – George Northey, MA of Clare Hall, Cambridge, whose candidacy was supported by the college fellows. Northey got a stipend of £40 per annum and the widow Challoner, whom he married. He proved more than a merely serviceable preacher, so that ministers in parish churches found it hard to fill pews when Northey was speaking elsewhere. The alderman respected his scriptural and social engagement, and when his Presbyterianism got him a suspension in 1583 they worked unceasingly for him to be reinstated – difficult with Whitgift at Canterbury, and the first churchman since Cardinal Pole to have a seat on the Privy Council. Still, preaching was thought so beneficial to the town that community leaders wanted their friends in high places to assist Northey, so the bailiffs wrote appeals to Walsingham, Leicester, Ambrose, Earl of Warwick, Sir Thomas Heneage, and Bishop Aylmer* of London, no friend of Puritans. One individual who was determined to have a say in the matter was a John Harrison, who contacted Walsingham, Sir Thomas Lucas and Sir Thomas Gawdie. But recipients did not always respond well to pressure, and in this case Heneage was irritated and Aylmer upset; but the hitch was overcome at length, and Northey got back his post. The town collectively took pleasure in this, for it saw the appointee as one element of good civic government.[7] Walsingham was also involved in the campaign to consolidate the foundation of the town grammar school, as was Leicester, both of them meeting Alderman John Pye when he was in London on town business in 1584.

Even the choice of the grammar school's schoolmaster could creep into his scrutiny when he was hugely over-burdened. So in 1588, when war threatened to swamp everything, Walsingham was involved in the appointment of a successor to Samuel Halsnoth (or Harsnett as he was later called). Colchester born, and educated at Pembroke College, Cambridge where he was a fellow, Halsnoth had been wooed back to teach, but after two years gave it up, choosing to return to Cambridge to study divinity rather than toil in the classroom in 'ye painful trade of teaching'. That bold choice led to the mastership of Pembroke, a brace of bishoprics and then translation to the Archbishopric of York. To succeed him as schoolmaster two strong candidates sought the post in a polite contest: Mark Sadlington and William Bentley. The former, from Peterhouse, Cambridge, had the support of Halsnoth, the fellows

* John Aylmer had been a Marian exile; in Zurich Robert Beale had been his servant, but on their return to England Beale complained of being ignored.

of Peterhouse, and most weighty of all, Walsingham, who wrote that he had heard good reports of his man's learning and 'sincerity in religion'. He added a sweetener that the town should again have him to serve them in the future if it made the sought-after appointment. Bentley mustered support from a range of sources, mostly academic and godly, so that it was he who carried the day.

While the bailiffs of Colchester considered Bentley they approached one outsider for an opinion, the Dean of Canterbury and noted Puritan diarist, Richard Rogers, also a preacher who could snare any congregation. When the post of dean became available there was a great deal of pressure for Rogers from local Puritan magistrates, and Walsingham was not to be excluded from the fray. The former suffragan Bishop of Dover (from 1569) had been a Marian exile, as had other men of Kent who advanced socially; a few lay exiles even joined the ranks of the country magnates. Edward Boys, who had signed the moderate 'new discipline' at Frankfurt in 1557, was acting for the Privy Council in Dover within weeks of his return, and as a kinsman of Walsingham and Peter Wentworth 'he was to be a leading figure in the godly cause in Kent for much of the reign'.[8] Amongst contemporaries like Sir Thomas Scott, Sir Moyle Finch (a friend of Philip Sidney) and Sir James Hales, there was a strong leaning towards a tougher Puritan line against Catholicism, and geography and ideology put them in Leicester's *kraal*. Yet the Lord Lieutenant of Kent, William, Lord Cobham, retained a crypto-Catholic – Peter Hendley – as his chaplain.[9] An isolated example to be sure, for in Kent Catholicism had shrivelled, and under increasing pressure in the 1570s the county gentry who held to it had dwindled. With the suspension of Grindal in 1577 the cause of the godly was for a short time enhanced, for as John Strype noted the Puritan grandees at court took the opportunity to advance 'their friends and their creatures' within the church. Alongside the earls, and a shade less prominent, was Walsingham pushing radical nominations in his county. A client of his – Robert Bishop – was for a time Official for the Archbishop.[10] So it was at a pivotal time that John Whitgift became Archbishop of Canterbury, a historic office in a diocese where Burghley in 1584 noted fifteen non-conforming clergy, with another four in adjacent Rochester where Bishop Yonge struggled to uphold the orthodox line. Nearly all the non-conforming ministers were graduates, mostly from Cambridge, powerful preachers whose mode of address to the congregation was clear and plain; radical preaching with an edge that could lead to parochial disorder.[11]

Also a former Cambridge academic, who had tutored Essex at Trinity College, Whitgift's appointment was intended to bring some order and discipline to a church that seemed to be on the brink of disintegration. So in January 1584 he called upon ministers within Kent to subscribe to certain articles of religion as approved by the Queen several months before. If they ignored the requirement it was proposed that they be ejected from office. The key requirement was that they move from occasional to continual use of the prayer book. A good few reviewed matters and gave way, but others resisted strongly, including some of the finest preachers, such as Dudley Fenner.[12] Eventually he retreated into exile in Middelburg, where he died in 1587. However, before leaving the country he and others confronted Whitgift, and the Archbishop refused to modify anything he had asked for. They responded by appealing to the rest of the Privy Council, and Whitgift felt aggrieved when his colleagues took issue with him. Theirs was not the only intercession, for the Puritan-inclined gentry of Kent also linked up to berate the Archbishop, and on 7 May thirty-eight landowners put in a petition against Whitgift to the Council. The group included clients and friends of Walsingham and Burghley: Thomas Wotton (father of the future diplomat Sir Henry Wotton); Sir John Leveson (whose second wife was Sir Walter Mildmay's daughter, Christian); Henry Killigrew and Thomas Randolph,* the diplomat and friend not only of Walsingham, but also of Walter Travers, fierce critic of church structure (and prime mover behind the Book of Discipline). On 8 May many of the petitioners travelled to Lambeth Palace for a meeting with Whitgift, whose attitude was stern – the ministers who chose not to conform were 'revolted altogether from the Gospel', and they disparaged the Book of Common Prayer. The heaping of insults on his listeners culminated in the accusation of Anabaptism, and the mild country gentleman Thomas Wotton was so angry that he argued with some frank rebuttals. By the end of the meeting the atmosphere was hostile.

This was not a struggle Whitgift could win single-handed, and at the strengthening of lay protest it became clear he had to make a truce at least with Walsingham and Leicester. And he got their support against unyielding Presbyterianism, while agreeing not to deprive ministers of their livings solely because they rejected his articles of faith. They in turn had to use the Prayer Book and not abuse it. Thomas Wotton delivered this message to Kent's

* Married to Anne Walsingham.

divines the following autumn, and almost all found the new formula acceptable. So what had this jousting between the two sides actually achieved? Whitgift might claim to have curbed radical Protestant notions (such as Presbyterianism), but by November 1586 the more extreme campaigners for it were voicing their beliefs in Parliament, and in March 1587 Peter Wentworth, MP and his fellow agitators were gaoled. The marriages of Wentworth are themselves of interest, for his first was to Lettice Lane, whose mother was a relative of Queen Katherine Parr, while his second was to Elizabeth Gates (née Walsingham and a sister to Francis). Moreover, Wentworth's own sister married Edward Boys, and it was as a couple they quit Marian England for exile. As for Wentworth's brothers, it was Paul acting in the role of recusant hunter who searched a house near to Staines in Middlesex where John, Lord Lumley was confined in 1570 before his period in the Marshalsea for involvement in the Ridolfi plot.

For Salvationist Protestants there was only one festival of the church and it was a weekly one – Sunday. The Lord's day was the pivotal day in Walsingham's calendar, and even during a national crisis he set aside his papers for a day mostly given over to religious observances. On this day every week the mighty acts of God in the creation, redemption and sanctification of man, through the life, death and resurrection of Jesus Christ, were celebrated. The whole drama of salvation was rehearsed each Sunday in its entirety. But this does not comprise all of their public religious services; they held lectures and prayers on weekdays and frequently met for special fasts and prayers on days of national emergency. But still these were the foothills of their public devotion, while the Sunday services were the peaks. The Walsinghams would have observed Sundays with family prayers, in English, not Latin, which hauled in many, if not all of those in service in the house. In like households it was not unknown for absentees to be fined with the deduction being made on quarter day from wages. God's covenant – invariably read at a baptism – was 'to you and to your children', and this welded family life into a solidarity in Christ. The head of the family who had promised to supervise the Christian milieu of his children, had a duty to immerse them in Scriptures, and if dutiful he would conduct family prayers twice daily. Given the relentless calls on Walsingham's time, his bouts of extended ill health and his absences on the Queen's business, I expect that with some reluctance he let the domestic chaplain, Dr Lionel Sharpe, profoundly anti-Spanish and anti-Catholic and later chaplain to Essex, do this. Or possibly even Dame Ursula, using the prayers collected by the Puritan preacher Henry Smith (d. 1591). It is also possible that such a scholarly humanist may have had his stepson read improving passages aloud to the adults present at a table; or perhaps say a Latin grace before the food was eaten. But not at breakfast, because those who took it generally ate in their rooms; it was not a family meal.

All the Walsinghams and the secretariat, as well as the domestic seniors, would each have had a personal Bible. A protégé of the family was a Christopher Barker, a member of the Drapers' company, who had for some years been trading as a bookseller and sought to translate to the Stationers. He secured the right to print the Geneva text of the Bible in England, and quickly afterwards purchased from the diplomat and a clerk of the Privy Council, Sir Thomas Wilkes, a patent which included the Old and New Testament in English, with or without notes, and in any translation. The full patent made Barker the royal printer of secular political items like bills and acts of Parliament, as well as religious texts. It was then a thriving concern, with father and son living at Bacon House in Noble Street, Aldgate, before Christopher Barker elected to retire to his country house in Datchett (Berks), where he died in 1599.* In Armada year, when the presses were frantically busy, he appointed George Bishop and Ralph Newbury his deputies, and in 1589 son Robert got the renewed patent in a reversion for life. In barely twenty-five years Barker and his underlings had put out nearly seventy editions of Scripture that were accurate and well printed. The translator and reviser of the Geneva New Testament was Laurence Tomson, the polyglot Oxford graduate who had become an important figure in the Walsingham secretariat. Barker also printed Tomson's translation of *A treatise of the excellencie of a Christian man* by Pierre de la Place, murdered by Catholics during the Massacre of St Bartholomew's. The unfortunate Robert Barker got into financial difficulties, perhaps over the printing of the 1611 Bible. Between 1618 and 1629 he was meshed in lawsuits while retaining his office, and from 1635 to his death in 1645 Robert Barker was a debt prisoner in the King's Bench prison. His office during this time passed to assignees.

* The Crown relied on the Stationer's Company to bring decorum to printing, and Vautrollier worked on contract for Barker. Both men co-operated on government sponsored surreptitious political publications, and some of Barker's texts were either decorated with Walsingham's coat of arms or dedicated to him.

Chapter 14

TIDE AND TIME

For many years the great men of Tudor England (and lots of their juniors) had proclaimed their importance by building. Thomas Wriothesley, 1st Earl of Southampton was one of that quite small but very important group who rose from humble origins to great wealth and social advantage during the reign of Elizabeth's father. No sooner had he obtained Titchfield Priory than he began mauling the former monastic buildings, including the church, for conversion into a large and handsome country house.[1] On a much less grand scale than this, even a former Puritan academic like Francis Mylles had a build to refashion Pear Tree House, Bitterne (Hants). Unlike his secretary, Walsingham remained indifferent to the lure of property, and despite his hefty income declined to build. This may have been because he recognised in himself a yawning lack of interest in dynasty building – unlike Burghley, whose careful career building for his son Robert was sustained during the difficult 1590s. Walsingham, by the height of his power in the mid-1580s had one stepson and one surviving daughter, so the focus of his rebuilding was to benefit the nation, not his family. When he received Barn Elms as a royal gift he may have followed the example of Mylles, but without a miraculous find of papers we will never know. Rather than fret about this we can instead focus on a really grand project for the nation, for Walsingham became a key figure among the gentlemen of Kent seeking the essential reconstruction of Dover Harbour, which has recently been called 'one of the great domestic achievements of Elizabeth I's long reign'.[2]

Dover had for centuries been a primary point of entry for foreign goods from the north European trading centres, particularly the Baltic region, and it provided an essential naval base that only grew in importance as other places on the south-eastern coast visibly decayed. To maintain and improve Dover was vitally necessary (*plus ça change*) because of its advantageous position, but there were also real disadvantages that strained the ingenuity and skills of a generation. The project also tested the ability of the Privy Council to make decisions on best advice – and who was to provide this when skilled engineers were more elusive than gold dust? None of the Privy Council was an engineer, and before completion it would employ and then discard the duds who pretended to be experts. The collective level of exasperation soared over the years as representatives of the political class had to grapple with the financial effects of failing to find the most able men to do the work. And as the work did go on (albeit sometimes sluggishly and sometimes with greater insight and commitment) they had still to make technical choices without any purposeful training themselves, a method almost certain to cause fumbling and inefficiency in the employment of hundreds of day labourers, their supervisors and the self-promoting experts. And just when the plan sagged badly and schedules were abandoned, a Kent man well known to Walsingham took hold of the project and drove it forward to success: Thomas Digges.

The antiquity of Dover, in a scoop between two majestic cliffs sitting at the top of the funnel of the English Channel, did not make it a grand natural harbour. But Archcliff to the south-west and Castle Cliff to the north-east did offer protection from any storm surging in from the north or west. Generations of mariners appreciated this, but reflected ruefully on the tidal current. The configuration of the land, the prevailing winds and the sea currents accounted for the shifting of vast quantities of sand, silt, pebbles and shingle. It was this deluge of marine detritus that threatened the viability of Dover. By 1558 the harbour barely existed, and the entrance became impassable to any ship drawing more than 4ft of water. In the time of her father Henry VIII, even ships drawing over 20ft could safely negotiate entry, but now nearby Camber, Winchelsea and Rye were sunk by the cumulative effect of tidal silting, as was Harfleur in France. Dover was left to languish until 1575, when Elizabeth, while visiting Canterbury, received a petition on the problem from the mayor, and this resulted in a commission to investigate the state of havens on the Kent coast. The four 'men of experience' were chaired by William Borough, Comptroller of the Navy, and they had to deliberate on the causes of decay, the utility of repairs, and which haven would be best for future use. In their report of 20 May 1576 they favoured Dover over Rye and Winchelsea, its position unique in relation to Europe. But this effort was simply set aside, perhaps because these men had no patron in the Privy Council. Yet Borough did not throw up his hands in dismay, and between 1575 and 1581 he prepared illustrated memoranda accurately setting out the cause of decay of Paradise, suggesting a new haven with two jetties at its mouth.

The storms in February 1579, followed by a pivotal meeting in Dover on 17 August, meant that all opinions got an airing. The scheme presented by Borough was judged to be the best available, superior to that of the men who had come over from Flanders, skilled in sea defence, but hugely expensive at a total cost of £18,200. It was set aside, and national pride may have had something to do with the decision, with the upshot that the matter was stalled. But the key matter was financial and to fund the effort something significant would have to be done, to which end an Act of Parliament was passed to tax all ships above a certain tonnage entering and leaving the country – all proceeds to go towards harbour construction at Dover.

It is not at all surprising that Lord Cobham, the Warden of the Cinque Ports, was asked by the Privy Council to set up a committee of 'special and choice men'. This last cluster became a permanent commission with appointed members, and Cobham himself able to select commissioners subject to council approval. As a man of Kent he naturally trawled for local men, men of substance and the county, some specialists in fortification, others sailors, and even travellers who had seen such work abroad. Among the commissioners were the Mayor of Dover, the Lieutenant of the Castle, Richard Barrey, and the sole technocrat, Thomas Digges, a Cambridge-trained mathematician and man of Kent living at Wooton Manor, the estate bought by his father.[3] Even Digges jnr had no experience of harbour wall building, although as a cartographer and surveyor he had visited the Low Countries and had looked at harbour designs. The commissioners were engaged to act as the eyes, ears and accountants of the project, with every step vetted by the Privy Council, which got its direction from Walsingham. As the money became available there was the serious matter of finding an engineer with practical ideas, and John True (or Trew) emerged as a man familiar with the problems from his time working on the Exeter Canal in the 1560s. His flawed plan did not alert the Privy Council to potential for trouble, simply because it was enticingly cheap they embraced it with alacrity. On 15 August 1580 True was appointed the first master surveyor of the Dover works.

His pay of ten shillings a day was for work limited to the first two rods of the proposed sea wall, but very soon Cobham, as head of the commission, was writing to Walsingham that True was chafing under the limits. Apparently he claimed that he wanted to start building the whole of the wall, and seemingly uneasy about something asked that his toil be judged when finished, not during construction. On 11 September 1580 the Privy Council ordered the Lord Chancellor to give True his commission to act as master surveyor, with wide-ranging powers in hiring men and calling in materials. He even had the power to imprison anyone hindering his work – but where was it? True acted his part for the rest of the year and much of 1581; clearly a well-crafted turn, for while stone was prepared the wall remained a concept. A stubborn whisper went about that Borough and Digges were increasingly sceptical about a man who airily waved aside a Council request for a progress report. True declared they would get a good harbour, but by mid-1581 his position was shaky and consultants were drafted in – heavy-weights like Francis Drake, Borough, Richard Hakluyt and Digges – all Walsingham men of good standing. Some of the Flemings were called upon to return for a review, and by July the Privy Council had essentially stalled the project, with supplies of material to be stockpiled for the following year. The formal dismissal of John True was subsequently held up for his accounts to be submitted, but from this time he was the wasteful office-holder who had pilfered about £1,300 in a year.

The Privy Council was bruised and keen not to repeat its error. Competition for the available post came from the Flemings, Borough and Digges, who thought his brisk faulting of True gave his own claim to the task a hearty bump forward. During 1581 he produced a famous report, which Walsingham placed before Elizabeth to impress her. In it Digges sketched out a grand scheme of building and renovation to make the harbour far larger than had been envisaged. It was big and bold, so that during the enquiry of December 1581 smaller minds may have flinched. He wanted to build a sluicing reservoir, but some of the water would be filched by a channel dug out under the Western Heights into the upper end of Paradise. To keep it full as a floating basin required a master sluice at the entrance. Further, a breakwater was projected to enclose the whole lower part of the bay, a curved feature from the shore facing Woolcomber Street, round to Archcliff, 'with the opening for the harbour situated at a point opposite Dolphin Passage, near New Bridge'.[4] Land reclamation was part of this, and Digges argued that the leases on it would bring useful revenue for the future maintenance of the harbour. He might have won the day if a Dutchman named Ferdinand Poins had not also put forward a plan (since lost). Poins was an engineer whose professional skills had been developed building sea defences in the Low

Countries and on the Thames at Erith and Woolwich. Now he was hired to drain the lagoon in front of the town and to build reinforcing jetties the length of the sandbar. Still, the Privy Council had learned something from the True fiasco, and while Poins had control on site, Digges was the new master-surveyor. Nor was Poins entirely unfettered in Dover, because the Privy Council also hired the former Cambridge academic Thomas Bedwell (c. 1546–95) who became deputy to Poins and had the support of Burghley.[5] It was practical mathematics that won Bedwell this advance in his career.

It was intended that this difficult project should not crush an individual, nor allow him (like the feckless True) to manipulate it solely to his own advantage. This meant a division of responsibility. Digges was too much the gentleman to be daily on site, so the surveying part of his brief was edged aside to allow him to act as the expert mediator of the Privy Council in dealings with the Dover commissioners. Periodically he rode to the town to look at the work done by Poins and Bedwell, which allowed him to make a commentary on the reports of the commissioners. Ostensibly this was a seamless system, but actually there was a flaw in it. Poins was subjected to criticism from all sides, and could no more than fitfully defend himself; Digges, who had the clout, would not do it for him. In fact, by May 1582 he had come to the sharp conclusion that Poins would fail and would do so at a high price. To cap this was the absurd proposition by Poins that he was unaware that he should keep accounts.

Failure on the monetary targets and failure on site – it was a familiar situation. The level of lagoon water fell by a mere 2ft, and in bad weather (surprise: it rains in Kent!) not at all. So what would happen with the first winter storm – and subsequently? It seemed obvious to Bedwell and to others. Even those on the Council who had supported Poins found elements of his work to criticise, and the beleaguered builder took to blaming everything and everyone, including some of the commissioners, like Richard Barrey. The Council refused the pre-emptive offers of resignation and Poins fumbled on, with one or two local voices speaking in his defence, like Dover's mayor. And so another year passed, another £1,000 was spent to no purpose, and the harbour project seemed doomed to decay. By what they had done, the Privy Council had created the administrative equivalent of a sandbar with no one man with sufficient leverage or muscular energy to get beyond it – until, that is, early in 1583. The unlooked-for arrived. A solution was suggested by the deeply interested observers in the neighbouring town of Romney, where the local technique of building seawalls preserved the economy of Romney Marshes. Confidence that the technique was transferable spread to London, and the faltering project was saved.

The purpose of the Dover sea walls was twofold: to keep water in and seawater surges out. There was to be a long wall the length of the sandbar guarding the pent from the sea, and also a cross wall issuing from the long wall going across the lagoon to the mainland; on it was the main sluice. It was on the solidity of these retaining walls that the project's success was dependent. They had to be strong enough to retain tons of water and exclude tons more; above all, they had to be watertight and storm-resistant. Moreover, they were to be built on a bumpy, shifting foundation of bedrock, river mud and sand across a 12ft-deep tidal river. No leakage through or under the wall could be allowed, and this all had to be done on a budget. Poins reckoned to make the sandbar bigger and stronger so the lagoon would be permanent, and this low-cost notion was supported by Sir William Wynter, Surveyor of the Queen's Ships. William Borough supported the expensive plan of the Queen's master shipwrights, Matthew Baker and Peter Pett, who knew marine carpentry and suggested two rows of planking for the pent, with local chalk and gravel for the infill. Of course, saturated timber would eventually rot, however well seasoned, and there was the problem of much reduced local supplies. Maybe the stocks of the Russia Company were considered by Walsingham for the task.

As the debate began in March 1583 it was commissioner Thomas Scott who set out for scrutiny the Romney alternative. To protect arable land from floods the townsmen had built walls of compacted chalk (abundant locally) and earth, mixed then overlaid with a layer of mud beaten flat, and possibly itself overlaid with turf. Writing in 1586 Reginald Scot phrased his comments ambiguously, so it is possible the turf was left off. Low-cost and efficient, the walls became more watertight over time as they settled, and if suddenly breached they were easily repaired. Thomas Scott had a quarter of a century on the Romney walls, building and maintaining them, and this time the main man knew how to keep accounts. Evidence of success, a detailed plan, men with skills having easy access, and Poins gave the proposal his support, no doubt dancing a gleeful little jig when Romney men declared the lagoon need be drained no further. The Dover commissioner, Edward Boys, was wooed and won over by the evident success of 'honest, skilful marsh artisans'. Thomas Digges wrote to Walsingham in praise of the same men, hoping that they would be expertly supervised, and so the Dover commissioners approved. Pett, Baker and Borough could still argue the case for wood, but Scott smartly pointed out to Walsingham that shipwrights and carpenters were no more qualified to build sea walls and ponds than the makers of such things were qualified to build houses or ships. If left to the commissioners the delays would have ended, but the Privy Council was their superior, and although willing to listen it was unwilling to relinquish its control. Scott therefore found representatives from among the Romney men to make a presentation in London, and the councillors hauled in for this session put many questions. These were answered by the surveyor and common clerk of the Kent men, who sturdily held back on their secret skill in dealing with leaks and said nothing about costs. It was good that they had Digges on their side – the local man with the privileged position close to Walsingham. With expert knowledge and a disinterested concern for the project's completion, Digges sought to distance himself from any taint of seeking to line his own pockets by the renunciation of his salary entitlement of ten shillings a day. He noted cannily that any satisfactorily completed version of the plan would bump up the value of his Kent estates.

Lord Burghley was among that cluster convinced by Digges; ironically, Walsingham was more elusive, but could not appear too intransigent for too long, and so after more talks with Digges, Borough, Poins and the Romney men he retreated to supporting the Romney method after more talks with Wynter. Tasked with asking all the old questions, that is what he did, and it was during these close scrutiny sessions that Borough was finally convinced. Poins was demoted by Wynter and Walsingham, but retained a less demanding part in the effort. He showed his gratitude by quitting.

In April 1583 the Romney men were officially taken on to build the walls that would enclose the pent, considered by all to be the task 'of greatest difficulty'. A test of the building technique was essayed, and it worked – though the sluice soon broke. Starting in May when the weather held fair, in less than three months a wall was built nearly half a mile long and reaching up several feet above the high-water mark. This speed was achieved by the smart direction of Digges, who advertised pay of one shilling a day for each man with a horse and cart. They trundled in from as far afield as Sevenoaks and Maidstone, using this period of freedom between sowing and harvesting. Many hundreds arrived and some had to be turned away while the carts were loaded with building materials overnight; stone from Folkestone, chalk from the locale. At six in the morning hundreds of loaded carts were on site, ready with material for the day's intensive labouring. Thomas Scott was the acting head overseer, who not only had to pasture the animals but to use the flood of workers effectively. He did this by working on the long and cross wall simultaneously. Barrey got to take charge of the completion of the long wall and Scott dealt with the more problematic cross wall himself. Their sides were made up of faggots pinned into place by massive piles, then covered with earth and chalk, also forced into any cracks or spaces. 'Starting from shore at a point just to the east of the mouth of the River Dour, the wall then ran parallel with the beach as far as the pier which lay to the north of the harbour entrance.' It was the cross wall that had at its landward end a floodgate and sluice, and when it met the long wall at right angles the pent was made. From this came a flow of water to make eventually Great Paradise.

On 21 July 1583 Scott was able to write a notice to Walsingham that the walls were done and apparently watertight. Fine weather and the hearty participation of swarms of men had allowed the task to be done in a little over two months, and some £5,000 cheaper than the next-lowest estimate. For the next decade the work done was tweaked and improved, and during the time from 1586–94 that Digges was in the Netherlands, his deputy, Alexander Mindge, was in charge, receiving Digges's salary. So, after long delays, pointless toil, pernicious pilfering, monies wasted and meetings galore, the work was done to relief and satisfaction in Kent and London, and if not immediately perfect it did great service in future.

A local problem with national ramifications had tested administrative and financial skills almost to the limits of possibility. Remarkably, at the same time, the government found itself a national problem with international consequences; they began looking to (as it were) repair the future. The course they submitted to intensive scrutiny was a matter of particular political and diplomatic contention in much of Western Europe – the reform of the ancient and creaky Julian calendar.[6] The Christian church had adopted the Roman Empire's Julian calendar in 325 AD to ensure the collective observation of Easter, but without realizing that the year of the Roman calculation was eleven minutes too long. By the late sixteenth century this had grown to ten days, and the reform of Pope Gregory XIII was promulgated in 1582 to bring reform to the timing of Easter, to remove the ten days (so bringing the calendar back to Nicaean regulation) and to modify leap years to keep the whole in balance. The papal bull for reform was accepted by two key powers of Catholic Europe, France and Spain, as well as the Duke of Savoy. Another duke – Alençon (Anjou) also decreed acceptance of the Gregorian calendar where he ruled in the transitional Low Countries. The result was that in Brussels the new Christmas was celebrated ten days before the old Catholic Christmas of 4 January. The new reckoning was not just a Roman concern. Every country in Europe had to decide whether to follow the papal bull, a copy of which came to Walsingham in diplomatic correspondence.[7] Since 1570 and *Regnans in Excelsis*, publication of a papal bull had been illegal, and the copy sent to John Dee by the Principal Secretary may have been forwarded from Paris in mid-October. Despite the whiff of papal incense about it, Walsingham inclined to reform and wanted the most rigorous, informed scrutiny of the proposal. So by the new Christmas Day 1582 Dee was already working on the matter, and in January 1583 Walsingham wanted the bull back in his archives. Dee worked hard on the assignment, and on 26 February Burghley received a sixty-two page, illuminated paper with the shortened title that becomes *A playne Discourse*.

In this two-part document Dee opened with an historic overview of how the movements within the solar system were translated in the calendar into everyday use, and how it had slipped out of alignment by ten days since the council of Nicaea, and, as Dee emphasised, by eleven days since the birth of Jesus. Christians should regard this as the *Radix of time*. Dee proposed a royal decree to make the change not by hacking off ten days, but by slicing off days in batches from May to September. This mode of action would reduce secular problems, such as the timing of the law terms. England would still be out of step with papal usage, but this would hardly be England's fault – the error would be hung on Gregory XIII. The year 1583 required a special calendar – the *annus reformationis* – to be followed in 1584 by Elizabeth's perpetual calendar. There was also an appeal to Europe to follow a more precise reform than that envisaged by the Pope. In his response Burghley rumbled the limiting element in Dee's paper, which was the lack of alignment with Europe, and he visited Mortlake to get the proposer to concede on that point. Dee agreed to the reduction of eleven days to ten, and that the whole matter should be scrutinised by a committee that included Thomas Digges. Burghley, in some notes to Robert Cecil, acknowledged his own lack of expertise in such matters, and that John Dee was able to cite material that ought to satisfy conservative, resisting opinion. With time passing, Walsingham arranged for Dee to attend a meeting in mid-March on the subject, and the men of science to be consulted were Digges, Henry Savile, Greek scholar and leading Copernican, and Mr Chambers – probably John Chambers. They made only limited revisions to what Dee had submitted; it was on the balance of utility over the ten/eleven days' hitch and Dee managed to re-jig his 1583 almanac to remove the ten that would align England with Europe. The final thought on the process was that if Elizabeth agreed to it then a proclamation would be issued to effect the change.

To win the solid approval of the senior clergy, Walsingham had already written to Archbishop Grindal setting out the government's thoughts. He was asked to consult swiftly with any bishops who happened to be in London – the injection of speed was because the proclamation was to be made on 1 May, the first month to be pruned. This rather abrupt tone with stubborn, conservative churchmen was a tactical error. Grindal felt no urge to respond, and Walsingham was forced to write again on 29 March. He pointed out that Elizabeth too was irked by the collective silence of the bishops. The stalled reply from Grindal, Aylmer, Piers and Young put as its principal objection that the Pope was the Anti-Christ, 'therefore we may not communicate with him in anything'. However, beyond this sharp assertion lay more subtle arguments. Walsingham had intended that the state should have the final say in the calendar reform, but this cluster of bishops disposed of that, putting forward the view that to do as the government wanted would require a meeting of Convocation. And as for remaining out of kilter with continental Europe – wherein was the harm? After all, the Privy Council had yet to deal with the English custom of starting the year on 25 March rather than 1 January. The rapid change sought by Walsingham and Burghley was blocked, but they were unwilling to give up, with the proclamation ready and dated 28 April. In the preamble efforts were made to counter the objections of the bishops, and it was pointed out that other Protestant countries had accepted the papal package. There would be advantages in trade and diplomacy, and secular opinion was altogether favourable, but the bishops were steadfast and they won the day. The proclamation was shelved.

Chapter 15

RUINING ROANOKE

Newfoundland in Canada was the oldest colony established by English seafarers, an effort led by Sir Humphrey Gilbert. Initially the fishermen spent only summers there (wise considering the winters), taking great hauls of cod from the seas and salmon from the rivers. We know that as early as 1574, when Gilbert petitioned the Queen to be allowed to undertake a voyage of discovery in western waters, among the gentlemen who countersigned was George Peckham of Denham, Buckinghamshire. A kinsman of the Wriothesley earls of Southampton, with a recusant brother who had died in Rome in 1569 after a self-imposed exile, George Peckham was loyal to Elizabeth, who visited him in 1570 while still uncertain about her host. For her stay she had a new bedroom door made, heavily furnished with locks, bolts, staples and hinges, but need not have bothered, and for his cordiality Peckham got a knighthood. His loyalty was given emphasis by his appointment as High Sheriff of Buckinghamshire in 1573, and in 1580 the building of Denham parish church.

Even so, although there is no evidence of an open profession of Catholicism, there are hints of a shift in sympathy in the late 1570s, and active involvement in Catholic relief. It was through the influence of his second wife, the daughter of his recusant neighbour David Penne, that Peckham gave funds to the keepers of London prisons for distribution to religious captives, and the even weightier crime of sheltering Edmund Campion, SJ. In March 1581 Peckham himself put up a bond of £1,000 for his own release from a short incarceration. Moreover, his daughter was now married to a son of Sir Thomas Gerrard, a notable papist family, and the respective fathers-in-law became close associates. The time in prison and the 1581 anti-recusant laws frightened Peckham – hence the very early manifestation of America beckoning to the oppressed. On 6 June 1582 Peckham and Gerrard signed articles of agreement concerning their proposed expedition with Gilbert, whose prospects of sailing were now altogether more immediate. He was not much concerned with the faith of backers – more their money bags.

Walsingham had knowledge of these dealings weeks before, and there is even the possibility that they had been nudged to assembly by his keen hope to evict at least a portion of the Queen's enemies.[1] Moreover, if intention and money did cohere then the patent of American lands granted to Philip Sidney on 7 July 1582 became a blue-chip holding for the impoverished would-be husband of Frances Walsingham; pert, pretty, but with no great dowry. To give the effort the Walsingham seal of approval, his stepson Christopher was involved. At least one German metallurgist sailed with Sir Humphrey, suggesting that the secondary aim was to locate and remove precious metals for the investors. Peckham and Gerrard did not participate in the journey, and on the return leg Gilbert went down with the 10-ton *Squirrel*. Peckham's tribute to Gilbert in 1583 was the publication *True Reporte of the Late Discoveries* with commendatory verses by Drake (his only known poem), John Hawkins and Martin Frobisher.

What was secondary to Gilbert became the primary matter for Ralegh in the attempt to establish a permanent English presence at Roanoke Island, beginning in 1584. The vast quantities of treasure seized by Philip II's soldiers and sailors underpinned a global empire linked to the papacy, and an English challenge to it would need resources on a heroic scale. These could either be wrested from Spain by hijacking her shipping or by the founding of new territories; Richard Hakluyt wrote 'the Spanish King . . . will in short pace become a laughing stock for all the world', and despite the hoarse edge to this it was close to what happened. After the return of the first Roanoke voyage it was Hakluyt who presented the Council with a keenly instructive position paper, *Discourse on Western Planting*, urging the Queen to underwrite Ralegh's future efforts. Remarkably she responded by assigning the *Tiger* to her Devonian champion, and in February 1585 Captain Ralph Lane was recalled from Ireland, where he was widely detested and his superiors could not get rid of him fast enough, to head the land forces. The general in fleet command was Ralegh's cousin, Sir Richard Grenville, one of the anti-Spanish tribe, bold in battle, ruthless in politics 'and compulsive killers as well as habitual liars'. Nor would the squadron sail without its company of experts and subsequently Lane made clear he had really only two interests – precious metals, and the discovery of a passage to the Pacific ocean from Pamlico

Sound, in present-day North Carolina. To gauge mineral finds they took Joachim Gans of Prague – surely the first Jew in English America, and present under the aegis of Walsingham. Gans did the journey across the Atlantic with a great deal of heavy equipment stored on the *Tiger*. On 29 June the flagship's pilot tried to squeeze her into a safe harbour, but misjudged the depth of water so the ship ran aground. She had to be refloated, and this meant jettisoning provisions and some of the equipment Gans had brought over.

The loss of supplies was not immediately serious, but it did mean that after sailing south and eventually settling on Roanoke, Grenville determined to sail home to regroup for the following year. Ralegh, had he been in Grenville's place, might have made a better fist of dealings with Lane, but it is doubtful, since the latter was stubborn, greedy and violent. Writing accusatory letters to Walsingham, he cast Grenville in a baleful light, and a strong written defence was necessary because Grenville would be in England and he had elected to remain in Roanoke. Lane wrote four letters to Walsingham, and Ralegh got what amounted to the book of the voyage, which would also be passed in a copy to the Principal Secretary. His spies, Atkinson and Russell, also returned with Grenville on the repaired *Tiger* – a journey Walsingham would have defended on the grounds that he was protecting the Queen's investment.

The first of the returners to reach London was John Arundell, who was immediately set before the Queen at Richmond Palace, where on 14 October he was knighted. Ralegh had of course used his expedition as a means of underpinning his court career, and with Arundell back he travelled to Plymouth to greet Grenville, who arrived on 18 October, not on the *Tiger* (already safely in port), but the *Santa Maria de San Vicente*, the flagship of the Santo Domingo treasure fleet, laden with sugar and ginger valued by Grenville at 40,000–50,000 ducats. His enemies whispered counter-claims, saying the manifest included gold, silver and pearls as seen by a Portuguese merchant, and an anonymous report (likely penned by Walsingham's former spy William Herle) sent to Elizabeth suggested a soaring value of more than 1 million ducats.[2] Ralegh believed family and scorned Lane's calumnies, so that Grenville was nominated to lead the return squadron. Before that Grenville had to defend his own conduct to Walsingham, and with the hold of the *Tiger* stuffed with items from this new, hugely promising world one wonders what (if anything) he sent to Barn Elms; some precious plants, or perhaps saplings?

Whatever Walsingham got for his investment, it would not have smothered his interest in the fortunes and fate of Joachim Gans, who remained in America. Some few years before this the clerk of the Society of Mines Royal, George Needham, had persuaded this clever, inventive polyglot Jew to come to England to advance himself and the science of metallurgy. Needham, who spoke German, was eager to improve the working methods of the Society and to enhance his standing with the Governor – Walsingham. From Bohemia to Keswick (the centre of the Society), where Gans did some trials at the smelters, and in 1581 wrote a proposal to the Governor for the improving of copper production. The immigrant's expertise in the smelting and refining of copper, lead and silver almost certainly came from working experience in the Ore Mountains that formed the border between Bohemia and Saxony. Others from that region had already made the journey to England, and those closest to Elizabeth (including Walsingham) urged her to ask the Elector to make more available. Needham could be pleased that his trawl for suitable people to employ came up with Gans, because in considering the operations of the Mines Royal he saw at once the wasteful firings (sixteen to eighteen) over the same number of weeks for ores to be worked into copper. He did some tests in Keswick and put it to Walsingham that the firings could be slashed to four and still produce rough copper. His offer was that he would produce 100 pounds of it for five shillings less than one Mark Steinberger, with peat to do the heating, not expensive wood.

Gans was a good linguist, but not yet at this time fluent in English, and so Needham translated items prepared for Walsingham. The innovation that Gans brought to Keswick was originally described in *De Re Metallica*, by Georgius Agricola (George Bauer), the father of mineralogy. Copper ore was reduced to a powder, then heated and water passed through the result, so that, as Needham explained, the water carried away vitriol, iron and sulphur. What Gans did was suggest that the vitriol (a mixture of iron and copper sulphate) could itself be used as a dye for textiles. On his move south to Neath near Swansea, Gans surely had amicable input into the building there of the Mines Royal smelter, which was ready just prior to his going to America. It was on his initiative that the Society reopened mines in Cornwall, where in July 1584 Ralegh became Lord Warden of the Stannaries. To become permanent governor of Virginia as his vast grants were named in 1585, Raleigh had to establish a permanent colony before his royal patent expired in 1590. If mining and smelting could be started the settlement would be given an immediate economic boost – making its survival more likely. Only Gans and his fellow German miners of the Society had the knowledge to determine if there were within the settled area valuable ores that could be commercially exploited. The assay oven seems to have been among the items jettisoned to refloat the *Tiger*, but Gans was an improviser as well as an improver, and archaeological evidence shows he built his own brick furnace.[3]

Roanoke Island became a base for exploratory outings, and having a naturally inquiring spirit Gans went along with as many as he could to search for natural resources. In the winter of 1585–6 one such push in boats went some 136 miles to the north, but sandy coastal plains were not going to yield anything significant. Lane became so taken up by the idea of mineral riches that he besieged the local native chief and kidnapped his son to elicit information. The journey up the Roanoke River that originates in the Blue Ridge Mountains, made in the spring of 1586, was also a flop and nearly ended in disaster. When they did get back to Roanoke the colony ran into serious difficulties – a war with the natives – and when no supply ships arrived, the appearance of Drake's fleet, after his Florida foray to attack the Spanish, must have seemed like prayers answered. Getting safely back to England, the odious Lane began a self-promoting campaign and attacked Grenville. For a more balanced discourse on future prospects, Walsingham could turn to Gans, who on his return settled in Blackfriars, London.

Ralegh was a belligerent dandy who never became a Privy Councillor: Elizabeth adored his looks and vivacious wit, but distrusted his judgement; Burghley looked on him with no favour, even with hostility, and Walsingham was alienated from him as his own loyal and intelligent stepson Christopher was pushed out of the limelight. Royal generosity to Ralegh by a menopausal woman of uncertain temper was so giddily stupid that Walsingham's dignified loyalty was badly bruised. The absurd expense of subsidizing Ralegh was insupportable to him when the 1585 commitment to the Dutch placed significant financial obligations upon the English state. While Walsingham elected (perhaps unconsciously) to mark Ralegh as the enemy at home, the unspoken, deep-buried feeling was flickering into life that it was Elizabeth whom his policies would have to shackle, albeit clandestinely and with the maximum cautious dissimulation. He would take her on in his last years, and he would rule despite her Tudor blood for she was powerless as a virgin to advance the Tudor dynasty, 'powerless to achieve salvation without the ministry of male preachers, powerless to govern effectively without male advice and guidance'.[4] If Walsingham wanted a text to underpin his deeply buried views he could find a passage in Peter Martyr's *Commentary on Romans* (English translation 1568) on the empowerment of inferior magistrates 'putting down' princes who transgressed the limits of power; making them do their duty.[5] The Queen needed to be made to do her duty, and he was the 'inferior magistrate' to do it, taking power invisibly and directing the country to the policies he had so patiently advocated. No woman, even a queen, could be allowed to stand in his way. So, for example, in 1584 when Merchant Adventurers violated Ralegh's licence to export cloth and Elizabeth sanctioned the arrest of their ships, it was Walsingham who defended them and accused her of damaging the collective trade of the company to privilege one man. There were individuals who in Walsingham's opinion deserved so much more from her – especially his son-in-law Philip Sidney, whose marriage to Frances Walsingham led to the all-too-predictable royal disapproval that was their stale marriage gift from the sour old virgin.[6] The sense that his son-in-law's rightful place in court and council was being usurped by those with little more than a handsome presence and smart wit was galling.

To deflate Ralegh and wreck his grand project for 1587 – the colonial cluster of men, women and children to be shipped under their governor, John White, to Chesapeake Bay, calling only briefly at Roanoke – needed a collaborator, and the seething Walsingham, who had seen his greatest triumph of 1586 (the destruction of the Babington Plot) degraded by Elizabeth's bizarre response to the snaring and execution of Mary, Queen of Scots, found one, as it seems, in Simão Fernandes, the Portuguese-born navigator. By now, of the triumvirate, Walsingham was absolutely the most dangerous to Elizabeth, because the core of beliefs he held was not subject to revision. Burghley could trim; Leicester too when he saw he had gone too far in his abundant risk-taking; but Walsingham had his vision, and his heroic inner strength kept him going despite poor general health. In March 1587 Walsingham was once again back in the heart of government, and was seen to be active on all matters. One ambition was to ignite a rebellion in Portugal on behalf of the exiled claimant of the Portuguese throne, Dom Antonio. Fernandes (born *c.* 1538) was an Azorean immigrant to England with a huge range of maritime experience, and was a loyal supporter of Dom Antonio. Although not totally trusted by those who sailed with him, the gusty personality of Fernandes and his hatred of the Spanish won him the protective encouragement of the powerful, including Walsingham. For a time Fernandes was imprisoned, satisfying the Portuguese ambassador, but

Francisco Giraldi was soon protesting to Walsingham at his release. Fernandes was identified as a rough spirit, and he entered the service of the Principal Secretary in 1578.

It took Walsingham some three months to get Privy Council agreement to the plan he had pitched on behalf of Dom Antonio. Just when Drake was ready to sail his crew fled, scared away according to Mendoza (Spanish ambassador in Paris) by Ralegh. Why would Ralegh be so keen to sabotage something that brought Drake and Walsingham together again? The answer must be that he wanted to eliminate anything competing for ships, men and resources while furthering the English settlement in Chesapeake Bay. When Richard Hakluyt the elder wrote an essay on colonization in 1585, he made the error of assuming that regions within similar latitudes must have similar climates (clearly he never went from London to Moscow), so he expected the Bay area to produce Mediterranean commodities highly sought after and at premium prices in England. Colonization was evolving, and was no longer to be in tandem with piracy, in which Ralegh had invested heavily, owning and operating a private man-o'-war.[7] Which is why Ralegh's disastrous error was to take on Fernandes, for all that he was untroubled by vast distances and little ships. By Ralegh's charter the settlers who would go were incorporated as 'the Governor and Assistants of the City of Raleigh (sic) in Virginia', with John White, the artist, as governor and Fernandes as one of the twelve assistants. This was a position of responsibility for one of the most highly regarded western navigators.

Three ships were equipped for the 117 settlers who sailed on 8 May 1587; John White and Fernandes were both on the *Lion*, and they may have gone together with a purpose, but this cracked as the old privateering imperatives seized Fernandes again and White, fearful for his settler charges, including his own daughter, resisted. When they had crossed the Atlantic as far as the West Indies, the Portuguese pilot fumbled their island-hopping so that they failed to get salt on Puerto Rico, and there were no sheep on Vicques Island despite his claim that it was alive with them. The primary plan had been to call at Roanoke, gather up the small group left by Grenville in 1586, and then move on to Chesapeake Bay. But Fernandes effectively hijacked the operation and brought down the plan by refusing to go beyond Roanoke, where they found signs of the former settlers and then, shockingly, skeletons, saying it was too late in the season to make for the Bay. White gave way and agreed they would stay, despite the foreseeable problem with food supplies. Late arrival meant late planting and little hope of a real harvest. This meant someone would have to return to England in the fly-boat, and since everyone deeply distrusted Fernandes the assistants chose White to represent them, his daughter remaining in Roanoke with her own baby daughter. White left at the end of August, reluctantly making what turned into a miserable crossing. Fernandes followed him in the *Lion* and failed to take any prizes as the ship's company fell sick and dawdled into Portsmouth in October. Fernandes had no further part to play in the ruin of Roanoke, but ruthlessly Walsingham did. In October the rescue pinnace for the settlers was stayed by the special Council of Shipping and Mariners because an invasion scare was on, and several months later when Grenville was about to sail from Bideford he too was commanded to remain. By panicking Elizabeth in his daily briefing conversations, and by setting the conciliar agenda, Walsingham saw to it that Roanoke became an archaeological site rather than a thriving settlement. Ralegh's ships were to be delivered to Drake, and the fumbling John White could do nothing until the Armada emergency was over. Still, he did try and was brutally thwarted by French pirates out of La Rochelle in the spring of 1588; they descended on him near Madeira, seeing not an ally but an opportunity for plunder.

Chapter 16

ALL AROUND THE HOUSES

former law student at Barnard's Inn who for two years from 1581 served as a soldier in the Spanish armies, John Savage entered the English College in Rheims in May 1583, and remained there for just two years.[1] He was an excellent recruit to the opposition, as his former colleague in arms noted; a well-educated soldier and linguist who believed that the killing of a tyrant was lawful. The professor of theology at Rheims at this time was Dr William Gifford, son of Catholic parents (his mother was a Throckmorton) who after time at Oxford moved abroad to study in Paris, Louvain, Rheims and Rome.[2] Savage would later name him the initiator of the Babington Plot, but Gifford's dealings with Walsingham and his leadership of the anti-Spanish cluster at Rheims suggest that Savage was deliberately misleading his interlocutors, or that he had misunderstood Gifford. But then Savage's allegation does refer to the summer of 1585, and the link to Walsingham comes in the spring of 1586, so Dr Gifford could have said something. A rather murky business, but we have a much clearer picture almost immediately. It sharpens to our advantage as Walsingham has delivered to his agent Solomon Aldred a letter and passport for return to England to be given to Dr Gifford. Another letter from Walsingham went to Father Edward Grateley at Rouen, and he in turn wrote to William Gifford seeking to persuade him to quit Rheims. This three-sided correspondence became four-sided when William's nephew Gilbert Gifford, also an agent for Walsingham, joined in. Gilbert, smooth of tongue as of face, a blue-eyed boy in every way, had a bumpy seminary career before being ordained as a deacon in 1585, by which time his hold over his uncle, strong and mysterious, was revealed by him to Walsingham. His joint letter to William Gifford was sent to Grateley, who put it with his own letter for delivery to Dr Gifford in the hands of Aldred. When he reached Paris Aldred approached Stafford, who found a messenger to deliver all the letters in Rheims and carried 10 crowns for Gifford to make the journey to Paris. When the messenger arrived on Sunday 10 April he found Gifford preparing to preach, and it was the next day that the professor set out for Paris, where Grateley had arrived to be lodged secretly with Aldred. By the Wednesday and Thursday Gifford, with much on his mind, was in conference with Aldred, willing also to talk to Stafford, but nervous at the possibility of being observed. So to slide round this Stafford came secretly to a rendezvous and the result was a boost to Gifford's confidence. He even gave optimistic voice to the notion of splitting Dr Allen and Robert Persons – putting them at variance would certainly have been in Walsingham's thoughts. Stafford tried to persuade Dr Gifford to return to England forthwith, with the passport already available from Aldred. However, he failed, and Gifford explained why to Stafford in a document to be sent to Walsingham. Being an intelligent man Dr Gifford must have seen the future – him in England as an active double agent betraying Catholicism.[3] The convergence of the English Catholic mission and Walsingham's intelligence network left undiscernible points of rupture within the country.

While Aldred was the 'facilitator' for all this, the idea that Stafford should meet Gifford came from Morgan, who knew that losses at cards were compromising Stafford. And why was Morgan prodding Gifford? Two reasons put themselves under the spotlight: first, any activity by Gifford might mislead Walsingham when plans were afoot for Mary to renew her European correspondence; second, by returning to England under government protection after creating a schism at Rheims, he had camouflage for spying to advantage the exiled secular Catholics. The senior Gifford could never be persuaded to set his moral principles aside, much to the irritation of Walsingham, who fared vastly better with Gilbert Gifford, the chancer who arrived back in England around December 1585 and got warm attention from the spymaster. He landed at Rye, thus putting himself in the way of Walsingham, carrying letters of recommendation from Morgan to Mary. We know now that the choice of Gifford as messenger was freighted with risk, but at the time, with his Catholic past and connections, he fitted perfectly the profile of a personable and trustworthy gentleman who could be relied on to deal faithfully with her. When Mary had been held at Tutbury she had been a few miles from the Gifford family home, so from Walsingham's point of view the young man had great potential, perhaps more; he seemed like someone of the calibre of Thomas Rogers (alias Nicholas Berden) who had spied in Paris and yet retained the confidence of the clandestine Catholics of London. To prepare Gifford, Walsingham put him in company with Thomas Phelippes, then residing in premises in Leadenhall market. The brilliant polyglot decipherer could work on Morgan's letter to Mary, then on the brink of being moved to Chartley, and scrutinise the new recruit. Phelippes visited Chartley as the guest of Paulet in the holiday season of 1585–6.

Back in September Walsingham directed that Mary's official correspondence should be transmitted through him and Paulet, rather than the French ambassador, Guillaume de L'Aubepine, Baron de Châteauneuf. For her secret missives Mary needed another route, and Gifford made the key suggestion to the ambassador on a visit to the embassy in Salisbury Court, briefly a marriage property of a Paulet. The idea of using the beer delivery to Chartley was likely that of Phelippes, who persuaded Paulet that it could work. The house had no brewing facility but regularly received supplies from Burton; inside the barrel stopper in a waterproof package letters to and from the royal prisoner could pass under the watchful Catholic eye of the brewer – a known partisan of Mary. Yet he could be bought, another pocket for Walsingham's gold, wherein it could mingle with Mary's, and for a price he agreed to carry letters in the cask passing 'out' items to the 'secret party': Gilbert Gifford. Apart from Morgan's letter, Gifford had others for Châteauneuf, which were handed over to the secretary designated to deal with Marian matters, Cordaillot. In flawless French Gifford explained his courier mission, and to give a gloss to his presentation he declared that his absence abroad for over a decade had effectively made him invisible to the English authorities. Cordaillot had to be cautious and wait for evidence that the 'invisible' man who sat before him actually had links to Mary.

Gifford had done some of the preliminary work for this and took himself off to the neighbourhood of Chartley, apparently to renew contacts with his father. He did not stay in the parental home but settled into a house formerly used by the steward of the Chartley estate. Then he ventured over to Burton, to meet the still anonymous brewer, handing over Morgan's letter with a covering note. Declining to work on the Sabbath the brewer made his delivery on the following Saturday, declaring his intention to return the next day to remove the emptied cask – apparently no one asked why he was accelerating the delivery system. Mary's household must have been galvanised by this sudden worldly breeze from beyond the walls, and there was little time for secret letter-writing and ciphering. But the arrangement was followed and worked sweetly, so that at a respectable distance from Chartley the wagon was halted and the brewer, or possibly an excited Gifford, retrieved the reply packet in pristine condition. He rode then to London in two or three days, and Phelippes set about deciphering what proved to be items of no consequence. One letter was an acknowledgement of Morgan's letter, and there were two more that merely conveyed that Mary was interested but properly wary. When Phelippes had done, all the seals were counterfeited by the master in wax, Arthur Gregory, and so Gifford was set to deliver to the French embassy.

Cordaillot shivered at his own involvement, but he had no option but to hand over a letter from his ambassador to Mary. It was in cipher but remained as innocuous as the first letter from her, and since Gifford had nothing to keep him in the city he left for Chartley. Paulet was expecting him for Tuesday 25 January, the brewer having made a weekend delivery of ale, and the 'out' missive from Mary was already being carried to London. It was now that there came a little jolt to the apparently smooth-running system. Paulet had to wait until 3 February, a whole nine days, before he received a note from Gifford asking for a trusted messenger who could collect a packet which the brewer had delivered to him. Gifford was presumably at the estate house, which explains how the brewer knew where to find him. As for the messenger, Paulet found a man to undertake the task, and Gifford swiftly penned a note as well to say he would be at Chartley on Saturday 5 February. Darkness hid his arrival from the part of the household for whom he had two packets and two additional letters. There was also a cipher previously received from Gilbert Curll, Mary's Scottish secretary. Gifford asked to keep this for an acknowledgement of the packets now handed over.[4]

Advances in cryptography and analysis had mostly been made in the fifteenth and sixteenth centuries in Italy, but in effect this was only catching up. The greatest experts had been Arabs, and the technique of frequency analysis was first described by the ninth century Iraqi philosopher and scientist Abu Yusuf Yacub ibn Ishaq al-Sabbah al-Kindi, in *A Manuscript on Deciphering Cryptographic Messages*, a text rediscovered in the 1980s which classified ciphers and described the use of several statistical techniques for cryptanalysis. Mary used a nomenclature cipher, and it was frequency analysis by Thomas Phelippes that was her undoing.

The lure of London to a young man so long absent from the country was strong, and Gilbert Gifford had it in mind to spend some time exploring it. If he was there then the French ambassador was going to get the mail faster and this should win praise. Like every double agent, he had to calculate the moves that would win the approval of both sides. While away from his Chartley bolt-hole a substitute would take his place and he would leave a 'counter-paper' with the brewer when next they met. This troubled Paulet, who thought he saw the original system of letter swaps shrivelling, and who in any case had no opportunity to leave Chartley even if his quotidian tasks took their toll. His very young daughter Elizabeth had probably been born at Tutbury, and in a letter to Walsingham he referred to her as 'my little jewel'.[5] Walsingham was her godfather, and in a household well peopled with women no doubt she was much petted and praised. As for Gifford, Paulet elicited some unease, for the young man occasionally gave him contradictory answers, and the brewer too had a breezy attitude that irked Paulet.

Walsingham, in regard to these two critical agents, was less concerned for the time being with Gifford than he was with the brewer, who had much more access to the household servants, and it is possible that he liked to sample his own brew a little too often. Moreover, there was now the need to nudge him further into the operation, with payments for first delivering any 'out' letters to Paulet before barrelling them away, and vice versa. The secret post was now in its definitive form, and it carried the intense hopes of Walsingham and his cadre.

So Gifford made his way to London. By the time he had arrived the letters forwarded by Paulet on 6 February had been deciphered by Phelippes and resealed, so a packet was ready to be passed to Châteauneuf. To the satisfaction of Walsingham and the team working to his orders it contained much of what had been hoped for, including authority for Châteauneuf to hand over to Gifford all the packets that had come in over six months. When Gifford went to him on 1 March, the key letter had been a month in transit; what he got in return was a major clutch of letters – a paper deluge that tested Phelippes. But he tackled the twenty-one packets with gusto, and by 4 March had deciphered the first batch. It was impossible to get them all into the barrel tube in one go, so Paulet had to arrange for delivery by instalments. Gifford was actually free from all this, able to throw himself into metropolitan diversions because the substitute who had been found was judged sound: he was an employee of Leicester, and Paulet and the brewer both approved of him. The next meeting at the barrel was to be on 20 March.

Gifford did have some assignments in London. One was to assimilate himself with an increasingly enthusiastic clandestine community of papists who would draw inspiration as readers from a tract like *De Persecutione Anglicana*, the work of Robert Persons and printed for export in Rouen. Walsingham had an informant there called François de Civille, agent for the Duke of Bouillon who considered the Jesuit (actually expelled from the town for hatching plots for the Holy League) one of the Principal Secretary's 'greatest enemies'. But not all were as ardent as Persons, and it was in company with Gifford that John Savage got a pointed reminder of the freely taken vow he had made to kill Elizabeth, and with burgeoning resolve came his declaration of intent to the Catholic priest John Ballard, an MA (Cantab) with a cluster of aliases who had fled to Rheims, was ordained at Chalons in March 1581, and then came to England. Visiting the Gatehouse he made the acquaintance of the agent for the government, Ballard's friend Anthony Tyrell.[6] When he escaped (the reader will wonder if this was a set-up) the two travelled abroad. They were tracked by Walsingham's agent (so likely it was) and Thomas Rogers was one who thought Ballard dangerous. Late in 1584 he travelled from Rouen to Southampton and linked up with the only known Jesuit in the country – Father William Weston – and from late 1585 to June 1586, with the involvement of a clutch of other priests, they began public exorcisms which achieved an underground notoriety. There were Puritan exorcisms as well, and both sides made it dramatic and contentious: 'it was performed through a series of prayers, conjuration of devils, and ritual instructions to the evil spirits to depart . . .'. On one occasion at Denham House five coaches bearing Catholic gentlemen arrived to see Ballard at work, for in company with them was a servant of Anthony Babington, deemed to be in the grip of malevolent spirits. With Marwood's young and impressionable employer came the men who were so soon to be hauled into the Babington Plot: Robert Gage, Charles Tilney, Thomas Salusbury and Chidiock Tichborne of the huge Hampshire Catholic family.

The pugnacious Ballard had gone once again to Paris to confer with Mendoza, Paget and Morgan. Later, to Savage and Babington he made the claim that a large continental army would be ready to give backing to their domestic efforts. He was back, in his disguise as 'Captain Fortescue', cutting a dashing figure, but lacking the smart discretion needed of the best clandestine operators – hence his tracking by one of Walsingham's agents – a purveyor of fact, hearsay and speculation intermingled. This was the man Ballard trusted with his travel arrangements, especially the getting of passports that could bear scrutiny, the slippery and disreputable Barnard

Maude, whose sneaky attempt to blackmail Archbishop Sandys after his dismissal by the ecclesiastic cost him a period in the Fleet. Towards the end of May 1586 plotters and potential plotters met at Babington's lodgings in Hern's Rents, Holborn. Given the fantastic news of the dukes of Guise and Parma preparing an invasion force of 60,000 troops, much preparation had to be done immediately. 'Black Foskew' (Ballard) would travel with Maude to Scotland and the north of England to ignite the ardour of as many Catholics as possible. Mary was simultaneously making defiant contacts with Mendoza – sometimes more sceptical than supposed, but who wanted the venture underwritten by Philip II. She pledged to override James VI's right of succession to the English throne, and would declare Philip her successor. The formerly hesitant King found his ambassador twitching with excitement about this new slant, and at length assigned Mary 12,000 escudos, with a payment to Morgan to be made from Mendoza's own expenses.

It was Ballard who now sketched out for the lightweight young Babington what was needed in England, as Europe looked on with high expectations. With his wide range of Catholic contacts about the country he must give prophetic voice to their future, and so bring about an uprising that would mesh with the great invasion. Mildly, Babington rehearsed the essential thing militating against the success of any such plan. The indifference of so many to Elizabeth's rule was by now greatly countered by those who would praise and cheer her. Ballard responded that this could be undermined – 'taken away by means already laid'. Her life was forfeited (in the project) and the man to effect this was John Savage, who himself visited Babington. Having returned from Rheims in the autumn of 1585, he took up his law books again at Barnard's Inn, and it was this quiet period into which burst the ebullient Gilbert Gifford – he knew exactly how to goad to a purpose and Savage would listen.

Chapter Seventeen

THE POPE'S WHITE SONS

March 1586: The Plough Inn outside Temple Bar in London's legal district. Close by was Lincoln's Inn, the latest place of study for Anthony Babington, gent, born October 1561, the third child of a wealthy Catholic gentry family of Dethick, near Matlock in Derbyshire. As the oldest son of Henry Babington, who died young, Anthony inherited the family estates as the ward of his mother and his guardian Philip Draycot, and despite the legislation of the government intended to punish Catholic recusants in their pockets, Anthony remained a privileged member of the *jeunesse dorée*. To give himself a sense of purpose he undertook to sell Catholic books for Girault de la Chassaigne, butler to the French ambassador, who with the embassy cook, René Leduc, ran an import/export business out of the embassy. They imported French Catholic books and exported second-hand Catholic church items which they bought cheaply and sold for a good profit.[1] Walsingham's embassy spy, known by his pseudonym 'Henry Fagot', called Girault 'a plague in the kingdom'.

Also present at the Plough were the Irishman of distinguished family, Robert Barnewell; Henry (Harry) Dunne, a gentleman of Kent; Chidiock Tichborne and two others. But the greatest of these were Babington and Ballard. And with the latter about to leave for France in his disguise as Captain Fortescue, the conversation over dinner must have been periodically coded for the sensitive information not to alert any listeners. The wealthy Babington was not always cash-rich, but now he probably gave a dole to the impoverished Ballard for the Paris stay and conference already mentioned. While waiting for 'newes from France' Babington decided to move into Hern's Rents in Holborn, and with little thought to his own security continued with tavern meetings. Among the cluster drawn in, apart from those already named were Thomas Habington, Robert Gage (a cousin of the Jesuit Robert Southwell), Thomas Salusbury, and Edward Jones of Plas Cadwgan. The

Salusbury family of Lleweni had already conformed, however Catholic they might remain in their sympathies, until Thomas veered the other way after the example of Campion. If disposed to prayer by him, it was through their devotion to Mary, Queen of Scots that Babington *et al.* came together to plot. She was the supreme symbol of their beleaguered faith, and had she been a Protestant with a claim to the throne it seems likely that the conspiracies through Elizabeth's reign would have occurred just the same.

Thomas Salusbury had spent some terms at Trinity College, Oxford before entering the service of his guardian, the Earl of Leicester. Married at the age of 10 years, his bumpy relationship with his child-bride (his stepfather's daughter) had been repaired, and at 22 he had himself just become the father of a daughter. There was once a Lleweni portrait of him showing his short, bushy black beard, carefully trimmed side-whiskers and a jewel earring, marking out a dandy. Portraits of those engaged in clandestine actions were not infrequently commissioned by them as a reminder to posterity of what they looked like, and Babington and his companions had theirs done so that eventually prints of these were taken and used to track them when they were hiding in St John's Wood.[2] Babington had acquired (how and when?) the personal devotion of Salusbury, just as the latter had that of Edward Jones, a young gentleman of means who had been taken into Leicester's entourage by the efforts of his father, a Master of the Wardrobe to Elizabeth. This homo-social attachment drew in Tichborne, John Travers, Thomas Habington and John Savage as well. Babington's wealth, of course, may have helped (he was said to have an annual income of £1,000 – modern equivalent roughly £500,000), but he also won praise beyond the pocket for a deep charm that escapes us now, and however splendid and worldly he may have seemed to Salusbury, it is also possible to glimpse something sentimental and passively mild. Easy game for the hyena-like Robert Poley – resourceful, greedy, self-promoting and ever snapping at the brocaded heels of the wealthy and weak. He came out of the shadows, a phoney Catholic and a phoney gentleman, recruited by Walsingham who knows when? Taken into the household at Barn Elms first, he was then dropped into the seething surroundings of the Marshalsea in Southwark. There he veered between close confinement and 'the liberty of the house', in a prison that at any one time held between twenty-five and thirty priests.[3]

Poley's reward for a grubby assignment was a trip abroad, and early in 1585 he returned to England, this time to be in Sir Philip Sidney's employment as a finance clerk. Sidney had tax debts dating back some years, as did his father, Sir Henry, noted in an original Latin certificate by Thomas Morrison, deputy Clerk of the Pipe in the Exchequer, late in 1585.[4] Sidney's deep reluctance to pay his tax suggests how little there would have been for Poley to steal at a time when he was deliberately cultivating a reputation for extravagant hospitality to Catholic priests in the Bishopsgate house that Burghley had set up for him. This brought him into contact with other Catholics, and it was through one of them – Tindall – that he slid into Babington's circle. For now his conduit to Walsingham was the cousin of the Principal Secretary, Thomas Walsingham of Chislehurst, Kent. The situation of Poley within the Walsingham household was actually a fact to recommend him to Thomas Morgan, whose initial suspicions had been replaced by warm approbation. Morgan wrote to Mary intimating that, it would advantage her to have Poley so placed.

Babington became the insect in amber, trapped inside the opaque ooze of the plot, aching at the possibility of success and the rapid extinction of an oppressive regime, yet still quaking with the damnable sense that it would all come to nothing. He put it to his posse and two more young Catholic courtiers, Charles Tilney and Edward Abingdon; none felt able to pledge their aid to killing Elizabeth despite a willingness to join in a revolt. Salusbury was even insecure about this, and thought to ease Babington from his leaning to Ballard by reviving a stalled intention to travel together in Europe. If their quitting the country was not to be misconstrued then they had to get government licences, and with this bureaucratic quest Tindall might help with his Poley connection to Walsingham. To secure Poley's intervention was soundly maintained, Babington thought to set up funding amounting to £400, and also added the rider that in the event of permission being granted perhaps someone should be employed to follow him closely. The hint was blatant but Walsingham allowed it to drift away, and no passport was yet forthcoming, so Poley went back to Tindall with a sweet revision: he (Poley) should go along on the journey and Babington would pay him a stipend and all his travel costs – a tweak that Babington did not reject.

The postman, meanwhile, was in Paris, where his uncle William had recently conferred with Stafford. The two Giffords and Fr Edmund Grateley (code name Foxley) were collaborating on a book defending Elizabeth's policy towards Catholics. In late May 1586 Gilbert wrote to Walsingham: 'The book is in hand and I doubt not will be of great importance.'[5] Morgan was delighted to see him but commented that he would rather he was in England, apparently believing that the postal system established for Mary would falter without him. In fact, as we have seen, the substitute was satisfactory and the post continued in the following manner: the anonymous brewer received Mary's letters via the barrel bung and handed them over to Paulet, who sent them at once to Walsingham. His operative Phelippes opened and deciphered them, before returning the carefully re-ordered items to Paulet. He returned them to the brewer, who handed them to the stand-in for Gifford, and he returned them to Paulet for forwarding to their named recipient. The kink in the transmission was Walsingham's method to prevent collusion between his two agents that could lead to him being defrauded. When the letters reached him second time around on the loop, Gifford would have delivered them to the French embassy in Salisbury Court. When he was absent another London postman had to be found and Gifford put up two men for the task, conveying to Mary that they were his cousins. Her secretary, Gilbert Curll, called one of them Barnaby, and it was he who said the second post was his brother.

Thomas Morgan had written to Mary about Babington as early as July 1585, and not quite a year later Walsingham and his aides were expecting her to write to her bemused admirer in her Whitsun mail. Morgan had intended she write before this, and he had the temerity to draft a letter for her, but Walsingham had pulled it from the system until June 1586, when Poley reported that Babington was discussing the matter of violence to Elizabeth with his friends. Salusbury rejected the notion; Henry Dunne was unenthusiastic; Tilney and Habington opposed it. The stop on Morgan's letters was now lifted, and on 25 June Mary responded, and Curll sent a note to Barnaby requiring its delivery to Babington *tout de suite*. Although the letter routine just outlined was followed, Paulet missed reading it because it seemed too small to be of importance, and it went from him to Walsingham on 29 June. Barnaby saw to its delivery to Babington after Phelippes had seen it on 1 July.

All this – the burning of candles late into the night in London and the Midlands, the pouring over ciphers – was done as Poley brought Babington to Walsingham for their first meeting, during which the Principal Secretary intimated to the young man that he should benefit himself by reporting on his confessional colleagues. He did not harangue him or make angry accusations, if anything his mode was temperate and he hoped tempting, because his intention was to fix Babington inextricably into the inchoate plot. Poley's task was to appear to lean to Babington while actually leaning *on* him, becoming in the process a confidant. Babington's resolve was still too brittle for him to be certain of his future actions, and he gave thought again to leaving the country, making another approach to Poley with the agreement of Salusbury. According to Tindall their intermediary with Walsingham was minded to travel with them, but lack of money pinned him down. As a Catholic he was bound with two sureties to present himself on a three-weekly calendar at court. To overcome this Babington offered him £50 and indicated he would be pleased to travel in his company. Poley responded with another Walsingham summons – this time to Barn Elms on 3 July. In an interview purged of warmth but still not menacing, it was allowed that Babington should have an interview with Elizabeth. Still thinking about travelling Babington considered selling some Derbyshire holdings as he sat reviewing the meeting back in his lodgings. Walsingham now called in Gilbert Gifford for a crisis meeting held before Phelippes, and when this was over Gifford had a crucial assignment – to meet Babington and get him to write in detail to Mary of what was taking shape. During this meeting Gifford asked Babington if he had a cipher, and when it was confirmed he sturdily proposed Babington should prepare a draft scheme of action, turn it into cipher and await the messenger. And the following day, 4 July, as Gifford left for Chartley with Mary's letter to Barnaby, Babington wrote the letter that would bring a startling number of people to an early death. He had hitherto held back, with scruples and from a foggy state of mind. Some of the writing flows, but there is a stuttering form to some of the paragraphs that suggests a man under pressure, and this increased as he had to cipher the whole thing. The letter adds a postscript to Claude Nau asking how far he should trust Poley. *Le pauvre Babington*.

Walsingham and the adept Phelippes reckoned with brilliant accuracy that Babington would be occupied for two days on this letter, so the royal letter from Chartley was stalled until the evening of 6 July, when Phelippes sent George Gifford with the item marked -). He was told to collect another letter and return with caution (presumably to Seething Lane) when certain he was not being followed. Holborn to headquarters in the dark took several hours, and Gifford sidled in after midnight with three packets. The one signed -) seemed likely to yield most, and so it proved; to a cipher master like Phelippes phrases like 'tragical execution' must have seemed like red-hot sparks. To Walsingham went the copy text, and to Chartley the original carried by Phelippes himself and delivered to Mary by the usual route.[6]

While she pondered her response, Babington found himself in company with Poley, nudging, tweaking, irritating. The decay in Babington's attachment to 'sweet Robin' was noted by Phelippes even before he left the city, but he was hopeful 'Poley may yet last', and the agent had hung about scattering thoughts on what service Babington could do Walsingham. Very little time elapsed before Poley reappeared with a commanding message that the young gentleman should present himself again at Barn Elms in a week's time. For John Ballard, whose extravagant optimism about another northern revolt was ebbing, this was a disturbing ripple, and the conspirators tight or loose in the fold could sense that Walsingham (whose emblem was the tiger's head) was on the prowl, and so dangerous. To cast this meeting in a more optimistic light (no doubt Ballard again) they made pretence to themselves that their adversary might actually reveal something of what he knew. Some hope! On Wednesday 13 July Poley and Babington were rowed to Barn Elms, and with the splash of oars and the sudden flap of water birds from the reedy banks, the two men stared out and at each other, hoping for the truth to be made visible.

An interview with Walsingham in such circumstances was liable to weld tongue and palate, for all the unrevealing politeness. And he had lighted upon a way to test Babington's faith and resolve. The Principal Secretary had already used Nicholas Berden (Thomas Rogers) to track Fr Robert Southwell and Fr Henry Garnet, and, unwilling at this point to rely on Poley, he wanted Babington to take on the task. It should not prove too strenuous because Southwell's cousin, Robert Gage, lodged at Southampton House, a short stroll from Hern's Rents. If, as it seemed to Walsingham, the young man happened upon the two Jesuits, or more actively managed to ferret them out before handing them over, he could have no other plot in mind. This corralling of two of his faith would sign his intent. If the Jesuits betrayed themselves to him that would be their fault, and Berden the veteran agent would be ready to make the arrest. Babington went back to the boat to return to London with Poley, and the powerful unspoken unease was at last given voice:

Babington: How is it your credit grows with Mr Secretary?
Poley: By my dealing with him in some business of my
                 master, Sir Philip Sidney.[7]
                 (Perhaps he meant the still outstanding tax debt?)

It will be evident by now that Anthony Babington was not someone of smart wisdom, or even intuition. He struggled to make sense of what was taking shape and needed to talk further to a convivial spirit, so he sought the London hiding place of Fr William Weston, who knew nothing about the putative Babington Plot but plenty about the two Jesuits named by Walsingham, since to give them respite he had them in another room in his lodgings in Hog Lane, Norton Folgate, the property owned by Mrs Frances Browne. Did they hear their names mentioned in the conversation that followed between the priest and the conspirator? Babington blurted out his desire to go abroad, but to obtain the necessary passport (essential to protect his patrimony) he was required to perform certain services for the government. How far could he go in giving superficial information about fellow Catholics without utterly compromising his integrity and special well-being? Weston baldly affirmed that any surface breach of confidence would lead to his doom, and after some general spiritual advice hustled Babington from the premises. Weston, Garnet and Southwell grabbed missals and the paraphernalia of worship for immediate flight from London, managing to elude an off-guard Berden, who got a summons to present himself to Walsingham on 18 July. While the agent shifted uneasily under the Secretary's dark-browed scrutiny, Babington delayed saying or doing anything until a request for full authority to deal with his co-religionists. This was granted, and Berden was instructed to join up with him; Walsingham's team were now preparing to swoop on Ballard and all the associates of Babington, ranging from enthusiasts to the much more detached. Only Poley was missing, having taken to his bed for three days of invisibility.

Thomas Phelippes carried the letter from Babington to Mary, leaving London on the evening of 7 July and arriving on Saturday 9 July. Since it was a delivery day the letter probably reached her on the same day, and nine days later a reply was ready; Phelippes had hold of it before alerting Walsingham to its existence, and it seems he contemplated sending the original to Babington without delay.[8] That he did not arises out of the response of Walsingham on 22 July, when he told Phelippes to return to London and bring the original; Phelippes actually left Chartley on 27 July, and it was not until two days later that the letter, in its original form or doctored, was delivered by the serving man in the blue coat. Despite the injunction to burn the ciphered letter quickly, Phelippes was optimistic that Babington would overlook this. Because the letter was pivotal to the case Phelippes also hoped that Elizabeth would hang Nau and Curll.

Trusty and well-beloved, According to the zeal and entire affection which I have known in you towards the common cause of religion and mine, having always made account of you as of a principal and right worthy member to be employed both in the one and the other: it hath been no less consolation unto me to understand your estate as I have done by your last, and to have found means to renew my intelligence with you, than I have felt grief all this while past to be without the same. I pray you therefore from henceforth to write unto me so often as you can of all occurrences which you may judge in any wise important to the good of my affairs, whereunto I shall not fail to correspond with all the care and diligence that shall be in my possibility.

For divers great and important considerations (which were here too long to be deduced) I cannot but greatly praise and commend your common desire to prevent in time the designments of our enemies for the extirpation of our religion out of this realm with the ruin of us all. For I have long ago shown unto the foreign Catholic princes – and experience doth approve it – the longer that they and we delay to put hand on the matter on this side, the greater leisure have our said enemies to prevail and win advantage over the said princes (as they have done against the King of Spain) and in the meantime the Catholics here, remaining exposed to all sorts of persecution and cruelty, do daily diminish in number, forces, means and power. So as, if remedy be not thereunto hastily provided, I fear not a little but they shall become altogether unable for ever to rise again and to receive any aid at all, whensoever it were offered them. For mine own part, I pray you to assure our principal friends that, albeit I had not in this cause any particular interest (that which I may pretend unto being of no consideration unto me in respect of the public good of this state) I shall be always ready and most willing to employ therein my life and all that I have or may ever look for in this world.

Now, for to ground substantially this enterprise and to bring it to good success, you must first examine deeply:

What forces, as well on foot as on horse, you may raise amongst you all, and what Captains you shall appoint for them in every shire, in case a chief general cannot be had.

Of what towns, ports and havens you may assure yourselves, as well in the North, West as South, to receive succours from the Low Countries, Spain and France.

What place you esteem fittest and of greatest advantage to assemble the principal company of your forces at: and at the same being assembled, whether or which way you have to march.

What foreign forces, as well on horse as foot, you require (which would be compassed conform to the proportion of yourself), for how long paid, and munition and ports the fittest for their landing in this realm from the three aforesaid foreign countries.

What provision of money and armour (in case you want) you would ask.

By what means do the six gentlemen deliberate to proceed?

And the manner also of my getting forth of this hold.

Upon which points having taken amongst you (who are the principal authors, and also as few in number as you can) the best resolution, my advice is that you impart the same with all diligence to Bernardino de Mendoza, ambassador lieger for the King of Spain in France, who (besides the experience he hath of the estate of this side) I may assure you will employ him therein most willingly. I shall not fail to write unto him of the matter with all the earnest recommendations that I can; as I shall also to any else that shall be needful. But you must make choice, for managing of this affair with the said Mendoza and others out of the realm, of some faithful and very secret personage, unto whom only you must commit yourselves, to the end things be the more secret, which for your own security I recommend unto you above the rest.

If your messenger bring you back again sure promise and sufficient assurance of the succour you demand, then thereafter (but no sooner, for that it were in vain) take diligent order that all those of your party on this side make (so secretly as they can) provision of armour, fit horse and ready money, wherewith to hold themselves in readiness to march so soon as it shall be signified unto them by their chief and principals in ever shire.

And for the better colouring of the matter (reserving to the principal the knowledge of the ground of the enterprise) it shall be enough, for the beginning, to give out to the rest that the said provisions are made only for fortifying yourselves, in case of need, against the puritans of this realm: the principal whereof, having the chief forces of the same in the Low Countries, have (as you may let the bruit go) designed to ruin and overthrow, at their return home, the whole Catholics, and to usurp the Crown; not only against me and all other lawful pretenders thereunto, but against their own Queen that now is, if she will not altogether commit herself to their only government. The same pretexts may serve to sound and establish amongst you all an association and confederation general, as done only for your own just preservations and defence, as well in religion as in lives, lands and goods, against the oppression and attempts of the said puritans, without touching directly by writing anything against that Queen, but rather showing yourselves willing to maintain her and her lawful heirs after her, unnaming me.

The affairs being thus prepared and forces in readiness both without and within the realm, then shall it be time to set the six gentlemen to work; taking order, upon the accomplishing of their designing, I may be suddenly transported out of this place, and that all your forces in the same time be on the field to meet me in tarrying for the arrival of the foreign aid, which then must be hastened with all diligence.

Now, for that there can be no certain day appointed for the accomplishing of the said gentlemen's designing, to the end that others may be in readiness to take me from hence, I would that the said gentlemen had always about them (or at least at Court) a four stout men, furnished with good and speedy horses, for – so soon as the said design shall be executed – to come with all diligence to advertise thereof those that shall be appointed for my transporting; to the end that immediately after they may be at the place of my abode, before that my keeper can have advice of the execution of the said design, or at least before he can fortify himself within the house or carry me out of the same. It were necessary to dispatch two or three of the said advertisers by divers ways, to the end that, if the one be stayed, the other may come through; and at the same instant were it also needful to essay to cut off the posts ordinary ways.

This the plat [plot] which I find best for this enterprise, and the order whereby you should conduct the same for our common securities. For stirring on this side before you be well assured of sufficient foreign forces, it were but for nothing to put yourselves in danger of following the miserable fortune of such as have heretofore travailed in like occasions. And to take me forth of this place, unbeing before well assured to set me in the midst of a good army, or in some very good strength where I may safely stay on the assembly of your forces and arrival of the said foreign succours, it were sufficient cause given to that Queen in catching me again to enclose me forever in some hole, forth of which I should never escape (if she did use me no worse), and to pursue with all extremity those that had assisted me – which would grieve me more than all the unhap [which] might fall upon myself. And therefore must I needs yet once again admonish you, so earnestly as I can, to look and take heed most carefully and vigilantly to compass and assure so well all that shall be necessary for the effectuating of the said

*enterprise, as (with the grace of God) you may bring the same to happy end:
remitting to the judgement of our principal friends on this side, with whom you
have to deal herein, to ordain [and] conclude upon this present (which shall serve
you only for an overture and proposition) as you shall amongst you find best:
and to yourself in particular I refer to assure the gentlemen above mentioned of
all that shall be requisite of my part for the entire execution of their good wills.*

*I leave also to your common resolutions to advise (in case their designment do
not take hold, as may happen) whither you will or not pursue my transport and
the execution of the rest of the enterprise. But if the mishap should fall out that
you might not come by me – being set in the Tower of London, or in any other
strength with greater ward, yet notwithstanding leave not, for God's sake, to
proceed in the rest of the enterprise; for I shall, at any time, die most contented,
understanding of your delivery forth of the servitude wherein you are holden as
slaves.*

*I shall assay that, at the same time that the work shall be in hand in these
parts, to make the Catholics of Scotland arise and to put my son in their hands,
to the effect that from thence our enemies here may not prevail of any succour. I
would also that some stirring in Ireland were laboured for, and to be begun some
while before anything were done here; to the end the alarm might be given
thereby on the flat contrary side that the stroke should come from.*

*Your reasons to have some general head or chief, methinketh, are very
pertinent; and therefore were it good to sound obscurely for the purpose the Earl
of Arundel, or some of his bretheren, and likewise to seek upon the young Earl of
Northumberland, if he be at liberty. From over sea the Earl of Westmoreland
may be had, whose house and name may [do] much, you know, in the North
parts: as also the Lord Paget, of good ability in some shires hereabout; both the
one and the other may be brought home secretly: amongst which some more of
the principal banished may return, if the enterprise be once resolute. The said
Lord Paget is now in Spain, and may treat there all which, by his brother Charles
or directly by himself, you will commit unto him touching this affair.*

*Beware that none of your messengers, whom you sent forth of the realm,
carry over any letters upon themselves; but make their dispatches be conveyed
either after or before them, by some other. Take heed of spies and false brethren
that are amongst you – especially of some priests, already practised by our
enemies for your discovery; and in any wise, keep never any paper about you that
in any sort may do harm. For from such like errors have come the only
condemnation of all such as have suffered heretofore, against whom could there*

otherwise have been nothing proved. Discover as little as you can your names and intentions to the French Ambassador now lieger at London; for although he be, as I understand, a very honest gentleman, of good conscience and religion, yet fear I that his master entertaineth, with that Queen, a course far contrary to our designments; which may move him to cross us, if it should happen he had any particular knowledge thereof.

All this while past I have sued to change and remove from this house; and, for answer, the Castle of Dudley only hath been named to serve the turn. So, as by appearance, within the end of this summer I may go thither. Wherefore advise, so soon as I shall be there, what provision may be had about that part for my escape from thence. If I stay here, there is for that purpose but one of these three means following to be looked.

The first that at one certain day appointed, in my walking abroad on horseback on the moors betwixt this and Stafford (where ordinarily you know very few people do pass), a fifty or threescore men, well horsed and armed, come to take me there; as they may easily, my keeper having with him ordinarily but eighteen or twenty horsemen only with dags [pistols].

The second means is to come at midnight (or soon after) to set fire in the barns and stables, which you know are near to the house; and whilst that my guardian's servants shall run forth to the fire, your company (having everyone a mark whereby they may know one another under night) might surprise the house; where I hope, with the few servants I have about me, I were able to give you correspondence.

And the third, some that bring carts hither ordinarily coming early in the morning, their carts might be so prepared and with such cartleaders that being just in the middle of the great gate the carts might fall down or overwhelm, and that thereupon you might come suddenly, with your followers, to make yourself master of the house, and carry me away. So you might do safely, before that any number of soldiers (who lodge in sundry places forth of this place, some a half and some a whole mile off) might come to the relief.

Whatever issue the matter taketh, I do, and will, think myself obliged, as long as I live, towards you, for the offers you make to hazard yourself, as you do, for my delivery; and by any means that ever I have, I shall do my endeavor to recognise, by effects, your deserts herein. I have commanded a more ample alphabet to be made for you, which herewith you will receive.

God almighty have you in protection.
Your most assured friend for ever, [Marie R.]
Fail not to burn this present quickly.

I would be glad to know the names and qualities of the six gentlemen which are to accomplish the designment, for it may be I shall be able, upon knowledge of the parties, to give you some further advice necessary to be followed therein, as also from time to time particularly how you proceed, and as soon as you may (for the same purpose) who be already, and how far, everyone is privy hereunto.

This letter was sufficient to bring down Babington and his cohorts, a case satisfactory to Walsingham who would have been one of the dead if Babington had actually gone ahead with a previous plan to massacre the Privy Council in Star Chamber. But the Principal Secretary wanted more, Mary, the great victim destroyed, hence the addition of the postcript which was likely devised by Elizabeth and Walsingham in tandem.

Chapter 18

CRADLED IN THEIR GRAVES

Instead of just drinking and dining together, sharing conviviality and confessional miseries and then setting them aside to get on with their lives, the young men of the Babington conspiracy (or Ballard's Barricades) allowed themselves to slip into calamity in service to a pale, unvirginal self-made martyr. These maudlin admirers found in Mary a project for undirected, privileged but marginalised lives, and they appear to have been emboldened by alcohol, holding their meetings in public ordinaries or inns like The Three Tuns, The Rye, The Plough, or near to the Royal Exchange, Ballard's haunt, The Castle. Compare the pointless, almost whimsical acts of violence dreamt up by these men – an arson raid on the Queen's ships anchored on the Thames; the kidnapping of Elizabeth and the simultaneous seizure of the huge stockpile of weapons kept by Leicester at Kenilworth (didn't they know Leicester was fighting a war in the Netherlands?) – with the peaceful group activities of those about George Gilbert. He was Suffolk-born of a Protestant family and, like Babington, when very young he succeeded to a rich estate. He was to prove an exceptionally handsome man about town and a sportsman, but he had too a spiritual yearning that led him first to Puritanism and then in 1579 to the Church of Rome. His range of study was still multi-faceted and he gave thought to a pilgrimage to Jerusalem – an exceptionally rare and dangerous activity that was risked by one Henry Timberlake. But Gilbert was persuaded out of the notion by Robert Persons, who had him return to England to use his position and wealth in helping the Catholic cause. When back in London he formed an intimate friendship with Thomas Pounde, then a religious prisoner, and between them they created an association of young men of birth and property, unencumbered bachelors who agreed to devote their time, gifts and means to the service of the faith – not only in bringing about conversions, but also by aiding priests and arranging for their landing; meeting them and securing safe conduct; finding them hiding-places, and also providing them with means, food and clothing fitted to the circumstances of their mission. Their objective as 'Conductor Companions' or 'Comforters of Priests' was so entirely spiritual that Pope Gregory XIII gave it his blessing. They drew their members from the highest of the old Catholic families: the Vaux, Throckmortons, Tichbornes, Fitzherberts, Stonors, Abingdons and so on.

How much more realistic and useful than the fantasy of Elizabeth being herself held a prisoner until she sacked her ministers and adopted Catholicism as the state religion again. It seems almost a quaint oversight that these men did not envisage the demolition of the Queen in Parliament by that old Marian favourite, a detonation of gunpowder. When Robert Catesby plotted in 1605 to kill James I and VI, the Queen, several royal children, lords and commoners, he did it within a tightly controlled family environment that sought to exclude outsiders for as long as possible, and so Sir Everard Digby only joined the gunpowder plotters late, and then only because they needed his wealth. Babington and Ballard sought to widen the scope of their plot by sounding out potential sympathisers like Edward Windsor, brother of Lord Windsor, and despite his ardent Catholicism, one who responded ambiguously that he would 'endeavour what he could'. Most discouraging; above all to the increasingly deflated Ballard (or Mr Brown, as he had been known to Henry Dunne's father Christopher Dunne of Addington, Kent), the man who sought out the well born, those of ancient lineage, the man who hated being contradicted, and when the plot had been swept aside found few demurred when he begged to have the blame for the whole calamity attached to him. By now even Babington, the would-be *chevalier sans peur*, could envisage an extreme proposition – sacrificing Ballard's plot partly so that the greater strategy of releasing Mary could be fulfilled. Time was running out for the plotters.

Before it did, Robert Poley sauntered back into the conspiracy, so Babington had a last chance to get an interview with Walsingham. To obtain this Babington had to buy dinner for the man from whom Fr Weston recoiled 'as at an unpleasant smell'. Thomas Rogers found out about this, but having been assigned to arrest Ballard, on whom he had a lead, the counter-spy elected to stay at home, as he informed Francis Mylles. Known to Catholics as Nicholas Berden, their trusted agent with some court influence, Thomas Rogers was half expecting that his two papist supper guests, who had sent him a capon and two rabbits, would bring Ballard along, and if he did not appear then attention should be focussed on his favoured haunt – The Castle. Not able to be there in person, Rogers arranged for a young man called

Painter to stand in for him and watch those who came in to eat. He suggested
too that since Mylles had no ciphering to do he should be at the Royal
Exchange to meet someone reporting on behalf of Painter. If Ballard did turn
up at The Castle he could easily be arrested there – 'most safe though it have
two doors'. But if he went to dinner with Rogers/Berden, then Mylles would
get a message at the Exchange, and could after the meal have him followed.
As it happened Ballard was missing from both meals, although Robert Gage
did turn up to confirm he had seen him recently and given him shelter.

The man in the blue coat was dismissed on delivery of the packet, with the
request that he should return in four days. Babington's levels of energy were
flagging and he had no illusions about his deciphering skills for the two main
items from Nau and Mary. That from the secretary at Chartley was blessedly
short and, with a pinch of mistrust, gave Babington support for his trust in
Poley. Then came the taxing royal missive which proved such a challenge that
when Tichborne turned up to see him he was persuaded to take over the
yawning task. While the work was in progress Ballard arrived and presented
a picture of some misery, since it was becoming clearer than ever that
provoking a northern uprising, let alone a national one, was beyond the
efforts of the plotters. How could they convey that to the letter writer when
her letter 'contained a complete ratification of his plans for rebellion and for
her own liberation'?[1] Indeed, how could they convey anything safely to her if,
as we may now suppose, Ballard told his co-conspirators what he seems to
have known for some time – that there was tampering with the packets.
Walsingham knew that Ballard knew – Gilbert Gifford had met with the priest
twice in two days some sixteen days before, and reported then that Phelippes's
movements were known. Walsingham had thought to have him (Ballard)
arrested then, but the man was elusive, and what was worse had somewhere
obtained an official warrant to leave the country. It was having it that allowed
him to make the apparently grand gesture of self-exposure, but just as
Walsingham delayed the timing of the arrests Ballard mistimed his escape.

The next day brought a surprise – the agreement of Walsingham to a
meeting with Babington – delivered by Robert Poley to a man whose capacity
for decision making had never been very robust, and who now dithered at the
thought of revealing more to the Principal Secretary. Instead, in company with
Poley he blurted out that he could bring down the government. The spy
wanted to know the means for all – as he put it delicately – he could not think
it lawful. Even so, if Elizabeth was not hurt he was ready to join them, and so

Babington should advance the coup and they would meet again at Hern's Rents the following morning. As they walked in open fields on 31 July Poley declared with no trace of irony that Babington should reveal the entire matter to Walsingham. This artless candour actually disguised the advantage Poley would take from such a declaration, for unless struck down by a paranoid conspirator in a rage, he was in a happy position and on the brink of a triumph. They walked then together to The Rose at Temple Bar to meet with Ballard, Savage, Henry Dunne, Robert Gage and one or two more. Poley now left them for Hern's Rents, saying to Babington that it was very likely under surveillance. To avoid arrest before the crucial meeting on Friday 4 August it was agreed that Babington would stay overnight with Poley at the house provided on requisition by Burghley, probably The Gardens, near the further end of Aldersgate, where Tichborne had a house. Supper that evening was a group affair at The Castle paid for by Poley – an expense he had later to justify.

Meanwhile, Walsingham and Phelippes were trying to remain calm, as circumstances seemed to change by the hour and the whim of traitors. They were waiting for Babington's answer in particular to Mary's letter and the infamous postscript, which increasingly Walsingham was regretting. By 2 August Phelippes was dismayed by a rumour (or real news) that Babington had ridden from London. The tension was so acute that Phelippes even offered to go after him to Staffordshire if Walsingham would arrange a bodyguard. If the imagined fugitive turned up in Lichfield the arrest would be left to Paulet. Walsingham too was deeply concerned, but not enough to send out his right-hand man.

On 3 August Phelippes got a letter from Walsingham in which the great projector began to suggest that the whole operation be ravelled up as quickly as possible. If the man in the blue coat 'receive not answer this day at Babington's hands, there were it not good to defer the apprehension of him, lest he should escape. If you hope by giving of time, that an answer may be drawn from him, then wish I the stay'. Note the little shove back to Phelippes for the final decision, because as Walsingham goes on to say if the delay in Babington's reply to Mary is caused by a meeting of the conspirators 'then were it a great hindrance of service to proceed over hastily to the arrest. These causes are subject to so many difficulties as it is a hard matter to resolve. Only this I conclude, it were better to lack the answer than to lack the man'.[2] The following day he was due to meet Babington but decided to postpone it until Saturday 5 August, by which time the plotter could be arrested; a sequence that depended on Poley finding Walsingham at court at Richmond for further instructions. As it happened, Poley was rowed downriver to the palace, unaware of the growing edge of panic in government decisions; Walsingham even fleetingly wondered if Elizabeth had let slip something to alert the enemy.

Before Poley made his excursion he had talked with Babington, who sent a serving boy to Hern's Rents to redirect any friends waiting there for him. The lad was soon to return with Savage and Ballard for what became another crisis meeting. They all agreed that the grand notion of invasion and deposition was collapsing, and that the invasion element would have to be trailed in front of Walsingham. Poley did this for them and Walsingham set it up that Babington should present himself on the Saturday – one day after the proposed arrest of the same man. 'I do not think good, notwithstanding, to defer the apprehension of Babington longer than Friday.'[3]

Having to wait for what they considered a climactic meeting did not bring cheer to Ballard and Babington as they went to join Gage and Dunne that evening at The Castle, for they now intended to turn Queen's evidence, safeguarding each other and delivering up to justice Barnard Maude and George Gifford – the core seeking to isolate themselves from the periphery. Gifford ended up in the Beauchamp Tower.

The melancholy mood would have slipped another notch had they known that, alerted by Phelippes, their surveillance had been restored – Mylles was at the Poley house environs during the day, and at the tavern came the night watch under Berden/Rogers. He followed them when they left the premises, and from a deep shadow observed a serving man call at Poley's to collect a packet. Babington had written two days before to Mary and now fatigue (emotional and physical) kept him from doing more than add the date, 3 August, to it. The letter carrier went off into the night without fuss, and their patience was rewarded on the morning of 4 August when Ballard turned up even before Babington had quit his bed. Mylles carried the warrant signed by the Lord Admiral, and the actual arresting officer was a deputy alderman, Mr Casty, along with Berden and the young Thomas Walsingham, who had met with the early-rising Poley.[4] Between sleeping and dozing and dreaming, Babington heard people entering the house, the buzz of voices with the content lost, a door closing and then silence. Ballard was taken under escort to the Wood Street Counter. And as Mylles wrote it 'was handled so circumspectly' that neither Walsingham nor his agents 'need be known in the matter'.

Babington's retreat under the covers could not stall the day. Poley burst in with news to galvanise a narcolept: Ballard was taken and the gloss he put on this was that an eager secretary of Walsingham had acted independently of his master. Their contemporary William Camden tells that Babington wrote a letter of complaint to Walsingham for whom the postman was Poley come to court to find out what was going on. In his absence Babington quit the house hurriedly to try to meet with Tichborne at his nearby residence. Having missed him, he dived into a barber's shop outside Bishopsgate and then, refreshed, hurried through Smithfield, only to find on meeting his friend that Tichborne had injured his leg.[5] Babington poured forth the predicament they were in, especially if Ballard blabbed, and then raced back to Poley's to meet John Savage, now fired with the active belligerence he had so long lacked and proposing an immediate attempt to assassinate Elizabeth. To get access to court he needed court clothes, and to cover the cost Babington handed over jewellery and cash. With Tichborne lame, someone had to step up to replace him, and it was Charnock, traced to St Paul's churchyard where we may guess he was browsing among the booksellers. On the bemused, conflicted Babington's return to Poley's, the absence of 'Robyn' led him to write the famous, haunted note beginning in Latin for the former student of Clare: '*Sollicitae non possunt cure mutare aranei stamina fusi.*' The shift within a sentence from English to Latin suggests the two minds Babington was in – one hopeful, the other resigned. 'I am ready to endure whatsoever shall be inflicted, *et facere et paci Romanorum est.*'

Robyn –

Sollicitae non possunt cure mutare aranei stamina fusi! I am ready to endure whatsoever shall be inflicted, *et facere et paci Romanorum est.*

What my course has been towards Mr Secretary you can witness, what my love towards you, yourself best can tell. Proceedings at my lodgings have been very strange. I am the same I always pretended. I pray God you be, and ever so remain towards me.

Farewell, sweet Robyn, if as I take thee, true to me. If not, adieu, *omnium bipedum nequissimus.*

Return me thine answer for my satisfaction, and my diamond, and what else thou wilt. The furnace is prepared wherein our faith must be tried. Farewell till we meet, which God knows when.

Thine, how far thou knowest,

Anthony Babington

As for his other letter, the one to Mary collected for Phelippes, it proved rather a thin item when deciphered. He ignored the infamous postscript, and with regard to his associates nothing was given away. His anger was chiefly directed at the discovery of Maude as a double agent, and he said he would keep Mary informed of the danger that arose from it and the subsequent efforts to quash the danger.

Babington was becoming increasingly exposed, and the temptation at this point to flee must have been surging through his head. No Ballard, no Poley, no pull or push. With a smart understanding of his psychology, Walsingham and Phelippes knew they had to have him under a watchful gaze, and the man chosen was John Scudamore. An explanatory letter was prepared for Babington saying that Ballard's arrest was a by-product of an unexpected surge of anti-Catholic zeal in the local justice Richard Young. Advised to remain in company with Scudamore to avoid the same fate, they went from Poley's to take supper together. As they finished the food Scudamore was handed a note, and despite the drink and calamities of the day, Babington was alert enough to recognise Walsingham's undisguised and inimitable hand. Rising to pay the bill (nothing new) he ducked out of Scudamore's sight and fled, leaving his cloak and sword on the back of his seat – two items a gentleman would not willingly forgo. His dilemma in the street was where to go; Ballard had been sharing rooms with Robert Gage, and so in his jumpy state Babington went there, to find on arrival that John Savage had turned up, but as Babington and Gage changed their clothes, he left in a hurry. The panicking two now moved on to Charnock's, where Gage thought to change again before they headed for a temporary wild sanctuary in the remnant of ancient forest, St John's Wood. Under examination later Gage was asked why he took to the forest, and he snapped in reply, 'For company.'[6] In fact they were joined by Henry Dunne and Robert Barnewell, the armed man who got closest to Elizabeth *en plein air* at Richmond, but who lost his nerve under her unflinching scrutiny and could but slink off.

To prevent their escape abroad, port authorities were alerted, although this action was not a guarantee of success. As they lurched through the forest, dirty and hungry, the government had messengers fanned out over the south-east of England. Remember that most of these fixated gallants had court connections: Babington himself had been a page in service to the Earl of Shrewsbury; Edward Abingdon was the Under-Treasurer's son; Tichborne served Hatton; and Charles Tilney was the son of Philip Tilney, a distant cousin of Elizabeth, who had entertained her at his Suffolk home. As for Mary and her entourage, 'to abate the sails of her royal pride' Walsingham had his assistant on hand to corral her safely. William Waad (Wade), the clerk of the council, had already conferred with Paulet in an outdoors huddle away from listeners. When Waad got back to London instructions were sent to Paulet for the temporary removal of Mary to Tixall, the home of Sir Walter Aston. There was to be a strict guard to prevent news reaching her, and in some measure her immediate circumstances grew worse, for in her absence Curll (newly a father) and Claude Nau were arrested and taken to London to produce confessions. This they did, although, as Read has pointed out, the value of such a thing made under these circumstances is open to question. Chartley was searched and probed until the walls groaned, and every scrap of paper was located for evidence in future trials. After a fortnight at Tixall, Mary was returned to Chartley, although the Privy Council wanted her in the Tower – a choice unacceptable to Elizabeth who refused to allow such an indignity to be heaped on an anointed queen – and at length settled on Fotheringhay Castle in Northamptonshire.

By 9 August the first cluster of plotters, including Tilney, Tichborne and Savage, had been arrested, and the last named was induced to write a confession. With the 'wanted' posters up for Babington and company (images taken from their conspiracy portraits) they stumbled into Uxendon Hall, ancestral home of the staunchly Catholic Bellamy family. Jerome and Bartholomew Bellamy fed them, provided fresh clothes and housed the fugitives in a barn where long, matted hair was roughly cut, and walnut juice gave them all a fake tan. But the gentlemanly pallor soon returned when Uxendon was raided on 14 August; a suspicious local constable had for once done his work conscientiously. Family and fugitives were gobbled up and Bartholomew died on the rack, so it was given out he had strangled himself, and Jerome was executed.[7] By the end of August a highly motivated government had seventeen men and one woman in the Tower. Thomas Salusbury was one who made a temporary escape and Burghley, rather aggrieved that Walsingham had carried this off without informing him, wrote to the Principal Secretary on 10 August 1586 to remark on the general level of stupidity among the ill-informed watchmen, who said they would know the young men 'by intelligence of their favour', for 'marry one has a hooked nose'.

Ballard was one of those who suffered physical torture, but Babington escaped it because he was not a priest, and in triumph Walsingham wanted a memory unfogged by pain. The conspirator was lodged with Hatton at Hatton House, and Walsingham spent a great deal of his time examining him and his smitten friends; by mid-September the vice-chamberlain was ready to conduct the Crown case against them, heard at Westminster. By then Babington had written two confessions – long items, of which only the second has survived; supplementaries came in a deluge from Phelippes and Walsingham.

Once he had the incontrovertible evidence, the plotters could be tried and executed as the preliminary to a special tribunal to investigate Mary's part. There was also simultaneous hectic state activity as Catholics realised with horror how they had been baited; even someone as well protected as the great recusant Catholic composer William Byrd had his home searched. Father Weston had been taken, but Southwell and Garnet remained free. Walsingham had Mylles keep a close eye on Nau and Curll. Many of the items they had drafted for Mary which had been seized at Chartley (a task for which Waad was remitted £30) went to Windsor Castle, where they were poured over by Phelippes. At the same time the legal moves to bring Mary to execution were begun, and this barely a month after the signing of the treaty of Berwick and the formation of a defence pact with James VI. With the ink barely dry, Walsingham and Burghley were confident that the son of such a mother would do nothing to jeopardise his own future. They would not have heard anything different from Archibald Douglas, now the resident ambassador in England and one almost entirely acquiescent to English wishes, who had his own agenda which included the elimination of his King's mother.[8]

The trial of the Babington plotters came as a great blow to loyal Catholics, who recoiled as their co-religionists appeared before a commission of Oyer and Terminer charged with high treason. Ballard had to be carried into the court on a chair, being quite unable to walk. For the patriarch of the Gifford family, old John, there was bitter distress when the Crown clerk named Dr William Gifford and Gilbert Gifford as conspirators when he read out the indictment of John Savage. And where was Gilbert Gifford? Still in Paris, from where he had written a long apology for his flight to Phelippes. Walsingham was, of course, not pleased that an important agent was absent without leave, but eventually Gifford (now Jacques Collardin) got a royal pension of £100 a year. For the main conspirators the trial was a swift means to find them guilty. The young men of good birth, of 'youthful ambition and high spirit' were, according to their prosecutor, Hatton, seduced by devilish priests and seminarists. By the evening of 16 September all were found guilty of treason and condemned to death. They had not long to reflect on their actions, which the nation called treachery, although Tichborne summoned the inner strength to write his famous 'elegy', which has won him an anthology immortality if nothing else. The sentence was carried out on a specially built gallows at St Giles Fields on 20 and 21 September, after the bumpy indignity of being hauled on hurdles to the place.

Walsingham had, among other things, thoroughly frightened Elizabeth. Formerly he had often complained of her casual, even robustly sneering attitude to her councillors' warnings of threats against her life. This time, perhaps because of that numbing moment of encounter with Barnewell, the plan shocked her out of complacency into a tyrant's cruelty. She asked Burghley if some punishment more cruel and plenary than the usual for treason could be devised, as if her contacts with Ivan the Terrible had given her a hint; Burghley, not himself squeamish, replied that the ordinary procedure was enough for any criminal. Ballard, Barnewell, Tichborne, Tilney, Habington, Savage and Babington were hanged before being butchered; so throttled, but not yet dead, their genitals were severed, their bowels hacked out and burned, and then the remnant body quartered. It was a bloodbath, and the watchers could not stifle a gasp when Babington murmured as the executioner, like an Aztec priest, groped for his heart. Savage, being a big man, broke the rope of his noose, and he too was conscious for the major part of the ritual. The following day Salusbury, Dunne, Jones,[9] Travers, Charnock, Gage and Jerome Bellamy followed their friends and associates but this time the hanging was not abbreviated. The account by William Camden in his *Annales* seems to be first-hand, but was not generally available, unlike George Whetsone's *The Censure of a Loyal Subject* (1587), dedicated to Burghley. Interestingly, Whetstone, who had been at the fatal skirmish at Zutphen during which Philip Sidney was mortally wounded, and who wrote Sidney's Life in verse, goes to great lengths to contradict the view that the large crowd of onlookers was disgusted or recoiled from the state's annihilation of the plotters: '. . . the odiousness of their treasons was so settled in every man's heart as there appeared no sadness or alteration among the people at the mangling and quartering of their bodies; yea the whole multitude without any sign of lamentation greedily beheld the spectacle from first to last'. Whetstone ends his pamphlet with the demand that Mary, Queen of Scots should die as her papist followers died. Walsingham took the same view; his work was not yet finished. The triumph was postponed; at least it was for him. For his countrymen there was rejoicing that the plot was thwarted, and the citizens of London lit bonfires and rang church bells in celebration. Holinshed in his *Chronicles* noted that even 'the meaner sort of people' unprovided with firewood 'parted with a penny or two to buy a few sticks by retail'.

The matchless efficiency of Walsingham's irresistible efforts to crush the Babington Plot was remarkable, but even he and his sturdy cohorts could not immediately haul in everyone touched by, or sympathetic to, the treason. The northern journeys of Ballard had brought him into the company of the seminarist John Boste, informally the leading figure among the clutch of priests serving the Neville affinity. Continental papists thought highly of Boste for his encouragement of recusancy and open support for the deposing power claimed by the papacy. The Earl of Huntingdon reported in November 1586 that Boste was still proclaiming 'the day of triumph' to come, despite the autumn executions and government movement to counter Mary's influence. Boste managed to remain at large until September 1593 and when Richard Topcliffe got time with him the charge was made that Boste had been alongside Ballard just before the latter's arrest – 'and he could not deny it'. The capture of Boste and a cluster of others was to be the belated triumph of Topcliffe's friend Anthony Atkinson, a man not afraid to challenge local grandees, and even James VI.

Association or kinship with the plotters could cost an individual dear – weeks or months in captivity. The spy Thomas Rogers (Nicholas Berden) had written four pages in invisible ink in 1585 to Walsingham reporting on various Englishmen abroad, all Catholics and mostly traitors anticipating the *impresa*. Rogers mentioned the poet George Turbervile as a sympathiser who counselled the bringing to England of Roger Yardley. Wrong Turbervile. Walsingham knew better from his 'Russian' contacts like his kinsman Thomas Randolph, who had himself travelled to the court of Ivan IV with George. But right Yardley, 'vehemently suspected' by the privy council (i.e. Walsingham) of Babington links overseas and of coming over to England 'for some evil purpose'. So if not George – then whom? Almost certainly the suspected Turbervile was cousin Thomas of Bere Regis, whose wife Thomasine was a strong recusant, because these Turberviles moved within the wide Arundell circle. It was actually Henry Brune, half-brother of Thomas, who was arrested in 1586 and taken to the Tower for examination when his brother-in-law Chidiock Tichborne was executed, but he escaped any further punishment because of lack of evidence, and he was released.

Chapter 19

OFF WITH HER HEAD

With the collapse of the Babington Plot in the late summer of 1586, all the hopes for the future of Mary, Queen of Scots were destroyed. When Sir Amias Paulet and Sir Thomas Gorges required her to go to Tixall, leaving Chartley to be thoroughly searched in her absence, she slumped to the ground and refused to move. This passive resistance got her nothing but a threat from Paulet that if she would not ride of her own accord she would be bundled into her coach when it arrived, and taken by force to Tixall. She had no option but to agree, and when she got there she asked to be allowed to write to Elizabeth. This was refused – Paulet would not supply the paper she required. Her doctor Bourgoing was sent back to Chartley, and to attend her she was allowed two ladies and an equerry; Paulet was looking to make cuts in her staff, suggesting that if such employees as coachmen were removed, the number could be reduced from thirty-eight to nineteen. When she did get back to Chartley she took to her bed. All that was left her after the search was a bag of money still in the cupboard where she had left it, and intended for her own necessities and for paying her servants. Directions came from London that this too should be removed, and despite her protestations Paulet and Richard Bagot did as they were commanded. The letter he received from Elizabeth was fulsome and highly charged in her rhetorical manner:

Amias, my most faithful and careful servant, God reward thee treble-fold in three double for thy most troublesome charge so well discharged. If you knew, my Amias, how kindly, besides dutifully my grateful heart accepteth and praiseth your spotless actions, your wise orders, and safe regards, performed in so dangerous and crafty a charge, it would ease your travails and rejoice your heart. In which I charge you carry this most just thought that I cannot balance in any weight of my judgement the value that I prize you at, and suppose no treasure to countervail such a faith; and shall condemn myself in that fault, which yet I never committed, if I reward not such deserts. Yea, let me lack when I most need, if I acknowledge not such a merit with a reward, *non omnibus datum*. Let your wicked murderess know how with hearty sorrow her vile deserts compelleth these orders; and bid her from me ask God forgiveness for her treacherous dealings towards the saver of her life many a year, to the intolerable peril of her own; and yet, not contented with so many forgivenesses, must fall again so horribly, for passing a woman's thought, much less a prince's; and instead of excusing (whereof not one can serve, it being so plainly confessed by the authors of my guiltless death), let repentence take place and let not the fiend possess her, so her better part be lost; which I pray, with hands lifted up to Him that may both save and spill. With my most loving adieu and prayers for thy long life, your most assured and loving sovereign, as thereto by good deserts induced. E.R.

Mary left Chartley on 21 September for her last place of restraint. With Paulet heading the party they made a brief stop at Lord's Place in Leicestershire and the house of the Earl of Huntingdon, one of the chief male English claimants to the throne so coveted by Mary. Here local people demonstrated their affection for her, and Paulet and his coach had to be protected when the crowds became hostile. They reached Fotheringhay castle in Northamptonshire on 25 September, and the apparatus for a public hearing of the case against Mary was established so that Paulet could inform her on 1 October. He now took it upon himself to try to get her to confess her crimes and to repent them, an effort by an inferior that she easily rejected. Meanwhile Burghley and Walsingham collaborated, and the notes made by the Lord Treasurer make it clear that if the Babington Plot and its demolition had been Walsingham's triumph, Burghley was now going to make his mark in the aftermath, planning the hearing, giving directions to Mary's gaoler, possible sites for it, travel distances and the summoning of Parliament.[1] Pressure on Elizabeth came from Parliament, when she had hoped the execution of the Babington plotters would be more than enough to satisfy the nation. That was her miscalculation. On 11 October the commissioners who would sit listening to the evidence began arriving at Fotheringhay. On 12 October a deputation from them waited on Mary, including Sir Walter Mildmay; the Usher of Parliament, Mister Stallenge; Elizabeth's notary,

Mr Barker; and Paulet himself. Just how long she made them wait is not clear, but in her own mind Mary held that an English court, even such a special one as this, had no jurisdiction over her. She would not appear on 14 October; but given the assurance that she would indeed be allowed to register this caveat, she reversed her decision in order to clear her name of plotting to kill Elizabeth. She did, however, admit that she had sought to escape her detention. Reporting to London on her demeanour and speeches before the hearing Paulet evidently found her irksome, straining to charm her auditor judges by 'long artificial speeches' and trying to throw all blame on Elizabeth and her councillors. She confidently expressed her belief that nothing could be found written in her own hand that could prove her complicity. She wrote to Beaton in Paris: 'As to my having plotted, counselled or commanded [Elizabeth's] death, I had never done so.' Surely Beaton identified the casuistry in this; that notion borrowed from St Thomas Aquinas distinguishing between lying and concealment. She might never have 'plotted, counselled or commanded', since those about her and her supporters in the outside world understood that only violence could change her position. Nothing in her own hand to convict her – so what, when she had secretaries to write for her and keep her secrets? Except that Nau and Curll were induced to blab.

For fifteen years at a minimum Mary had been associated with papist insurgents, constantly threatening the stability of English political life. Holding her tiny rival court in a series of heavily guarded manor houses and castles, she attracted men to conspire and rebel for her. She claimed a status equivalent to the woman she would have driven out if geography, demography and the triumvirate of sturdy Englishmen had not thwarted her. Mary's claim of royal sovereignty was inviolable, and by disputing or discrediting it Elizabeth was subject to an accusation of betraying the divine right of monarchs, to which she frequently alluded as proof of her own authority. The rider to this was that Elizabeth was putting her immortal soul at risk, and in the 'court of conscience' before God her actions would be reviewed. Before and during the trial Mary thrust this notion at the commissioners, through whom she spoke to her royal 'sister'. She tried to get closer to understanding them by questioning Paulet, but he was relieved that they heard her with indifference. Walsingham responded calmly to provocation, as if he had his Maker waiting behind an arras or invisibly sitting in the symbolically empty 'chair of estate for the Queen of England', 'I call God to record that as a private person I have done nothing unbeseeming an honest man, nor as I bear the place of a public person, have I done anything unworthy of my place.' Trained in civil law, Walsingham had the support of other civil lawyers who flatly refused to acknowledge Mary's royalty. They argued that she had already been deposed by the 'three estates of Scotland', effectively reducing her from monarch to subject. Sir Christopher Hatton, representing 'the holy conscience of the queen' was himself quite willing to allow Mary's pretensions, since they meant nothing. Burghley had worked hard to get a reliably anti-Marian Parliament, and they agreed with Hatton because everyone was subject to the authority of the common law.

Elizabeth had insisted on revising the terms of the commission, an intervention that pained Walsingham, who had hoped her absence from the forum would accelerate matters. It did not prevent it, but she required a daily digest of the proceedings by express post. When the forty-two participants, including Lords Lumley, Zouche and Montague of the Catholic affinity, ended their hearings, they returned to London to deliberate, and thirty-six gave their final verdict in Star Chamber on 25 October. Tried under the statute called 'the Act for the Queen's Safety', which had been passed in the previous Parliament as the necessary legislative replacement for the Bond (or Act) of Association with Mary in mind, she was found guilty in a unanimous verdict. In accordance too with Elizabeth's wish they confirmed that this did not prejudice in any way the claim of James VI to the succession, although the Bond might well have excluded him. After the death sentence against Mary had been passed and made public, Parliament required only one act of Elizabeth – the signing of the death warrant to chime with the will of the national majority.

During this time Paulet was fairly frequently in company with her, although it made him uncomfortable, for he had his instructions to secure her full confession. On the Feast of All Saints, 1 November, he went to see her, and finding her day of prayer not quite ended waited politely for her to finish. When they did talk she proved too nimble of response for the dour Puritan, and he wrote to Walsingham asking if he could reduce the number of times he had to see her because 'I do not see that any good can come of it'. He went on to order the removal of her billiard table, finding it altogether too frivolous. Then there was a minor flap at the thought she might escape, and Paulet requested more foot-soldiers and bowmen be sent to raise the garrison numbers to seventy and fifty. Then in November, after months of painful gout,

Paulet got a very senior aide, Sir Drue Drury, which as he recorded in a letter to Walsingham was a great boost, since the two men were good friends of long standing. They jointly decided that a letter from Mary to Elizabeth should be held back until the time of the execution was known, for Elizabeth was fighting the insistent waves of anti-Marian pressure. Leading her opponents were Burghley and Walsingham, the former having made sure that in the House of Commons the members elected again as Speaker Sergeant John Pickering, for the fifth Parliament of her reign. That Burghley took the lead at this point is not strange – Walsingham was stricken by the death of his son-in-law and the life-threatening pregnancy of Sidney's widow, Frances.

Instead of being present at the opening ceremonies of Parliament as was her custom, Elizabeth kept her distance by remaining at Richmond, sending instead three commissioners, Burghley, Archbishop Whitgift and the Earl of Derby, to present the case against Mary. Petitioned twice by Parliament to sign the death warrant, in two speeches given in November she refused to give a direct answer to them using language so opaque that the meaning had all the purposeful clarity of smoke from a bowl of tobacco. One speech, as Burghley noted, 'drew tears from many eyes', but then so did smoke. Walsingham grew more and more exasperated with her dithering over the execution, and because she signally failed to grieve over Sidney's dreadful, slow demise. For giving his life in her service she later called him 'that inconsiderate fellow' – a truly unforgivable comment. No wonder that Walsingham withdrew from the court in mid-December; but before he went there was the public proclamation of the sentence: a proclamation written and re-written by Elizabeth with Burghley at her elbow as editor. The warrant for the sentence was drafted by Walsingham, leaving Burghley to prepare the letter-patent to Paulet and Drury. These two were still hoping the execution would be carried out before Christmas – the perfect gift for the season. Mary, meanwhile, got her bag of money returned to her, and returned too was her priest de Preau, who gave Paulet further cause to express his fears for Mary's immortal soul. Then Paulet's mortal body kicked in and he was sick with gout for over two weeks, which excused him from those verbal jousts with Mary that she actually rather enjoyed and he hated. She missed meeting with one contact with the outside world, for all that she detested him, especially when she wrote again to Elizabeth, only for Paulet to halt this letter too. Nor did he endear himself when he told de Preau and her steward, Melville, that although they too would remain in residence their quotidian dealings with Mary were ended. From now on she would only be permitted to see Bourgoing. In her gloomy days Mary wondered if she would be assassinated and she said as much to her physician, who in turn spoke of them to Paulet. He was shocked by such a notion; as he said, he was 'a man of honour and a gentleman' – hence not disposed to behave like a Turk. Yet some of the formalities that had been allowed her, such as her butler carrying the rod of office before meat dishes, were now stopped, on the grounds that she had been convicted and condemned.

As for Walsingham, suffering physically and emotionally, nothing would release his pent-up distress and anxiety other than the execution. To achieve this he seems to have put together another plot against Elizabeth's life, or at least reviewed the mechanics of a possible plot in such a way as to suggest her only safety lay in acting against Mary. The culprit was William Stafford, the wayward brother of Ambassador Stafford in Paris. Sir Edward was having a rather torrid time, for in December Gilbert Gifford had been arrested in Paris with some old letters from Phelippes in his possession that encouraged him to spy on the envoy. Also involved in William Stafford's clumsy attempt to blackmail Châteauneuf was Michael Moody, the unruly recusant former servant to Sir Edward. Chamber accounts show Walsingham signing warrants to pay Moody for carrying letters between London and Paris, but by 1586 he was in Newgate, where amongst the squalor of ruined lives he was visited by William Stafford. His plot to murder Elizabeth pivoted on Moody, who was then visited by the French ambassador's secretary, Léonard des Trappes. The plot to blow up Elizabeth in her bed with a bag of gunpowder was apparently revealed to her by William Stafford, and on 12 January 1587 Burghley called a meeting at his house attended by Leicester, Hatton and William Davison, the second Principal Secretary appointed in September 1586. Châteauneuf was required to attend them, and when confronted by Stafford (who was still in the Tower in August 1588) he made a vehement denial of the charges made against him. But he agreed, acutely embarrassed, that Stafford had spoken of a plot, and hence was confined to his residence.

By the end of the month, in which no reports came from Fotheringhay, rumours of the escape and rescue of Mary had London agog. Paulet had to write to reassure Davison that no such disaster had occurred, or would.

You may see by these letters inclosed, with mine answer to the same, that the report of the Scottish Queen's escape, or of her making away, as it is now termed, carrieth much credit in these parts, as it is followed with hue and cry. And although considering my later letters to like effect, I did not think it needful to advertise you thereof with speed, yet I would not hide it from you, and therefore do send it by one of my servants repairing to London about his own business, not doubting but that the same will come as speedily to your hands as if it had been sent by the post. These seditious rumours are not to be neglected, in my simple opinion, and indeed there is not a more ready way to levy forces to the achieving of that which these lewd reporters pretend to fear. I cannot let them flatter themselves with vain hope, but by the grace of God I will not lose this lady, my charge, without the loss of my life, neither shall it be possible for any force to take her out of my hands alive.

All this stir provoked a crisis of conscience for Elizabeth. She wanted Mary dead but recoiled from being the instrument to that end, so she consulted William Davison about the terms of the Bond of Association to which Paulet and Drury were signatories. Were they not obliged by it to kill anyone seeking her murder? Davison evidently thought not, and tried persuasion, but she insisted that Walsingham should write to upbraid them for failing to relieve her of a great burden, and a letter was sent on 1 February, arriving the next day at about five in the afternoon.

After our hearty commendations, we find by speech lately uttered by her Majesty that she doth note in you a lack of that care and zeal of her service that she looketh for at your hands, in that you have not in all this time of yourselves (without other provocation) found out some way to shorten the life of that Queen, considering the great peril she is subject to hourly, so long as the said Queen shall live. Wherein, besides a kind of lack of love towards her, she noteth greatly that you have not that care of your own particular safeties, or rather of the preservation of religion and the public good and prosperity of your country that reason and policy commandeth, especially having so good a warrant and ground for the satisfaction of your consciences toward God and the discharge of your credit and reputations towards the world as the oath of association which you both have so solemnly taken and vowed, and especially the matter wherewith she standeth charged being so clearly and manifestly proved against her. And therefore she taketh it most unkindly towards her, that men professing that love towards her that you do, should in any kind of sort, for lack of the discharge of your duties, cast the burthen upon her, knowing as you do her indisposition to shed blood, especially of that sex and quality, and so near to her in blood as the said Queen is.

These respects do greatly trouble her Majesty, who, we assure you, has sundry times protested that if the regard of the danger of her good subjects and faithful servants did not more move her than her own peril, she would never be drawn to assent to the shedding of her blood. We thought it very well to acquaint you with these speeches lately passed from her Majesty, referring the same to your good judgements. And so we commit you to the protection of the Almighty.

Davison wanted this letter burnt, but Sir Amias was too upright and canny to do this, and to protect his good name for all time had copies given to members of his family. The reply he and Drury sent to London was hot with indignation, as evinced by his speed of reply:

Your letters of yesterday coming to my hands this present day at five in the afternoon, I would not fail according to your directions to return my answer with all possible speed, which shall deliver unto you with great grief and bitterness of mind, in that I am so unhappy to have liven to see this unhappy day, in the which I am required by direction from my most gracious sovereign to do an act which God and the law forbiddeth. My good livings and life are at her Majesty's disposition and I am ready to lose them this next morrow if it shall so please her, acknowledging that I hold them as of her mere and most gracious favour, and do not desire them to enjoy them, but with her Highness' good liking. But God forbid that I should make so foul a shipwreck of my conscience or leave so great a blot to my poor posterity, to shed blood without law or warrant. Trusting that her Majesty, of her accustomed clemency, will take this my dutiful answer in good part (and the rather by your good mediation), as proceeding from one who will never be inferior to any Christian subject living in duty, honour, love and obedience towards his sovereign.

And thus I commit you to the mercy of the Almighty. From Fotheringay the 2nd of February 1587. Your most assured poor friends

A. Poulet

D. Drury

Your letters coming in the plural number seem to be meant as to Sir Drue Drury as to myself, and yet because he is not named in them, neither the letter directed unto him, he forbeareth to make any particular answer, but subscribeth in heart to my opinion.

No wonder he balked at this mode of securing Mary's death; imagine the possibilities for him if after the murder Elizabeth had changed her mind – she could say she had been misunderstood. Her hesitations having been chivvied and blocked by Burghley, she now gave way and summoning William Davison signed the death warrant. He was then instructed to have it endorsed by the Great Seal and when it had acquired its huge roundel of wax it was to be shown to Walsingham on Elizabeth's orders, for as she remarked sardonically it 'would go near to kill him outright'. Next morning Davison got word from her to delay going to the Lord Chancellor Bromley until she had spoken to him again. But the task was done and he told her so in an interview later that day, allowing her to ask indignantly what occasioned the hurry. This rowing back on intention would have warned Walsingham, but Davison was so taken aback by her minatory tone he overlooked the chance to get her written agreement that matters should be allowed to take their course. Instead he went to Hatton to unburden himself, and together they went to Burghley, who alerted as many Privy Councillors as he could that a secret meeting would take place the next day. These men now seized the initiative, swore an oath to deal no further with Elizabeth in the matter, took the warrant, wrote the letters to accompany it and sent Robert Beale, Clerk of the Council, along with the executioner to Fotheringhay.

All the representations of royal conscience from James VI and Henri III could not bring a reprieve for Mary. The last effort of her son was a personal plea to Elizabeth, having no power to make it more forceful, and in any case he had recent experience that 'forceful words tended to antagonise rather than appease'.[2] Not that this concerned some of his nobles, Catholic and pro-French, like Lord Claude Hamilton, who wanted to inflame public opinion against Elizabeth and to wreck the terms of the treaty of Berwick. But in England they heard only the voice of Sir Alexander Stewart, who claimed to know the King's mind in this matter – an indifference that could be blotted out with gifts of dogs and deer.[3] At least one dog seems to have been present in the chamber wherein Mary was clumsily executed by sword on 8 February

1587. Denied the presence of her own servants, she was taken to the scaffold by Sir Amias Paulet, for which he was thanked by her – a contemporary drawing suggests a raised platform approached by three steps. After the three strikes of the executioner, he had the unnerving experience of picking up her head by the hair only for them to separate, since like her cousin in her latter days she wore a wig. Her little dog provided one further moment of almost comic horror by licking at the royal blood that had been spilt. Within weeks Robert Persons and William Allen, both in Rome, were putting forward a new possibility for the succession – Isabella, the Infanta of Spain.[4]

News of the execution reached London the following day and Paris on 18 February, when Arundel told Bernardino de Mendoza. When it got to Scotland the news provoked a reaction mixing anti-English feeling and some shocked distress. Robert Persons was to claim later that the young King spent a day laughing at the news, but that may have been in his chamber among intimates, and in public he adopted the conventional grieving son posture, dressing in mourning clothes and attending obsequies for her. The Scottish grinding of teeth at this offence was not heard in London immediately, for there general rejoicing swamped everything except the cascade of anxiety that fell on Elizabeth. This may have been triggered by long-buried distress at the shocking fate of her mother at the hands of her murderous father. 'What will [my enemies] not now say, when it shall be spread that, for the sake of her life, a maiden queen could be content to spill the blood even of her own kinswoman?' Anxiety about her reputation lurched into rage at every man about her: Burghley was wise to retreat from the court, Hatton was rebuked and the unfortunate Davison went to the Tower, the chief victim of the attempt to placate James. There he was later joined by Job Throckmorton, whose speech to Parliament on 23 February was judged to insult the King. In an attempt to soothe the hurt done to James as a blood relative (but with his characteristic unconcern for Scotland's honour), Walsingham, now back in harness, wrote at length to the King's Secretary, Sir John Maitland of Thirlestone, on 4 March.[5] With cool rigour, the man who had done so much clandestine work to bring down Mary put the case for James now maintaining the shaky Anglo-Scottish amity; anything else would make it impossible for the English to allow him to succeed. English good will should not be dissipated in pursuit of ties with Spain or France, and Maitland, who had himself been leaning to the latter, came to agree with the ever-eloquent Walsingham. Very quickly James came to see the sense of these propositions, even while he wished for alternatives to present themselves; the embassy sent to Denmark on 26 March was to speak not only of his marriage to a Danish princess, but also of aid against England.

Even in London there were still repercussions. By the end of March all the councillors who had met with Burghley were summoned before the Lord Chancellor Bromley, Archbishop Whitgift and the two chief justices, to justify their actions. This they did by quoting Davison's report of the Queen's intention to have the death warrant sealed; no one revealed the oath they had taken to keep the matter from Elizabeth. It was Davison's misfortune to bear the brunt of her ire, being tried before special commissioners, fined 10,000 marks (later remitted) and imprisoned until Elizabeth could be won over enough to release him. Nothing remotely disagreeable happened to Paulet or Drury; indeed Sir Amias did rather well, becoming Clerk to the Duchy of Lancaster and Chancellor of the Order of the Garter, taking over this last from Walsingham just before St George's Day, 23 April. Until Burghley trundled back from his enforced sabbatical, the weight of government fell on Walsingham and Hatton, who would soon replace Bromley as Lord Chancellor in May 1587. Leicester too was absent and ailing, taking the spa waters at Bath. With the grand old men absentees, the court began to notice the presence of younger men like the Earl of Essex, Robert Cecil and Charles Blount, who must surely be the subject of Nicholas Hilliard's most famous miniature 'Young Man among Roses' (*c.* 1587). One of the tasks that fell to Cecil was the compiling and editing of a pamphlet of parliamentary speeches and other official documents, which became the authorised reading in the defence of the government and Elizabeth, whose famed reluctance over twenty years to execute Mary was cited as a great virtue.

It was necessarily Walsingham who got the most difficult diplomatic assignment – defusing French hostility – doing so when the English ambassador there, Stafford, was regarded with proper and deep suspicion. When Babington and his accomplices were executed, Walsingham had sent Edward Wotton to 'lay open' the whole affair to the French court. This time the assignment went to William Waad, and it was bound to be a bruising experience, for the French reaction was passionately hostile. Parisian Catholics pressed for revenge to be meted out on the long-suffering Huguenots, and the *politiques* who offered some favour to them. The Guises had thought of Mary as their best hope for a Catholic succession, and they benefited from the surge of anti-Protestant feeling, putting pressure on Henri

III to abandon treaties signed with England. He held back from doing this despite feeling that he had been snubbed, and he rather quickly discouraged thoughts of revenge by James. As for the Guises, the passage of time with no response from them indicated that their attention was really elsewhere. It was François de la Noue, the Huguenot friend of Walsingham and Paulet, who thought Philip II an obvious ally for the Guises, having 'equity and holiness in his mouth, and injustice and hypocrisy in his heart'; the translation was by Anthony Munday, former *agent provocateur* in the English College in Rome, now part of Walsingham's secret service.

Chapter 20

THE AGENT OF THE CANALS

T he successes of the Elizabethan secret services of Burghley, Leicester and above all Sir Francis Walsingham depended for the most part on the pragmatic treachery of men like Maude, Tyrell and Gifford, Anthony Poyntz and others. They were specifically tasked and could therefore succeed or fail, win a reward or rebuke. Others whom it is better to term intelligencers generally could be in the field somewhere in Europe;[1] William Harborne did intelligence work in Constantinople while a diplomat and trade representative, sent there in the early 1580s after Walsingham's masterly position paper *Memorandum on the Turkey Trade* written in 1578. It was the hope of the Principal Secretary that the Turks could be incited to harry the Spanish navy, or perhaps mount an incursion on Spanish territories from north Africa. The intelligencer or agent on whom this chapter will concentrate was Stephen Powle, whose time in Italy for Walsingham was less exciting than that of Nicholas Faunt, hunted in Naples in 1581 and then arrested in Rome by the papal Inquisition. When he was freed, perhaps by the efforts of a double agent (someone planted in the English College?), he bobbed up again in Paris.[2]

In March 1586 Duke John Casimir of the Palatinate wrote a formal letter of commendation in Latin about Powle to Burghley, and the Lord Treasurer in June got a gift from the young would-be diplomat of a genealogy of the Duke – a very well judged item that chimed with Burghley's snobbish antiquarian tastes. As a reward for service he intended Powle to become Clerk of the Privy Council, but was foiled by Elizabeth promising the office to another candidate. By December 1586 Powle's circumstances in his father's house in Maiden Lane were decaying, and clearly he needed a post with a more or less regular income – as did so many educated young men. If a passport was provided he might improve his circumstances by travel, and he needed more than ever to escape Powle snr. The advantage to Walsingham of employing an enthusiastic young linguist was that a fresh, alert mind was put to work; and he was

English, not another Scot on the make (Scots in Venice in particular sent Walsingham news and intelligence). Now Powle got a £50 annual pension, the passport, and £30 in travel expenses, and in late March 1587 he set off.

On the boat crossing to France he met one of Burghley's aristocratic wards, Lord Zouche,[3] whose education with the young earls of Oxford, Essex, Rutland and Southampton was now being smoothed by travel in company with Claude Holliband, the well-known instructor in French, and they travelled together for safety to Hamburg and then to Frankfurt-on-Main, a key centre for European commerce and banking. It was there that Powle delivered a packet from Walsingham to one of England's most important men – Horatio Pallavicino, formerly of Genoa, businessman, ambassador and spy. In 1586, when he was in Dresden, Pallavicino had an unexpected meeting with one Walsingham agent; his hustling around Germany took him in and out of his Frankfurt house, as he was there representing Elizabeth in negotiations to recruit a German Protestant army to support Henri of Navarre.[4] One of the many visitors seems to have been Giordano Bruno, an Oxford contact of Alberico Gentili who was now very briefly Pallavicino's personal aide; Bruno found shelter with the printer Johannes Wechel. Another visitor was Walter Williams, who had letters for him from Walsingham and was heading for Geneva.[5] In July 1586 Pallavicino was in Luneburg, for what amounted to a Protestant grand council of war – princes and electors, and representatives of Navarre, and the King of Denmark; having met with the Elector of Saxony in the previous month, he was on excellent terms with him. As for Gentili, in November 1586 Walsingham offered him the chair of regius professor of law at Oxford, and the official appointment was made in June 1587.

Powle's progress saw him in Venice in April 1587, when he reported the increasingly difficult circumstances of many as they came under pressure from the city's Inquisition. To Walsingham he sent his man Daniel Simpson with a newsletter telling of the mélange of continental reactions to the execution of Mary, Queen of Scots; some highly perturbed and others finding it a sovereign remedy of the ills assailing Protestantism. Among the princes in Italy who wished Elizabeth well in her sturdy resistance to Spanish domination he noted the dukes of Ferrara, Mantua and Florence, as well as the Venetian Signoria. The temper of the Doge towards England was also mild because of the volume of trade between the two countries. In fact, if he had chosen, Powle could have sailed between London (or Southampton) and Venice; the year before he arrived two English merchant ships, well-laden, had made the journey in the remarkable sailing time of twenty-nine days.

If the assignment was to provide Powle with a future career in government he needed to show attention to detail, and he did this in part by his cautious treatment of the transmission of letters, which might pass through many hands and be scrutinised many times. He would first of all hop between English and Italian, writing innocuous details in the latter in the reasonable hope that a reader might not bother to translate (or have it translated for him) when mastery of English was so rare in Europe. When he wrote to Walsingham on 30 May 1587, he mentioned that his letter of 16 May had been given to Hieronimo di Bonna and was enclosed in a letter to Niccolo di Gozzi. Three weeks later, when writing to his older brother Thomas, he said that he was then in Strasbourg (this was false) and expected to be in Frankfurt the next September. The language shift is noticeable in letter five to Walsingham, in which Powle gave details of letters delivered from Rome. Within the English College there was a well received rumour that James VI was minded to retreat from the terms of the Treaty of Berwick, change his religion and recall to Scotland three exiled bishops; the execution of Mary was an affront to many in that country, and given her French status James was apparently taken with the idea of regenerating the 'Auld Alliance' with an approach. In March, the late queen's ambassador representative to France, the Archbishop of Glasgow, was restored to his bishopric by Act of Parliament and given the role of resident ambassador for James in Paris.[6] The talk now became quite animated about those who might be raised to the college of cardinals. One candidate was supposedly Richard Shelley, now Prior of the Knights of St John, a company of international adventurers, and the man who had once had the temerity to petition Elizabeth for religious toleration as she strolled through the palace gardens at Greenwich.[7] Exile had not made him more diffident, since he asked Powle to request of Walsingham and Burghley that he be paid his annuities and rents from his London properties. He drew attention to his refusal of a Spanish pension to underscore the idea that he was loyal to Elizabeth.

The follow-up letter of 24 July 1587 was the sixth, with more than half in Italian. In the English remainder he refers to the Altanni brothers, picked out by Philip II to take letters from Venice to the Spanish ambassador resident in Constantinople, concerning 'the enterprise of England'. However, the brothers stalled their mission and just vanished for five months so that the letters lay waiting. Contrast this with the energetic enthusiasm of William Harborne representing Walsingham in the same city, an inventive diplomat, whose activity grew in intensity as war between England and Spain became unavoidable. Philip II was angry that such a simple assignment had stalled, and he pressed the Venetian authorities to apprehend the idle brothers, on the grounds that he supposed them to have allowed the letters to stray. The worst thought was the English had them, thus allowing the mighty and feared Drake a huge advantage. The brothers were subsequently prosecuted by the Spanish Secretary of State, but on his death they were tried and freed to enjoy their liberty as usual. As for Shelley, according to Powle's report he had been in conflict with certain Jesuits who supported the now deceased Babington plotters, and ill with stress he collapsed and died on about 12 July. Most of the financial arrears of pension and rents which he had been keen to collect from his three London properties he bequeathed to his servant John, who had been in his service for some twenty-eight years. John made a decision to travel to London to secure Walsingham's help in getting his inheritance. How secure this was remained to be seen, given Shelley's large debts to certain merchants resident in Rome.

Powle was still fretting about his letters, their delivery and the extent to which their content was useful when he himself thought on occasions that his employer was getting something stale. When letter seven was written on 1 August 1587 Walsingham was a-bed with his recurring kidney infection, but by mid-September he had recovered and had written to Burghley after Powle had sent a strong endorsement of Henri of Navarre with Pallavicino the money man for prompt action if Elizabeth agreed. There had been, as it seemed, a dramatic shift in Navarre's favour when in battle at Coutras, the King of France lost his favourite Anne, Duke of Joyeuse, in a pitched battle in July. A week later, however, Guise – sent by Henri III to fight the combined German forces, lose, and terminally embarrass the League – instead mounted an attack at Auneau and routed them. 'La Ligue, après Coutras se radicalise.'[8] For Walsingham the Guise were 'Spaniolated' and support for Navarre was 'apt to stop the Spanish preparation against this realm'. If Elizabeth deliberated for too long, or would not find the cash for her ally, 'she shall have cause, I fear, to say farewell my days of peace'. But she was a ruler tormented by the draining of her supply; back in January she had given John Casimir 100,000 crowns, and to little purpose when he fumbled the pro-Huguenot invasion of France. The nest-egg of the carefully accumulated surplus, which was some £300,000 in 1584, plus the payments on the 1584 grant of subsidy, tided the government over for a time, but subsidies to France, the standing costs of the Low Countries, and in 1588 resistance to the Armada, made a breach in the financial wall, and Elizabeth thought she faced bankruptcy. The moment the Earl of Leicester arrived in the Low Countries in December 1585 he had to use royal money to buy off the Estates garrison in Ostend, which was on the brink of mutiny. As soon as he made attempts to increase his revenues from the Estates-General he was in sharp conflict with them, and their embassy in London was repeatedly in discussions over costs and payments. Two kneeling representatives before an amazingly elongated Elizabeth giving an audience in the Privy Chamber appear in a strange naïve painting now in the Kunstsammlungen, Kassel, the town in which John Dee had found a temporary abode, and visited by Powle early in his peregrinations.

Early in November 1587 Powle wrote to Walsingham to warn him of a plan to assassinate Elizabeth. The source for this was Stephen Rodwey whom he had met three years before when in Bohemia. Rodwey could speak French and Dutch to native standard, and Powle noted that he had a quality of inner reserve that suggested his use as an intelligencer. So he sent him to Rome, full of Catholic exiles plotting against Elizabeth; a dangerous city where just a few years before a clutch of Protestant mariners had been burned in a public square for failing to abjure their faith. Rodwey could pass for a Frenchman or Dutchman and did so successfully. Travelling back from Rome – near Verona – he fell into company with four strangers, and began one of those travel conversations lasting for hours with the equally garrulous Guiseppe Giraldo, a merchant from Bergamo who related tales of his cousin Michele Giraldo. The latter was a middle-aged merchant who had just got back from Constantinople, and from Venice he had hurried to Rome in secret, before returning to Venice and taking ship to England. Cousin Guiseppe asked him the reason for this voyage with its attendant dangers, and Michele said that within a box he had a poisoned cake for the Queen – presumably the poison in the ingredients would keep it fresh for a ruler known to love her cakes and eating them. This weirdly inventive strike at her was papal-inspired, and it was such things that produced a contempt for Rome in the families of sometime Catholic English gentry, squires and yeomen, as well as the Protestant majority.

Being an agent of some diligence Powle could not let such a tantalizing narrative pass uninvestigated, and he looked up the summer sailings from Venice to England. Surprisingly only two ships had made the journey, and Michele Giraldo, the bearer of the poisoned papal pastry, seemed most likely

to have made the passage on the galleon *Tizzone* with its shipment of
Malmsey. Under its master Zuane Plaidemo the great vessel was attacked
below Cascais by a ship belonging to the Earl of Cumberland, and it was
wrecked while being hauled to England.[9] The other ship had left a little earlier
– the *Stella e Vidala* – with Giraldo on board, and this was shipwrecked off the
Isle of Wight around Michaelmas, meaning one less thing for Walsingham to
fret about. News about the papacy was given extra zest by Powle's report that
another order of excommunication of Elizabeth was soon to be published. At
the same time some counter-propaganda was issuing from Prague, the
Imperial city to which Dee had returned to spread prophecies about 'the
imminent fall of a mighty kingdom amid fearsome storms'. These reached the
Vatican via the wildly superstitious Emperor Rudolf II, but given John Dee's
huge reputation as an astrologer, alchemist and antiquarian, it was more
important that they also reached the Dutch almanac printers (did Rodwey
assist in this?), suppliers of almanacs to much of Europe. Appearing in such a
format at a critical moment, they helped to undermine Spanish morale.[10]

At about this time too Powle's own morale was clipped. He had
undertaken a risky assignment (as it seems from a letter to his friend Edward
Egerton – alas, no details) for Walsingham, but had not succeeded in every
aspect. Subsequently Egerton had gone back to England, and it is clear that
Powle now envied him; he was suffering from an acute bout of homesickness
for the language and the land: 'and the shadow of an English oak would
give a more perfect refreshing to my whole body than the stately Pines of
Ravenna'.[11] By the beginning of 1588 he had real reasons to feel jumpy
about 'this unpleasant liberty I enjoy . . .'; foreigners in the territory of
Venice found increasingly that freedoms that had been theirs hitherto were
now curtailed; so, for example, there were new laws against the close
scrutiny and reporting of changes in the politics of the Serene Republic, and
foreigners with no clear reason for being there were urged to leave. Powle
had a permit to remain, but it was not renewed for more than fifteen days at
a time and he became the only visible Englishman in the city. This made him
vulnerable, and he pressed Walsingham to get him some sort of protective
warrant or transfer him. While he continued to write at length on European
politics, and his views often chimed with those of the ailing Principal
Secretary in London, Powle was also beginning to fret about money. He was
now very much out of pocket as a result of his service and he wanted
Walsingham to augment his pay (such as it was) by one French crown per

day. The maintenance he had received from his father was now a trickle, and the family expectation that Elizabeth was paying generously and so excusing them made things even worse. 'I most humbly crave pardon for my importuning your Honour with my private suits in these general troubles whereabout your Honour is greatly busied.'

Waiting for a response, Powle sat down on Saturday 19 March to write to Master Kyrton at Ferrara. Being older, more conscientious and brighter than his young countryman, who had sought the correspondence but omitted to give him a particular address, Powle could not assume therefore that his letter would reach Kyrton. However, given that the few left in the area felt nervous about their isolation, they did try to write to each other in case something crippling, or worse, happened. Since 'Ferrara' was the maximum address he could muster, Powle's letter was rather bland, avoiding anything topical, but he did note he had not heard that week from Stephen Rodwey – a matter for concern. As for Kyrton's future, he wanted a position as a gentleman in service to the Duke of Ferrara, and Powle wished him well. Within a very few days his anxiety about an address dissolved – Kyrton wrote back with it, a fact that redounds to the credit of the messenger. When Powle wrote again to Kyrton on 23 March he chided him for a wasteful sprawl on his paper which had cost Powle more than he cared for; all his Venice letters are very closely written, to economise on postal costs. He made mention too in this letter that the following Monday 28 March he was setting out to walk to Verona, a distance of about sixty-five miles, and always attended at this time of year by the possibility of wintry weather, because he felt hemmed in by Venice and the lack of exercise. He planned to be absent no more than eight days, with a visit in company with Kyrton to Ferrara at Easter. In closing he mentioned greetings directed to Kyrton from a Miss Tayler, and barely a week later he wrote again and enquired about Kyrton's suit. He added other political news items such as the grief of Henri of Navarre over the death by poison of the Prince of Condé.[12] Rodwey was now in Frankfurt, and whatever news he sent by letters that Powle was keenly anticipating the following day, Kyrton was promised an update.

After mid-April Daniel, Powle's servant, arrived from England bringing with him the best of news. Walsingham agreed to the return to England of his prized intelligencer, and perhaps even better put up £50 at a time when his own finances had taken a mauling. Powle decided to remove himself from the no-longer-so-serene Serene Republic with all speed, travelling the rather familiar route to Hamburg, and hoping to be in England by the end of May. The letter to Walsingham signed with invisible ink (lemon juice?) on 29 April may have reached London after Powle himself, who had the dubious pleasure of returning to his testy old father's house in Maiden Lane after so many months of freedom. What would have delighted Powle was the news that in his absence a patron had seen to it that he received a coveted grant of arms from the Garter King of Arms. Did Walsingham push this through as a supplementary reward? Or was it Burghley, unusually responsive to the young man, who had sent him gifts?

Chapter 21

DAMNABLE LOSSES

In the aftermath of Sidney's death the Walsinghams were under great physical and emotional pressure. Frances Walsingham, who had gone to be with her dying husband, was heavily pregnant and grieving so that Leicester delayed her return to England, fearing a miscarriage and a premature death for his friend's child. Walsingham had a dead son-in-law to bury – but not immediately. The corpse was brought back to England on the *Black Pinnace* and lay in state at the Minories, headquarters of the Ordnance Office, Sidney's official bureau as intended successor to Warwick. Sidney was the heir to a very recently dead father whose funeral had cost just over £1,500, and an even more recently dead mother. Now the heir to the Sidney estates, Robert Sidney got large tracts of land from his father and brother, but much less cash to pay for funerals, debts and bequests. Because Frances Walsingham eventually had a stillborn child, she and Robert Sidney shared the lands until her death. Sales of estates provided the lawyers with years of business because of entail property restrictions, and since Walsingham was a lawyer he naturally defended the claims of his daughter, especially since by marriage to Barbara Gamage, Robert Sidney was the husband already of a south Wales heiress; she had been left her father's estate in 1584 and he had hurled himself upon her to win the prize which meant freedom from poverty. But now Walsingham calculated the dead hero's debts at £6,000, and Robert Sidney had the responsibility of paying them off and giving out the gifts, which were specified in the Will; but the sole executrix was Frances Walsingham. She had no interest in seeing her father impoverish himself prematurely, and the notion that Walsingham took on the entire £6,000 debt seems not merely unlikely but improbable in the extreme. It was Thomas Nevitt, Robert Sidney's accountant, who thirty-five years later pointed out that after the distribution to beneficiaries of money and jewels, any remaining goods were to go to Lady Frances, and that these items, including furniture, hangings, paintings and silverware, were taken from Penshurst by

Walsingham on his daughter's behalf, and the total value of what was removed was £20,000 (modern equivalent, *c.* £10,000,000).[1] This seems staggeringly high unless the house was stuffed to the eaves with treasure, and Nevitt was calculating their replacement cost.

The reason Walsingham wanted cash was because the funeral planned for the late Protestant hero was going to trump the beheading of Mary, Queen of Scots. Moreover, the cost of the burial could be used to twist the arm of Elizabeth, since he petitioned for the hugely sought-after post of Chancellor of the Duchy of Lancaster, an appanage formerly used to enrich the heir to the throne. If he could make it seem he had financial ruin parked on his doorstep it might sway her – especially if Burghley threw his weight behind the proposal. That would more than offset the fact that Leicester (with whom Walsingham's relations had become tense) had an alternative candidate to promote. The funeral was held on 16 February, a state funeral of a kind never seen before for someone not of the royal family, eye-poppingly grand with 700 mourners. Even Sidney's warhorse was in the procession, a huge *destrier* grandly turned out with little Daniel Bacheler riding, or at least sitting in the saddle, his legs too short to put feet in the stirrups, carrying a battle-axe. Quite a change from his usual lute for entertaining the Walsingham family at leisure. Long after the obsequies it was considered an affront to the memory of the dead man to appear at court or in the city in brightly coloured garments. Among the pallbearers were Edward Dyer and Fulke Greville, shown in one of the thirty-four engraved plates of the funeral prepared within a year for a memorial volume by Thomas Lant, a member of Sidney's household re-employed by the Walsinghams. Dyer and Greville, Gabriel Harvey and Edmund Spenser had been entertained by Sidney and his beloved sister Mary, Countess of Pembroke at Wilton House, Wiltshire, the home she very rarely left, although she was also at the funeral.

Initially, Sidney's grave, which had two volleys of shots fired over it by musketeers of the trained bands, had no tomb built over it. Robert Sidney and Walsingham were relieved of the burden of designing and paying for one by Greville, former schoolmate of Sidney and worshipper just this side of idolatry. He planned a tomb for old St Paul's that would hold both their bodily remains, and if his devotion needed any further proof it came surely in his 'annexation' of the *Old Arcadia*, because of what he saw as the threat to Sidney's reputation by a proposed pirated edition of a hitherto circulated but unpublished work. Concerned, in November 1586 he wrote to Walsingham of an approach by a man called Ponsonby, a bookbinder in St Paul's Churchyard, William Ponsonby, who asked Greville if the proposed printed edition of the *Old Arcadia* instead of Sidney's unfinished revision, of which the manuscript copy had recently been passed to his widow, was done with Walsingham's permission. Since it was subsequently stopped the answer becomes evident, and it was not until 1590 that Greville and Dr Matthew Gwynne oversaw the printed edition that Mary Sidney found too formal.[2] Under their preparation it became a moral allegory, when she preferred it as a romance written in her company. By the time of her own 1593 hybrid version, Ponsonby was selling books from the Bishop's Head premises in St Paul's Churchyard and may have been succeeded there by Edward (Ned) Blount, his former apprentice. Ponsonby thrived after his original intervention because he had won the trust of the family. In 1590, 1593 and 1598 he published *Arcadia* and thereafter according to Peter Lindenbaum 'became what amounted to being the Sidney-circle publisher'. In 1598 it was Blount who put out the first edition of the late Christopher Marlowe's unfinished epyllion, *Hero and Leander*, dedicated to the former patron of the dead poet, Sir Thomas Walsingham. In a decade his career had advanced, and like his old dead cousin he had been knighted.

Even longer delayed than Sidney's funeral was that of Mary, Queen of Scots. It took place five months after her death, and there may have been some foreign pressure on Elizabeth to hold it. Pope Sixtus V, who blessed Spanish preparations to crush England, wrote a poem on Mary's death in which he deplored the lack of formal obsequies. When the funeral was finally held in Peterborough (some eleven miles from Fotheringhay) on 1 August 1587, no foreign ambassadors were invited, but Elizabeth did send her officers and heralds to dignify the event with some royal pomp. It was staged using an empty coffin, since the body had already been put into the open vault the previous night, and it cost an unprincely £321 14s 6d. Up to the time of her execution Walsingham had never been entirely satisfied that his chief source of information concerning the intensifying Armada preparations, Anthony Standen, former page of Mary and employee of Philip II, could be trusted. But Walsingham sat on this unease because the exiled blond Catholic with a clutch of aliases (Pompeo Pellegrini, André Sandal and M. La Faye) had much to offer to advantage the English government.

One informer nurtured by Standen in a lengthy career was Giovanni Figliazzi, ambassador for Medici Florence to Spain, and well known to William

Waad. In a letter to Walsingham written in early February 1588 Standen (Pellegrini) remarked that Philip II was so taken with Figliazzi that he wanted to employ him himself. Figliazzi had meanwhile been emboldened to declare to Standen how 'addicted' he was to Walsingham, but how this admiration had come about Standen had no reason to record. Had Walsingham perhaps met Figliazzi in Paris, or at a later diplomatic conference such as the one in the Low Countries with Don John in 1578? It was an unnamed Fleming that Standen engaged to go information-gathering in Lisbon, for the brother of the Fleming was a servant to the Marquis of Santa Cruz, who urged Philip II that as the ruler of Portugal he should assemble his fleets for an attack on England. He urged the same in January 1586, and by that time there is good reason to suppose that Philip had made the decision to do so. His preparations were barely begun before the English government knew, but not because Anthony Poyntz had struck a mother-lode of secret information; in fact the Spanish made little effort to conceal what was going on.

Not so the English. As Philip made his decision just before Mary's execution, there were secret plans afoot in England to attack Spain, with the entire English fleet going after 'the provisions of Spain', and only at the beginning of March was Drake known to be the commander. A year or so before this Walsingham instructed William Harborne in Constantinople to incite the Turkish Sultan to attack Spain, and for the rest of his time there that was perhaps the key diversionary objective. But the Turks were preoccupied with a war with Persia, and Walsingham had no inclination to wait on their success. With the return of Leicester from his tormented time in the Low Countries, Walsingham in theory at least had another ally in Council ready to support an effort by Drake. According to Mendoza in Paris it was Ralegh who was 'very cold about these preparations and is secretly trying to dissuade the Queen from them'. No surprise then if Walsingham became exasperated with him and, as I have suggested before, decided the Roanoke venture was going to fail. All Walsingham saw was that in Drake he had the keenest partisan of his own fighting gospel, and for the great seaman his urgent desire to take on the might of Philip II had no stronger supporter than the Principal Secretary. 'It is hardly too much to say that taken together they stand forth as the great protagonists of militant English Protestantism.'[3]

Elizabethan England had never seen a stronger force than this. The fleet of twenty-three ships included four men-of-war put up by the Queen, with the *Elizabeth Bonaventure* given to Drake, and William Borough, Clerk of the

Queen's Ships, the Vice-Admiral, likely to be on a steep learning curve when it came to engagement with the enemy, commanding the *Golden Lion*. That they got to depart on 2 April was because Drake was satisfied with his orders, did not want them curtailed out of feminine timidity, and anticipated a royal message that would ruin his prospects. He was correct to do so, and as he outran the pinnace with her corrective instructions he wrote to Walsingham a message that tugs at the heart even now: 'The winds command me away. Our ship is under sail. God grant we may live in His fear as the enemy may have cause to say that God doth fight for Her Majesty as well abroad as at home' – a reference to the recent beheading of Mary and the rounding up of Jesuits. Imagine the anger of both men when Dr William Allen was that summer made a cardinal, months after Drake had laid waste Cadiz and destroyed thirty-one vessels with a vast amount of stores. The next target after Sagres Castle on the Algarve surrendered was to have been Lisbon, but Drake noted its fortifications, and in any case his fleet was hampered by light winds. Instead, he opted to slip towards the Azores, having heard while watering at Cape St Vincent that a great carrack from the East Indies was due. Such a mouth-watering prize was found sheltering in the lee of the island of Sao Miguel – it was the *San Felipe*, the property of the King himself, and after a cannonade that of Elizabeth. Drake put a crew on board, and the expedition was effectively at an end as the fleet returned to Plymouth with an amazing cargo from the carrack of silks, jewels and spices valued then at £114,000 (*c.* £57 million), with Elizabeth's share at an amazing £40,000 (*c.* £20 million). If anyone at court deserved a reward from this more than Walsingham it is hard to identify them, so perhaps it was now that he got the Walsingham Cup. English morale got a further fillip when the Marquis of Santa Cruz suddenly died, and it has been suggested that he was poisoned by one of Walsingham's agents based in Malaga – Nicholas Ousley (Oseley) – who had smuggled ciphered messages to England in wine-casks. Although regarded with suspicion in Spain he continued to report up to April 1588, and later that year, on his return to London, his reward was a lease on a city house.[4]

Walsingham lived with the constant expectation of war, as did mariners like Drake (and Hawkins) who wrote that 'Our profit and best course is to seek our peace by a determined and resolute war.' Yet even at this juncture there were many, rich and poor, who were deeply reluctant to give practical assistance in a foreign war, and many of those who had rushed to join Leicester in his efforts to prop up the Dutch resistance to Spain came to regret their martial ardour. During the winter of 1586/7 virtually everyone on both sides starved, and in the early months of 1587 Elizabeth refused the Dutch envoys more money. Further, she decided to send Thomas, Lord Buckhurst, an opponent of the war, to test in secret the Dutch about peace negotiations. This at a time when Philip's general, Parma, was so hard pressed that the greater part of his army stayed in Bimburg and Luxemburg for lack of forage until May 1587. To bring some order to a depressingly chaotic situation in the Low Countries, Walsingham took the straightforward view that Leicester needed to return despite hostility to him in some quarters, and Elizabeth had to pay her starving soldiers. And not only Walsingham, but Hatton and Burghley thought that Leicester could still accomplish something worthwhile – after all, so far the greatest general in Europe, Parma, had not achieved a superior position, and the old peacenik Burghley even thought that a better peace could be secured by arms: 'a demonstration in force under Leicester was the quickest way to bring Parma to reasonable terms'.[5]

Leicester was not a man to set aside a grievance when it was possible to go on recalling it. His first period in the Low Countries had begun on an optimistic high, but ended with frustration and bitter recriminations. The grievances were numerous – forty-two to be precise, which the red-faced Buckhurst had to read in Latin before the Estates-General on 14 April. Elizabeth had stipulated that this was to be done, for amity was restored with Leicester, and since Buckhurst was representing her he did try to soften Tudor asperities. As for Walsingham, he was resolute but glum, and when Leicester did return to the Low Countries in late June he was accompanied by two councillors, Henry Killigrew and Robert Beale, sent to replace Thomas Wilkes and Bartholomew Clark on the Council of State. Along with the two men from the core of the Walsingham affinity went a younger man, the equally trusted Francis Needham, placed as Leicester's secretary in order to observe and report on progress and failings. Leicester's attitude before he went slipped about as he talked at length to colleagues and read the correspondence flowing between London and the United Provinces. What exasperated him was the sense he took from all of this that Buckhurst, Wilkes, Norreys and the reconstructed Council of State were neglecting his interests and dignity. Walsingham did detect a leaning in the Queen towards his cousin Norreys, the man so hated by Leicester that the Earl had sworn never to serve with him again, so Norreys was shuffled off to another colonial war – the one in Ireland. Wilkes and Buckhurst were by now busy doing nothing, and Wilkes came back to London with a letter to the Dutch representatives from Oldenbarnevelt bitterly critical of Leicester and very likely meant to curtail his return.

But this became more difficult to achieve when there were significant shifts in London, where Elizabeth was creakily inclining to let her favourite courtier earl return to duty, and he was pronouncing his willingness to serve her. Some more royal funds would be paid out, lending him £6,000, with £30,000 for campaigning with 5,000 fresh troops. Burghley and Walsingham played pivotal roles in the endless discussions and revisions of how and when and to what purpose. It had become a given of Anglo-Dutch resistance that it needed a leader of national standing to hold the squabbling allies together. The final decision to opt once again for Leicester was very possibly taken in May, when at Barn Elms Walsingham had a royal visit. Among those awaiting Elizabeth with a petition was Lord Gilbert Talbot, son of the Earl of Shrewsbury, and on this occasion 'Barn Elms had become the clearing house for petitions', with Talbot one of many, and Walsingham performing an appreciated service for other courtiers also seeking access to Elizabeth. The aspiring courtier could certainly be eased into that bear-pit, the court, by Walsingham, who seems to have done this for Thomas Myddelton, a former factor for a sugar-trading enterprise in Antwerp,[6] who returned with riches that beautifully grew into a fortune after introductions to the leading seamen freebooters – men intimate with Walsingham. In 1595 Myddelton bought Chirk Castle, near Wrexham, built during the reign of Edward I.

So Leicester was back in the devil's playground, and Francis Needham quickly began to fret about having too little to do, 'for I am idle all the day'. He was not involved in military matters, which picked up once Parma had roused his army from its winter torpor. The general began an offensive that aimed to capture towns, and their vital food supplies were shipped from France, Holland and Zeeland, whose deputies then dominated the Estates-General, and thought it wiser to concentrate on their own defence. This meant they did nothing to assist the English when Parma began to lay siege to Sluys on 12 June and Sir Roger Williams moved from Ostend to aid the town. What this friend of Walsingham faced was Parma's force of some 6,000 infantry, and cavalry numbering 2,000, as well as the famous battering train of thirty heavy guns. These last Parma very nearly lost when a raiding party clattered out of Sluys and caught the guns on the river, driving off the escort, so that only the arrival of Spanish reinforcements prevented a notable and much-needed victory. Subsequently, although Williams squeezed into Sluys, he must have found it dreadfully uncomfortable, for by late June, as Leicester arrived back, Parma had captured a fort that allowed him to bombard the town. The indifference of the Dutch to the fate of Sluys was merely notched up by the recall of Norreys, and having saved 200,000 florins in extraordinary contributions they elected to pay the German cavalry of Count Mors. Only on 13 July did they vote 100,000 fl. for the relief of Sluys, and only a fraction of this was handed over. To Walsingham came a letter from Leicester saying that 'nothing is to be gotten but for money . . . use all your furtherance for the speedy sending of money'.[7]

Despite the best swimming efforts of a gallant Dutch sailor called van Trappen, who got into Sluys via the water way to collect information on a possible safe spot for relief ships, they dispersed in threatening weather, and six days later, on 26 July, short of gunpowder, the town surrendered. This was misery on a stick for the English, and Leicester quickly, and not too unreasonably, blamed the Dutch. He was very likely correct in thinking that the Estates-General sacrificed the town in order to prod Elizabeth to be more open-handed with subsidies, but it was unwise also to blame Buckhurst, Wilkes and Norreys, who would have told Walsingham of the raggedness of his colleagues' approach – the lack of sound strategic thinking. Certainly it was apparent that the differences between Leicester and the Estates-General were the core of the problem, and Needham pointed out that unless they were reconciled still more disastrous consequences might follow. And to this we can add the unanswerable question: if Philip Sidney had lived might not things have gone better? On 31 July Walsingham wrote to Beale and Killigrew that he was trying to rustle up a remedy for perceived ills, and he warned Leicester of the gravity of the situation. But then everything and everyone, as it seemed, exasperated the Earl, and the hint that Walsingham was not as hostile as he was to Buckhurst, Wilkes and Norris, proved another goad. Needham wrote to Walsingham just a few days before this that Leicester had heard that when Wilkes was imprisoned in the Fleet, Walsingham notified the warden that Wilkes was to be 'well used for that he was not to be a close prisoner'. Leicester felt very sore that someone he had accounted a sound friend had betrayed his trust, and Walsingham thought it necessary to write promptly to him to explain his protective stance for Wilkes, who was very unwell. It is not clear if Leicester's mood lightened, for all the clarification. Probably not, for at this time Leicester was hearing that Dutch officers from Sluys were blaming the Zeeland naval command and the regent burghers of Holland for the town's fall. They had actually wanted the Earl to attempt a coup and to rule directly, but Anjou had tried and failed years before, and Leicester saw the sense of not seeking to overturn history as well as his enemies.

Walsingham, Burghley and Hatton (but not Ralegh) all tried to give leverage to Leicester's rule and to bolster his confidence. They did this by trying to get Elizabeth to subsidise the war with more funds, but her instincts remained the same – hope to promote peace talks. Even Burghley's cogent notion that the best way to secure an honourable peace was to prosecute the war with all-out vigour got shunted aside. That track looked more and more impossible as English desertions mounted, the situation decaying so fast that Leicester seems to have been verging on a stress-related breakdown. In England Walsingham too was ill again and needed treatment for his autogenic malady. By November the debilitating fever had abated, but even holding a pen to write was too much for him – 'I write not with mine own hand'. Some seven or eight weeks prior to this Leicester had stirred the Estates-General with the stark warning that their cause was about to be lost if they did not come up with money and equipment, and that negotiating for peace might be a better solution. Imagine hearing this rasping truth if you were Dutch; a truth that chimed with Elizabeth's desire, so that as yet he was not recalled. At the same time it is very possible that not every colleague on the Privy Council wanted Leicester back in England to meddle again in daily affairs. Walsingham would hint that this was so, but the final decision lay with Elizabeth, and in November she made it. Leicester *would* be recalled and Dr John Herbert, Master of Requests, would go over on a peace mission, landing at Flushing on 16 November, whence came Leicester from Utrecht, via Dordrecht. Leicester's command, which had been such a torment (and for this he blamed Walsingham), passed to Lord Willoughby. Characteristically and without reference to anyone, Leicester held onto the new man's patent of office until he himself had returned to England. It was the act of a self-important man whose time had passed and was blemished with failure.

We have seen how frequently Elizabeth resisted or temporarily stalled when called upon to face the human and financial cost of war. Mercantile interests were her henchmen in such resistance, for the English cloth trade was suffering very badly as exports diminished. Spain, Portugal and the Low Countries were closed to the English, and Parma controlled the middle Rhine, blocking the ordinary trade conduit in western and southern Germany. Moreover, Spanish intrigues, joined with the efforts of the Hanseatic League, had all but closed Hamburg, the great outlet for cloth in northern Germany. It had been Machiavelli's contention that the prince who wanted an active, strong homeland had to be taken up by the absorbing matter of warfare, and Walsingham's associate Thomas Digges, looking at the broad sweep of history, concluded that military skill was the greatest natural cause of the rise and fall of all monarchies, kingdoms and empires. Yet even apart from the practical barriers imposed by a queen and her cautious chief minister, there were inhibitions occasioned by conscience to squeeze a philosophy of active militarism. Might a just government undertake wars of aggression? Could a nation apparently brimming with a surplus population justifiably discharge the superfluous? Walsingham would certainly have answered, as did Simon Harward in *The Solace for the Souldier and Saylor* (1592), that in general war was useful and lawful when directed against 'the professed enemies of God's truth'. The justification for piratical voyages against Spanish shipping and territories stemmed from more than merely economic rapacity – the Spaniard is 'an idolater, a pillar and prop of Antichrist . . . and a professed patron of truce breaking, falsehood and disloyalty'. His plan was global annexation.[8]

As it happened, Parma had stalled while besieging and then taking Sluys. The immediate effect was to dampen Elizabeth's ardour for peace, for all that she had appeared eager to take up the offer of mediation by the King of Denmark, Frederick II (d. February 1588), who was ailing during the previous summer as his diplomats also negotiated for the marriage of a daughter to James VI. But the see-sawing of Elizabeth's inclination to peace went on, and Walsingham wrote to Leicester on 7 August, 'I never saw her Majesty's disposition so unfit for the wars as at this present.' He thought the Dutch were tottering on the brink of annihilation, and when Philip II had them under his heel 'we are to look for a war at our own home; a matter fearful to think of, considering the corruption of this estate, the doubtful terms we stand in with Scotland and how unfurnished we are of martial men to make head to the enemy'.[9] From his own sickbed in September 1587 Walsingham devised a little stratagem that was meant to destabilise Parma's position and disconcert Philip II. To do this he had one of his secretaries write to one of his spies in the Low Countries. The proposition was that Parma should renege on his service to Spain and set himself up as the independent ruler of the Low Countries. According to the letter, Elizabeth would far rather have Parma as a latter-day duke of Burgundy for her neighbour that any Spanish monarch. Nor was this power scenario entirely new; the same secret agent had tried to make mischief between the prince and his employer with the thought a year before this bluff. The agent was perhaps Thomas Barnes, employed to go among exiled English Catholics in Paris after the execution of Mary. Rumours of rumours certainly got to ambassador Mendoza in Paris, and when Herbert went to the Low Countries in October 1587 on the peace trail he very likely nudged the matter before Parma. In an endeavour to bring down two high-fliers, Parma and Stafford, with one ambush, knowing that Stafford was selling information to Philip II, Walsingham surely revealed the bait for Parma to his ambassador, since it would then be passed via Mendoza to his king.

And Elizabeth? With the absence on sick leave of her Principal Secretary, she became addicted to the narcotic advice of Sir James Crofts, the Leicestrian who had turned on his leader to become his enemy, and another informer in London for Mendoza. Yet the commissioners for peace negotiations were not sent, as the Queen dithered in November about their despatch. According to a Spanish agent in London, on the seventeenth of the month she stormed at Burghley, Walsingham and Croft for the false path of dealing with Parma the eloquent. Walsingham was so irritated by this vexing nonsense that he wrote a paper defending his actions and those of Burghley. He reminded the Queen too that if Drake had returned to sea immediately after the capture of the *San Felipe* 'there was great likelihood to man's judgement that the West India fleet should have been intercepted, whereby the present storms that now lay over this realm might have been both cleared and prevented'.[10] This brisk rebuke to a ruler generally besotted with the idea of peace may have been good for Walsingham's morale, but it failed to swing Elizabeth round to his point of view.

Before the New Year she was calling for peace at any price, a notion risible to Walsingham, who was ordered to press negotiations forward with the help of Burghley. Actually, in tandem they kept her intention untethered until February 1588, because Walsingham now firmly held that all talk of peace with Spain at this time was hokum; negotiations simply masked their preparations for war, and the correspondence between Philip II and Parma shows how accurate was Walsingham's reading of the situation. The triumvirate in London, once again including a slightly chastened Leicester, regarded peace with a quizzical eye – or perhaps 'eyes wide shut'. Walsingham's God was the God of battles, and his prayers would not have been for diplomats but soldiers and seamen; in April 1588 an entry in the Privy Council register notes the supply of 'provisions' to Drake – among them

200 muskets, 1,000 arrows for the muskets with tamkins (wads), 500 long pikes and 300 short pikes.

By then Dr Herbert was back in England, and the Queen's five commissioners, headed by Derby, had gone to Ostend to negotiate with a great deal of latitude on most matters of substance, though not the repayment of all the monies Elizabeth had hitherto spent in the Low Countries, nor the retention by her of the cautionary towns until the huge capital sum was repaid. Of the five it is clear from correspondence that Cobham was in Walsingham's support cluster; the men of Kent thought alike on this. Parma's representatives were evidently there to fill in time, and perhaps even as a screen for his canal-digging near the coast of Flanders, and his collecting of flat-bottomed boats for the invasion of England once the Spanish Grand Fleet had gained command of the seas between Dover and Flushing. The only real enthusiast for peace was Crofts, and he had been sent because Walsingham had smartly calculated that his absence would make the Queen's ears deafer to his policy blandishments. As for his whispers in Parma's ears, an irate Queen commanded they should cease. Crofts then made a serious miscalculation; he took it upon himself to stretch her instructions in order to develop his own course for foreign policy. Crofts was galloping, as it were, feet out of stirrups, towards the cliff-edge, and Walsingham was there smiling and waving him through. This 'weak old man of seventy with very little sagacity' was Parma's thumbnail characterization, an acuteness in his opponents unknown to Crofts, who did not become more cautious but instead struck out independently. In May 1588, chafing at the dawdling of his colleagues, he set out for Ghent to make a private visit to Parma, and without reference to anyone made an offer of terms which Elizabeth would accept (so he said) if Parma negotiated directly with her. In sum, his offer was that if Philip II withdrew his foreign army of occupation from the Netherlands, restored the old administration there and allowed some elasticity in religious toleration to the Dutch, then Elizabeth would elect to make peace, would withdraw her troops and hand over to Spain the cautionary towns.

Once or twice in years before this these terms might have chimed with Elizabeth's actual intentions – in so far as she knew them. But the political milieu of the English court had shifted to favour Walsingham and her senior advisers who saw war as inevitable. Croft had gone beyond his remit, and the formal negotiations became dull little wrangles about diplomatic niceties until the English and Spanish commissioners finally met at the end of May 1588. They argued for another month about the cessation of the armed struggle, and as they did so the Antwerp presses were preparing thousands of copies of a new papal bull of excommunication. To ruffle things and confuse the Spanish, Walsingham fluffed up a modest peace froth of his own, and in a letter to Giovanni Figliazzi he protested:

> I know that I am reputed a principal nourisher of the discord between their Majesties yet I pray you assure yourself, whatsoever you hear to the contrary, that no councillor the Queen my mistress hath doth more desire a peace than myself, so far forth as may stand with her Majesty's honour and safety.[11]

Figliazzi had returned from his embassy to Spain, to his native Florence and through the previous winter had been seeking to arrange a marriage between Grand Duke Ferdinand and a Spanish infanta. Delivery of the letter was the task of Anthony Standen, and in a cipher letter of 7 June that fetched up in the Salisbury papers at Hatfield, the English spy wrote to Walsingham that Figliazzi had gone to the Spanish court to confer with Secretary Idiaquez when he got the initial communication from London. The Spaniard read it with a sneer and commented that it was 'an ordinary meal of Secretary Walsingham's corn', and so nothing came from the policy swerve. Yet even the scornful response may have been in a small way useful, for it added to the evidence of Spanish hostility resisting moderation. The notion of war as inevitable was anathema to Elizabeth, who would lose power to her fighting men; Burghley and Walsingham had managed after all to delay it for many years. But now, as a consequence of her ostrich posture, they had to make war preparations more or less in spite of her.

Chapter 22

DEFYING THE DON

In tandem Burghley and Walsingham constituted 'the active and yet steady hand of authority'. Secret activity to uncover enemy advances by the actions, intuitions and penetration of spies and intelligencers had gradually been taken over by Walsingham, so that the networks of the triumvirate fused under him. At the beginning of 1588 Walsingham had accumulated shelves of information because of his passion for detail, while Sir Thomas Gresham, Elizabeth's main economic adviser, had given her a surplus of £154,000. Between March 1587 and June 1588 Walsingham received £3,300 for the secret service, over which he now had total control, and it was the largest sum he ever got. Even so, it was not enough for his purposes, so his own personal wealth was used, as his first principle was always that 'knowledge is never too dear'. Spain, which was spending 10 million ducats on the Armada fleet when the English fleet cost around £150,000, was always the greatest intelligence problem for Walsingham, the most testing to infiltrate. Ambassador Mendoza was one to trumpet the view that all English traders in Spain should be regarded with suspicion; added to this trust deficit was the fact that in the first three months of the Anglo-Spanish war English privateers seized twenty-seven Spanish ships valued at nearly 295,000 ducats. Traditionally the north coast of Spain from La Coruña to San Sebastian was safer than Andalucia for English traders.[1] However, markets in southern Spain were more prosperous, so some merchants were prepared to factor in risks because the return cargoes were more varied, and provided they reached their destination safely made for a wider profit margin. Once Portugal had been annexed by Philip II, the Anglo-Spanish tensions grew amongst other things over the trade with the kingdom of Morocco.

One of the pivotal figures in this was Roger Bodenham, who lived in Seville with his Spanish wife, although he was frequently in San Lucar de Barrameda at the mouth of the river Guadalquivir, where the patron of the merchant colony was the Duke of Medina Sidonia. A kinsman of Sir James Crofts, Bodenham traded with Fez and was a prominent member of the Spanish Company when the Privy Council incorporated it in 1577. Writing in 1579, he predicated an agreement allowing the English to fortify Mogador. This would allow for protection of national shipping, and service an attack on the Spanish fleet returning from the West Indies via the Canaries. He even imagined that one day King Ahmed el-Mansour might invade Spain, although altogether Ahmed was very cautious in his dealings with the English, and he annoyed merchants, who did not trust or like him. Bodenham still believed passionately in joining forces with an Islamic state, and even cited the St Bartholomew's Massacre as sufficient to justify the use of any means to build resistance to Catholic tyranny. This would have brightened Walsingham's day, and it is no surprise that Bodenham, after offering his services to Burghley, regularly sent information to the Principal Secretary from 1581. Elizabeth's government needed saltpetre for gunpowder and el-Mansour needed military supplies. To effect this controversial exchange, both needed to swing past the official cloth-for-sugar trade.

Securing untainted and accurate information from hidden or embedded sources became even harder for Walsingham when Philip II suddenly closed all Spanish ports to English traders, protecting stores required to defeat England. One belief current among Spaniards was that Drake ('El Dracque') had a magic mirror that showed him the position of every ship in the world. By June Standen was convinced that Spain would have to stall the Armada, and when Walsingham passed this to Burghley a postscript said it was for his eyes only; he was naturally very protective of a key source: 'I would be loathe the gentleman should have any harm through my default.'[2] As for his pension, it was exactly the sum saved by Elizabeth when another spy – Gilbert Gifford – stumbled into his cell in Paris.

Walsingham not only benefited from good will and the payments he made to single spies in southern Europe. He had much closer to home, but equally at risk of the dagger or bullet, an outstandingly conscientious agent in the Low Countries, a grain and sundries merchant called Wychegerde, who had every reason to feel aggrieved, but did not, at Drake's storming into Cadiz, because corn he had bought went down in one of the sunk ships. Originally from Germany, so probably a Lutheran, he was constantly on the move in the Low Countries to glean information in towns, camps, markets and garrisons. The risks were high, and in one startling incident Wychegerde got snatched by pirates who stole his money, commodities and even the clothes he was wearing, releasing him in his underwear at Boulogne. It was at this period that pirates at home and abroad began to adopt flamboyant garb for their visits to terra firma, and Execution Dock, Wapping, saw some prettily dressed rogues hung in crowd-pleasing finery. As for Walsingham's courageous spy, he held to his task and with a new set of clothes (or maybe second-hand ones) he slipped across saturated fields, clambered over ditches and dykes, looking and counting so that in his ciphered reports to London he assigned to Parma a mixed force of some 5,000, whereas Leicester, probably to save face when he failed to overcome them, inflated the figure by a guess to 18,000. Wychegerde was actually rather impressed by the battle-hardened veterans; ironically no one in London was inclined to credit his data.

Nor could Walsingham back it from another source. He never managed by theft or the suborning of an aide to Parma to penetrate the general's correspondence. Instead, he had to make do with reported fragments of the dinner table exchanges of those about Prince Maurice of Nassau. But in any case, given his many sources, solicited and unsolicited, Walsingham anticipated the Armada, and month-by-month his analysis was given to a resistant Queen. To rouse her to face the shocking truth that her former brother-in-law was preparing a vast assault on her nation and her occupation of the throne was astonishingly difficult. It was as if some rare jungle soporific had been used to drug her small ale; she was in denial. And then in Italy and Spain things came to pass to bolster the prospect of enemy action against England: one was that Philip's ambassador in Rome, Count Olivarez, had negotiated Pope Sixtus V to a standstill, so that the papacy would hand over 1 million gold ducats; and the second was that the Plate fleet from the Caribbean got safely to Spain with 16 million ducats, of which Philip got 4 million. These golden enablers made the English extremely nervous in the summer and autumn of 1587, and Walsingham argued vehemently that the best way 'to bridle their malice is the interrupting of the Indian fleets'.[3] But Elizabeth pursed her lips and Drake was grounded, despite the rattle of heightened anxiety in October, so that despite a recovery from illness Walsingham's tone in writing to Leicester was extremely gloomy. The sea which had for most been seen as a defensive moat increasingly looked like a way of invasion, so of necessity England became a sea power. 'The transition of a country from a land to a sea power demands structural organizational modifications and results in great social changes.'

A good deal had been done over the years by tough, objective men like Sir John Hawkins, Treasurer of the Navy since 1578, and Dr Julius Caesar, judge of the Admiralty Court from 1583. A man of great vigour and sterling integrity, he made a powerful sweep of inefficient and corrupt local officials, and in 1588 a central Admiralty Commission was set up empowered to search out cases of piracy throughout England and Wales. On land too the forces the government could put up were in better shape than before, although military training was then in its infancy. The 'trained bands' (not of the music-making ilk) were formed in 1573, and every county was required to hold a general muster every three years, at which crown-appointed muster-masters would hold a general inspection. The pivotal task of the muster-masters was to pass on their knowledge of warfare to corporals, who did the same for the clusters of ordinary militiamen assigned to their instruction. These collective training sessions might be monthly, weekly or even daily, but the muster-master was required to call the 'trained bands' together at least twice a year to inspect weapons and assess training levels. When the Privy Council called for a general muster of the 'trained bands', the muster-master had his efforts inspected by the Deputy Lieutenants of the county, who were in turn answerable to the Privy Council.

Walsingham and Burghley had striven for a level of preparedness that by early December had the former advising Elizabeth with some pride as to numbers, and although the 'trained bands' drew some satirical comments from cynics highlighting bribery and corrupt patronage, serious training increased according to the level of threat. In May 1588 a London-based Spanish spy reported that the 'trained bands' of the city were drilling twice a week, and that considering they were recruits they were well-armed and very good troops. A kind eye here clearly, and one wonders how successful armed resistance would have been against veterans. The certificates of musters of the 'trained bands' held throughout England in April recorded a total of 156,000 men able to serve, and of these 85,000 were armed, and some 50,000 had had training.

The militia was clearly of national importance, but it should not be overlooked that the nobility and clergy escaped that comparatively lowly form of national service because they were still required by custom to recruit private clusters of fighting men. Even a lifelong Catholic like Viscount Montague raised 200 cavalry. The Earl of Essex put up 180 lances, 65 petronels[4] and 50 foot; and Walsingham 50 lances, 10 petronels and 200 foot, a personal total raised at great cost and only surpassed by Hatton and Essex. By Christmas 1587 Walsingham's servants saw him energised, and like Drake he wanted the war to be taken to the enemy rather than timidly wait. This notion was of course stifled by Elizabeth, who was unwilling to take such a high risk, especially while old Crofts jawed for peace and even argued that Drake should be forced to disgorge his Spanish plunder. Not much likelihood of that, to be sure, but lolling about in Plymouth did nothing for the health, wealth and morale of his crews. He did, however, send out some scout ships to the Spanish coast, and they returned with confirmation that 'we shall be stirred very shortly with heave and ho'. Burghley's absence from court in March 1588 left Walsingham and Leicester with a unity of purpose that had been fractured but was now mending, getting Elizabeth to shift purposefully. It seemed they had succeeded when on 15 March Drake got royal orders to reconfigure his squadron for a sharp offensive. Unfortunately, before he could put the supplies he needed in the holds the old timidity of the Queen had been revived by sibilant whispers from the peace brigade.

Drake may have been gnawing his knuckles with exasperation, but the sense that it was necessary to prepare was now fixed. At the end of March Walsingham was tasked to write to Lord Willoughby in the Low Countries, requiring him to request of the Dutch that they make ready the auxiliary ships they had promised in case of need. A little later Elizabeth was asking for sailors because of pressure on English recruitment. There was a demand gap because the fleet needed *c.* 16,000 men, and sourcing from inland counties was a poor option since it meant turning men utterly ignorant of sea life into sailors in an absurdly short time. In England a general embargo on shipping was put out, and the port towns were called upon to furnish men-of-war as supplements to the royal fleets. On 5 April Sir John Norreys was sent to the south coast to inspect the defences, and on 12 April the arms and armour of all recusant Catholics became subject to seizure, and were to be sold to benefit the loyal citizenry. Five days later and Lord Admiral Howard was directed to leave Queensborough with the fleet so as to join with Drake in Plymouth Sound. Out of Spain and into Walsingham's eager hand came intelligence that the Armada would leave Lisbon about the middle of May. And when did it leave? Between 18 and 20 May.

Buoyed up by his mission, strong in the belief that God was a Protestant, Walsingham became the administrative hub of the Kingdom, not only having to organise and supply the land forces, but also even consider broad questions of strategy. Every kind of question was referred to him, or the Privy Council through him; there was also Scotland to hem in, and the possibility of winning France to some kind of alliance could not be junked. He did this against a background of diplomatic dross, some treasonable, emanating from Stafford, who into 1588 went on repeating the line that the Armada had been disbanded. Not surprising then that Stafford's brother-in-law was bemused by these reports: he was, after all, the Lord Admiral Howard. Burghley may have leaned instinctively to the lies, because he was essentially a man of peace. But Walsingham knew the true state of affairs – Stafford, for a dwindling amount of money, was betraying his country. To counter this was a challenge, and every sinew of the Principal Secretary's ageing infirm body was given over to the struggle, so that he even ordered a new suit of armour from the Low Countries. It was there, of course, that the core of an improving second-rate fighting force might have been created to defend England. And with Philip absorbed by his vast investment in the Armada and its crucial linking with Parma, the Dutch could have struggled on without the English forces, although Elizabeth got a reminder from them that by treaty she was obliged to maintain 5,000 men for their support. As for Parma, a letter written in mid-April to Philip was clear and unambiguous:

> The enemy have been forewarned and acquainted with our plans, and have made all preparations for their defence; so that it is manifest that the enterprise, which at one time was so easy and safe, can only now be carried out with infinitely greater difficulty, and at a much larger expenditure of blood and trouble.

In the Spanish state papers (f. 278) is a document giving Parma's breakdown of one month's expenditure on the army in Flanders, and the total (which omits extras like the cost of messengers, spies and even gunpowder) was 454,311 crowns (equal to 370,000 gold crowns).[5]

On both sides of the Armada campaign there were men desperate for sustaining food and drink, and both sides found enormous difficulties in victualling. Like Hawkins, Lord Admiral Charles Howard recognised that healthy men were better able to fight effectively than the sick. His appeals for extra rations were, however, rarely successful, because the traditional supply chain was so creaky and wasteful. Even within her own palaces, vast quantities of food Elizabeth paid for were filched, lazily stored and rotted. The traditional supply routine was profitable to some, and so it was with the matter of provisioning the fleet. In fact, while Elizabeth and her government required fighting men, the daily experience marked them as mostly superfluous men who could be sacrificed rather than have every financial sinew disintegrate in any effort to feed them appropriately. For centuries ships in the Channel got only a month's victuals at a time – a system with some advantages: more room for powder and shot, fresher food and less waste. Still, Howard anticipated that his fleet would actually be short on rations, and there would never be any time to pick up more; as things developed his insight became a naggingly accurate assessment. If anything was worse it was the miserable situation of Medina Sidonia. After leaving Lisbon the great fleet took a sluggish thirteen days to sail 160 sea miles to Cape Finisterre, and in that time much of the food was spoiled and unfit for consumption. Even more dispiriting and potentially catastrophic was the shortage of potable water, when the quantities stored should have been enough for a voyage of two or three months. The reason was Drake's Cadiz triumph and his much less glamorous but vastly effective campaign against the coastal traders plying between Spain and the Armada's Lisbon base. Sunk or burnt by Drake were large quantities of barrel staves meant for food and water barrels. Loss of seasoned wood meant using green wood, which split and shrank, and their supply situation was so bad that it was decided to move into La Coruña harbour. Disaster struck when a storm scattered those that failed to get in quickly and drop anchor in the dark. It took weeks for the scattered, battered ships to return. Medina Sidonia martyred by sea-sickness, ached to give up now, but Philip ordered them to push on.

Chapter 23

THE LAST EFFORT

The prospect of the Armada and Parma jointly setting about the destruction of the last Tudor government gave hope in abundance to men like Cardinal Allen. He thrilled to see it as a passionate crusade for the true religion and galvanised by his fervent anticipation he wrote *Admonition to the Nobility and People of England* which was then squeezed into a printed broadsheet summarizing it, *A Declaration of a Sentence*, calling upon the Catholic nobility in England to turn on Elizabeth and tormentors like Walsingham. On 12 June a copy of *Admonition* was delivered to the latter, sent by Burghley, who read it as openly treasonable and ripe for suppression. At first the government handled this rather mildly, without any printed response, but then Walsingham grappled with it and decided that Catholics of ambiguous loyalty might need to be hauled into special areas of confinement, and the *Admonition* got rigorous attention in a belated effort to deny it circulation.

In mid-June Walsingham and some of the voices about him won a small but significant victory in preparation for what was to come. They persuaded Elizabeth to leave the strategy of the naval campaign to Howard and the war council he selected – that is, to the men of experience. Their relief must have been palpable, with the members of this ad hoc cluster all taking an oath of secrecy as the only ones consulted or given access to strategic planning. Of course, the first named of them was Francis Drake, and he was joined by other sailors and soldiers, as well as two young(ish) noblemen – Lord Thomas Howard, a cousin of the Lord Admiral, and Lord Edmund Sheffield, nephew of Howard and protégé of Leicester. The Lord Admiral had the towering responsibility for thwarting a terrible threat to the nation, and charged with such a burden he expressed his confidence with a weighty seriousness. A man with a strong streak of personal vanity, he was never stubbornly headstrong, and so was accepting of opinions given in good faith by experts.[1] While he was invoking God's assistance for a fair wind and fresh supplies delivered on it, Lord Henry Seymour was out with his little fleet of fifteen ships patrolling the Narrow Seas to hem in Parma. Eventually he came to the view that Parma had wearied of (even abandoned) the flat-bottomed boat-crossing from the Low Countries to England, switching his attention to attack Walcheren Island. The Estates-General agreed, and requested a preventative intervention by Seymour's ships. But Elizabeth daintily held off, and for once Walsingham's view chimed with hers. Writing to his cousin, Sir Edward Norreys, the commander of the English troops at Ostend, Walsingham showed an alert grasp of sea power (inculcated, no doubt, by those talks with John Dee years before), far beyond that of most landsmen. He was matched in this when the Armada was sighted and reported off the Lizard – the Lord Admiral quite correctly got his fleet out of Plymouth to manoeuvre it into a position to the rear of the enemy, despite the difficult winds prevailing.

Almost simultaneously land forces were mobilised in the south-east of England, and by bringing troops into the county of Essex Elizabeth undid the purse strings for spending. Walsingham was not complacent about debt (personal or national) and he wrote to Burghley about a money-markets conversation he had had with Horatio Pallavicino. The financier and speculator took the view that money could be fairly promptly raised on Merchant Adventurers' bonds, with very wealthy Flemings in Cologne, Hamburg and Frankfurt ready to loan great amounts. Such optimism when these alert, rich men would certainly have been aware of a widespread European opinion that the English Queen, a stiff-necked Tudor, was about to be trounced in war. Even in London a loan of £30,000 negotiated in March was paying 10 per cent interest. Burghley later calculated the estimated cost of keeping the fleet at sea for one month was £16,800 in wages (so rarely paid) and victuals (so disgusting). Just when he was sighing mournfully over the impossibility of meeting such charges and wishing that the enemy would engage now, he got his wish. The Spanish fleet of some 130 sail (about half of which were transport or victualling vessels, or pinnaces that took no part in the fighting) were off the Lizard, a sighting announced briefly by Howard in a note to Walsingham, and declared at court on 23 July. For the next ten days Walsingham and his colleagues met in council in one almost continuous session, with a torrent of administrative work for him and his assembled men. England, as Walsingham knew and said, was unfit for war at this time, but desperation and improvisation could achieve much when everything was in short supply.

The greatest hope of defeating Spanish might was in the turbulent waters of the Channel, the sometimes freakish wind, the sails, timbers, guns and powder, muscle and blood of English sailors. So the fleet correctly received most attention from the Privy Council as every letter from Howard pressed for more powder and shot. And after the frantic melée at Gravelines, when the Armada was scuttling northwards with Drake in pursuit, desperate to achieve its utter destruction, it was the powder-shot shortage that prevented this. If blame for this is to be allocated, the main culprits would have to be Elizabeth for her orders, and the Earl of Warwick, Master of the Ordnance, who followed them and lost the opportunity. Yet after Gravelines, when the huge importance of that success became clear to the Queen, she became testy about the lack of prizes other than the *Nuestra Señora del Rosario*, flagship of the Andalucian squadron and commanded by Don Pedro de Valdés, who surrendered to Drake. Now she sent an equerry to enquire among the English fleet the sum of the treasure taken, and she summoned Howard to Whitehall to order him to pay off the armed merchantmen. There are times when the historian longs to seize Elizabeth by her bejewelled throat preparatory to slapping her hard.

'The bullets fly at random where they list.' To the traumatised Spanish fleet quitting the English Channel in disarray, it must have seemed the worst was over, but in great measure they were wrong. To Elizabeth and the Privy Council the most pressing questions were: Where were they going? And would they soon return? In fact, Medina Sidonia was saved from complete disaster with a west-south-west wind that took the fleet into the North Sea. If the wind had changed favourably he was minded to fight his way back through the Straits of Dover to attempt to take an English harbour, holding it for Parma. But because the southwesterly held he was driven towards Scotland, the Orkneys and Shetlands, then the west of Ireland. As the Countess of Pembroke wrote, 'the very winds did on thy part blow', and on the Atlantic coasts of Scotland and Ireland as many as thirty-five ships went down. Many were salvaged or pillaged when the immediate opportunity occurred, and one, which attracted great attention over the centuries, was a converted merchant ship, the *San Juan de Sicilia*, which blew up in Tobermory bay, possibly at the hands of an agent working for Walsingham – John Smollett of Kirkton.

Howard and Drake had followed to see the Armada core pass the Firth of Forth some sixty miles out to sea. Then the victory was evident and they could turn back to the Downs, with Howard not unreasonably concerned that Elizabeth would be too hasty in relaxing the country's defences. Still sparking like a recently shut-down furnace, he was hot to do more and suggested a sudden attack against the Dunkirk privateers, but by 8 August he was with his ships back in Margate. Drake too had thought of a Dunkirk action to convince Parma that he really must abandon all thoughts of an invasion, which it seems Parma had done long before. It took the government a long time to realise just how powerless he was, a fact ascribable to Walsingham's failure to infiltrate a spy or buy a willing traitor. This led to the famous if pointless gathering at Tilbury, when men raised by the nobility, clergy, and the Queen's servants came together with the 'trained bands'. It had been thought that in total they would number about 50,000 men, but it seems unlikely that more than 10,000 ever reached this jamboree. No doubt in establishing 'Camp Royal' on the Essex bank of the Thames she acted on the advice of Leicester, who was staying not in his Wanstead mansion but in the camp. The whole thing was a source of huge confusion because of the numbers arriving – 870 horse at Brentwood on 27 July; 2,200 at Stratford on 29 July – and as ever a shortage of provisions, with the Lord Steward (Leicester) tasked to sort it all out. Pay records show 16,500 foot and 1,050 horse were gathered, with more men marching, scrambling and dawdling towards it.

Leicester was clearly optimistic that the cascade of problems would soon be sorted out, for he wrote to Elizabeth on 27 July suggesting she visit. Nearly two weeks later, on 8 August, she arrived by water barge, landing at Tilbury blockhouse at about midday. She stayed locally overnight, very likely at old Arden Hall, Horndon, which was demolished around 1730. At the time of the royal visit the house was owned by William Poley, who rented it to Thomas Rich (a kinsman of Lord Rich), who was paid to prepare the house. The following day Elizabeth inspected her assembled fighting men, accompanied by Leicester, his stepson Essex, six footmen, maids of honour, and her bodyguard. Then she went to stand at a favourable point for the march past, after which she delivered the famous speech with its crisp emphasis on her as the maiden queen of stout courage. The stomach of this particular Englishwoman was being placated with a cooked meal when the Earl of Cumberland arrived with despatches from the fleet telling of the engagement and subsequent north-west flight to Scotland and beyond.

To face the prospect of danger in the north, the Earl of Huntingdon had for months been mustering and training the county levies in northern England.

But there was general agreement in London with Walsingham that the best way to secure the north was to win over James VI – a task that as we have seen fell to William Asheby. His conversations with the King came as the Armada was within a few nautical miles, and on 5 August, with Asheby's generous clutch of remunerative promises to sweeten his mood, James declared his hostility to Spain. It was actually Walsingham who reproved Asheby for exceeding his ambassadorial remit, but James did get £3,000 as a *douceur*. It followed that he was annoyed with any of his subjects who might undermine his claim to succeed Elizabeth by meddling with the Spanish. So much so that he even sought English help (a huge cannon similar to 'Mons Meg' at Edinburgh Castle) to subdue Lochmaben Castle, where the Maxwells were holed up with some rescued Spanish troops. Unfortunately for them an English-manufactured bombard could smash castle walls, and the refuge was finally stormed. The Maxwells were a prize for James, and the Spanish who survived wreck and siege were taken in chains to England. Little spasms of apprehension went on, so that on 1 September the Privy Council in London wrote to Lord Willoughby in the Low Countries saying the remnant Armada was about to surge down from Scotland to the mouth of the Channel, and that he should urge the Dutch to keep their fleet at sea. By then, of course, Camp Royal was only a gusty memory, and its instigator Leicester, travelling slowly from the court, fetched up at Cornbury in Oxfordshire, where he died on 4 September, in his lodge as ranger of Wychwood forest.

When Elizabeth and the court should have been rejoicing at the defeat of the enemy, instead they were mourning variously the permanent absence of one of the great men; for Elizabeth this swipe from Fortune was deeply felt, and at Whitehall she withdrew to her apartment and locked the doors until Burghley, with other councillors to support his firm action, had them broken open. As she mourned one of the men who had figured longest and most prominently in her life and reign, she found some solace in heaping his debts onto his widow, so that Lettice Knollys Devereux Dudley had to auction the contents of her late husband's three great houses. A few months later the former countess took a little revenge by yet another marriage, this time to the darkly handsome and much younger Sir Christopher Blount. Years passed and in 1601 Elizabeth took her revenge by having him executed for his part in his stepson Essex's rebellion. Meanwhile, the news of the Armada defeat reached Rome, to be greeted with incredulity, while in the English college the students, it is reported, roared their acclaim and there was much hat-throwing.

When the ceremonies marking the defeat of the Armada were held, it is interesting to note the reluctance on all sides to lay claim to superior English nautical skill. Instead, the fact that the country had emerged as the vanquisher of the greatest empire in the world was attributed to the weather and luck (Fortune). The fact that England had benefited so immeasurably must mean that God had chosen deliberately the English side. To Elizabeth herself was attributed a song very likely sung as she made her way to old St Paul's, which developed the themes of benign meteorology, of England as the new Israel, and of its Queen as bride of Christ.[2] The relief crowned by joy was faltering, as we can see from the bitter frustration suffered by Sir John Hawkins, one of the true architects of victory. As Treasurer of the Navy it was his task to pay off the navy just at the moment when Elizabeth's parsimony began a general hurt. On 5 September he wrote to Walsingham saying he hoped God would soon deliver him 'for there is no other hell', a striking phrase suggesting he had already heard of Leicester's death and envied him.[3] Certainly Walsingham for the whole of this period was the advocate of caution when disbanding was the agenda topic, and he had Drake and the Lord Admiral on his side, while Burghley went along with the Queen and embraced passivity and retrenchment. While Howard and the sea captains about him got most of the nation's praise, the biographer of Walsingham can provide a little more balance, commending his continuous efforts to provide the government with accurate intelligence on all aspects of the Spanish fleet. Without his tenacity and complete devotion to defeating the enemy, as Drake and Lord Henry Seymour both testified with total conviction, things might have been intolerably other. And even Elizabeth, at length, came to see how much she owed personally to her great Secretary of State.[4] So much so that she did consider for implementation his project to intercept the Indies treasure fleet, a notion turned down by Drake and Howard immediately in favour of refitting the navy.

Early in September 1588 Howard's men-of-war, which had formed the nucleus of the main fleet, were laid up at Chatham, while Seymour's squadron was much reduced under Sir Henry Palmer.[5] Later that month, when off the west of Ireland someone spotted Spanish ships, it was proposed that a squadron under Sir Richard Grenville, with soldiers commanded by Ralegh, be sent to challenge them. But this effort was not realised when the timorous nature of the defeated was understood; Medina Sidonia shut up in his cabin, hopeless and inaccessible, leaving the management of details to others. By now most of the acute anxiety in England had been vented, but the English in Ireland were in a wild panic, uncertain of the strength and intentions of the Spaniards, surrounded by a subject people ready to join invaders if such they proved. The result was that English officers were much more interested in killing the intruders than recording the names of ships and the shipwrecked. The Viceroy later wrote that 1,000 fresh, armed Spaniards might have taken Ireland, since the country would have joined them and there was no English force to resist them. From the Armada of Biscay a cluster of fourteen ships, the *Gran Grin*, the second largest ship of the entire fleet at 1,160 Sp tons, and a ship's complement of 329, went down on Clare island. One hundred men struggled ashore only to be massacred, and among them was the brother of Don Pedro de Mendoza, which vexed the President of Connacht (Connaught), Sir Richard Bingham, since a possible ransom was lost. By the end of the month, writing to Walsingham about his province, Bingham estimated that 1,000 Spaniards had landed from wrecks, and all had been put to the sword. By the end of the year Fitzwilliam (the Viceroy) could write to Elizabeth that Ireland was free of Spaniards, save for a few naked stragglers, and as late as 1596 Philip II, who had visited this calamity on his own people, got a petition from eight mercenaries asking for aid to return to Spain.

Chapter 24

LAST ORDERS

Although Drake and Hawkins had beached Walsingham's proposal for the pursuit of the Spanish, they made a substitution hard on the heels of Sir John Norreys; the first official documents of 19 September assign the plan to him, with Drake's name added the next day.[1] Having conferred with Burghley, Walsingham, Williams, Ralph Lane and other important naval officers over a month, their plan that emerged had a three-fold objective: destroy surviving Armada ships at Lisbon and Cadiz; reinstate Dom Antonio; and use the Azores as a base for an attack on the treasure fleet returning from South America. Drake dreamed of an effort that with its combination of strikes would bring crashing down the wealth and residual power of Spain. It would, if successful, be the triumphant pinnacle of his career, even the culmination of his life's work. With Elizabeth putting up funds of £20,000, the Dutch £10,000, another £40,000 was required from private investors whose confidence was to be won by Drake, the man with gold in his hair colour and the real thing in iron-bound chests at his home. The combination of royal and private investment in such an effort made possible what the Queen could not alone seek to do. She would provide six ships of the second rank, while Drake and his investors would provide the crews. Some twenty or so further ships would be drawn from London and other towns. They were expected to carry 4,000 men for the land operations, with another 4,000 volunteers to be found by the efforts of Sir John Norreys, who would equip and pay them, aided by his father and the notorious captains denounced by Thomas Digges.

'Black John' Norreys, probably born in 1547, was one of the sons of Henry Norreys of Rycote and his wife Marjorie (née Williams), daughter of Sir John Williams of Thame, a strong supporter of Mary Tudor and Catholicism. Following Wyatt's Rebellion, Lord Williams (as he became) not only had his daughter and son-in-law staying at the Wytham (Berkshire) family home, but also he became one of those courtiers assigned to watch and control Princess Elizabeth. This brought the Norreys family close to her during the danger years and made for an intimacy that would dramatically affect the fortunes of John Norreys, called 'Black John' by his soldiers because he had inherited from his mother a head of glossy black hair. He seems to have got from her as well a hot temper and arrogant pride.[2] With the family home at Rycote it was convenient for the aspiring young man to go to Oxford's Magdalene College, but unlike two of his brothers he seems to have left without taking a degree. In the autumn of 1566 Sir Henry Norreys was appointed Elizabeth's resident ambassador in France, and when his son joined the family in the embassy the talk was of the young man learning to soldier. He began his military career with the Huguenots, and it is possible that his marked leaning to Calvinism was toughened by the incorporation of religious instruction into fighting discipline by François de la Noue.[3] Norreys (*père*) was ambassador until 1570, and when he was recalled his replacement was of course Francis Walsingham. Since John Norreys stayed on after his father returned to England, it seems possible that he did so at the behest of the new ambassador, who needed to saturate himself in French domestic affairs. Norreys like Walsingham spoke French and Italian, and he benefited for the next fifteen years from his patronage, directed to places such as Ireland and the Low Countries, where a Protestant soldier could show his skills.[4]

Norreys had reckoned to turn the campaign in the Netherlands into a family operation with his brothers (father and sons apparently all became involved in the international arms trade), but this drift was thwarted by Elizabeth. By December 1585, when Leicester arrived there with his forces, including Thomas Digges heading the engineers and surveyors, Norreys the seasoned campaigner was settling to become the enemy of both men. The soaring cost of financing the expeditionary force and those already there provided the financial background to the rift that opened up between Leicester and Norreys, the sort of subordinate who bridled at any correction and who became Leicester's designated failure scapegoat. Norreys and his corrupt captains may have been partially to blame for the parlous state of the English companies, but Leicester's fumblings (the disastrously ill-judged execution of the sometime governor of Grave, van Hemert) and his seething anger thereafter made matters worse. The English companies were severely reduced by starvation, desertion to the army of Flanders to try to avoid it, sickness and criminal violence, so that by June 1586 army discipline had evaporated, mocking the regulations Leicester had set out months before. After the calamitous engagement at Zutphen which wasted lives, including that of Philip Sidney, Leicester looked for relief to England by quitting, leaving the army to Norreys but seeking to make his position as exposed and difficult as possible. Somehow he managed to get the army through that winter, and even found time to write to Burghley and Walsingham for the advancement of captains displaced by Leicester. His care for individuals won him much respect. Yet when recalled to England himself he left his own companies unpaid, so that Lord Willoughby inherited a discontented rabble. Despite a revival of his career, aided by Burghley, Walsingham and Lord Admiral Howard, Norreys would never be allowed to return to this key theatre of war. This did not soothe his famous irascibility, but with the Portugal expedition he became a 'co-chairman of one of the greatest joint stock enterprises in English history up to that date'.[5]

By late September 1588 the plan had been fleshed out in its component parts, and on 11 October Norreys and Drake, both much beholden to Walsingham in their striking careers, got their royal commissions. They had now four months to make their preparations, and Norreys was assigned to securing the generous involvement of the Estates-General. Seeing that he was favoured by the Dutch, Elizabeth decided to repair strained relations with them by employing him as an ambassador extraordinary, and for a man of his choleric temperament he proved himself quite an adept. Even in his dealings with a suspicious Lord Willoughby he managed, though he warned Walsingham that cooperation on the Portugal expedition would be muffled, and thought a temporary recall of his lordship might help. Despite the rebuff he could return to England moderately well pleased, with at least promises of men, ships and gunpowder, and his brother Edward still there to smooth sharp edges and bring matters to a successful conclusion. This positive frame of mind was matched by Drake's successful fund-raising, his purchase of provisions for several months and the preparation of the royal ships. But as ever there was a cloud on the horizon.

It took the form of a deep Spanish reluctance to do as expected. Walsingham, through his spies on their ground, discovered that the Armada remnant had not reached Lisbon or Cadiz; a great many had put into Santander and San Sebastian, the northern Spanish ports. This put them in an area that English seamen regarded with particular unease, and if they did venture there it made a voyage to Lisbon difficult. Moreover, these ports had little plunder to entice the military entrepreneurs and were hopelessly positioned for any attempt on the treasure fleet. Norreys, with an army of some 12,000, would have too many men with little to do. This wretched turn of events led to the despatch of an investigative pinnace in early 1589, sent to try to find counter-evidence, but the scanners on board could not alter the facts. So it was necessary for the commanders to disengage the Queen's key element in the plan – the destruction of ships – from the expedition to Portugal. Their huge investment hung in the balance, and Burghley certainly noticed that Norreys and Drake were gradually sliding the cost burden down their decks to Elizabeth, who very probably could not afford an operation aimed only at Santander. Burghley was himself so uneasy that when he cautioned Walsingham to be very reticent on the matter, he penned the note himself, unwilling to let anyone in his handpicked secretariat know the truth.

By early February, as the Dutch and Willoughby made difficulties, Burghley was anxiously reviewing the whole matter in his head, and Elizabeth wanted to rejig the operation so that the commanders went without the ship-borne troops, because an attack on Santander made them superfluous, and for the Portuguese element they could be sent later. Norreys and Drake both squirmed at this, knowing that a rendezvous on the high seas was always difficult, and Drake anticipated losses at Santander that would make the forcing of Lisbon more dangerous. It is hard not to agree with the bitter comment made by Elizabeth that her sailors went more for profit than service. On alert that Portugal had seized their imaginations she repeatedly had them promise to go first to Santander. Only a national rising in favour of the heavy-drinking Dom Antonio would signal an intervention, and it was a sign of her disfavour that she refused him a galleon for his flagship and would not countenance the putting together of a siege train. This squeeze on the planning very likely increased his need for consoling wine, because the original proposal had offered him so much, and although he had no investment money he was lavish with promises, even agreeing that once safely home he would put up the cost of the whole thing. Drake might have paused to consider how likely this was. No wonder Elizabeth stalled on the passage of the final instructions under the great seal.

19 March 1589: with a requisition of sixty Dutch flyboats that arrived just in time in newly repaired Dover to be used as transports, the commanders moved their forces to Plymouth, leaving behind a chagrined Lord Admiral Howard. Once there the fleet was hemmed in by contrary winds and the

influx of men lured more, so that the local supplies of food disappeared, and
instead of adding to their sea stores they had no option but to breach them.
By 1 April (see how the timescale had stretched) one-third of the sea stores
had been gobbled up by an army Norreys thought swollen by 12,000
volunteers to 19,000 men. All this reeked of a future disaster, since nearly
£100,000 had been spent; some £25,000 more than the estimate of the total
cost. So nothing about organization had been learnt from the now minor-
seeming difficulties of the harbour repairs at Dover. Invoking a payment
clause in the original agreement with Elizabeth did not prod her into paying
any extra immediately, and driven frantic by the weather Norreys wrote to
Burghley that controlling the army was becoming an impossible task. Years
later it was the ebullient young Earl of Essex who claimed that Devereux
influence and arm-twisting secured the sizeable *tranche* of funds sent by
Burghley in mid-April, just as Drake and Norreys seized the day when the
winds veered at last to favourable. Yet even now their destination was
uncertain, for although the Queen's representative, Anthony Ashley, pushed
for attacks on Santander and San Sebastian, he was resisted in the planning
of Drake and his sailors. These ports were least favoured, and once at sea who
would have the controlling power?

This critically important unresolved problem came with supplementaries.
The outstanding figure among the volunteer soldiers distributed over the fleet
was Essex himself, a heavy investor who had used his own money to
advantage those who followed him. Yet he was only there having flouted
Elizabeth's command that another ornament of her court should not risk his
life by participating. He was fixated by war and notions of honour, desperate
to wield the sword inherited from Sir Philip Sidney, whose widow Frances he
was now wooing. He got himself on the Queen's galleon *Swiftsure* early in
April, joining Sir Roger Williams, colonel-general of the infantry, in Falmouth.
When his absence from court was noticed Elizabeth sent his grandfather, Sir
Francis Knollys (who had served under Drake in 1585) to scour Plymouth,
and then Huntingdon was told to secure the return of the young gallant. It
was too late to throttle his initiative, and Elizabeth raged not only at his
presumption, but also at Norreys and Drake as culpable in the matter. Her
fuzzy focus was wrong, because Norreys had nothing to gain from Essex's
wilful escapade, and possibly might lose much as fighting ambition seized the
Earl. Moreover, Williams had a personal history of strife with Norreys, and he
certainly favoured sailing directly to Lisbon, as was proven when the *Swiftsure*

headed in that direction. In the event, the command to court for Essex took two months to deliver, by which time he was risking his life in any exchange, large or small. Williams was supposed to be arrested immediately, and might have been executed. So to prevent this Walsingham calmly intervened and did what he could to soothe the extravagant royal tantrum. As usual he took a pen and produced a finely balanced letter to the clerk of the Signet, Thomas Windebank, acknowledging the Queen's urgency of feelings, while seeking to counterbalance this with the esteem of Drake (and supposedly Norreys) for Sir Roger, 'that the proceeding against him may breed a mutiny and division in the army, with the overthrow of the whole action to her Majesty's infinite dishonour'. It seems very likely that Walsingham wrote to the commanders to resolve the matter sagaciously – send Essex back to England with his ardour for fighting partly assuaged, and spare Williams. And so they did.

The absolute specificity of Elizabeth's instructions to the commanders could not be clearer – attack Santander and San Sebastian above all else. Instead Drake imposed his own slippery logic on their destination and chose La Coruña, hoping to pick up auxiliary supplies of food and any stragglers from the fleet. Towards the end of April the town was taken by the thousands landed by Norreys, but the castle above the town held out, and although it was a pointless operation he decided to besiege it. The reason seems to have been the corrupting of discipline occasioned by the soldiers not only finding food in large quantities, but also wine, which made them belligerent, dangerous and finally ill. The failure over days to take the castle should have sobered them, but the bungling attempt to mine the walls seems to have given the Spanish heart, and to the east a Spanish commander had put together a force larger than that of Norreys. He marched out to engage them, and wielding a pike saved his brother Edward when he took a head wound. It was a victory of hyperbole over fact that Norreys later reported: 1,500 Spanish killed; two English soldiers dead; four captains wounded. And the castle was still not taken.

This sideshow gained the English nothing; the Spanish now knew of the troubles ahead and the Governor of Portugal for Philip II, Cardinal Archduke Albert, was able to make preparations to repulse the enemy. Supporters of Dom Antonio were rounded up, the undecided expelled from the country, and an army began to take shape. When the English put to sea again on 10 May they should have sailed on the benign southwesterly wind to Santander. Instead they went westward, keen to meet supply ships and anxious to avoid sailing east into the Bay of Biscay, with its destructive reputation. It was a total violation of their sworn duty, indicating how mesmerised they were by the Portugal component of the expedition. What made it particularly shameless was their knowledge that within a month Santander would echo with the sound of ship repairs. However, when they met up with *Swiftsure* off Finisterre, Essex and Williams joined the council of war held on 15 May instead of being summarily punished; yet despite their recent experience at the mouth of the Tagus, the plan put forward by Williams for going up the river and past the St Julian's fort with the fleet for a combined assault was rejected. Drake and Norreys instead favoured landing the troops at Peniche, followed by a march of over 40 miles through the Torres Vedras hills. Perhaps they thought such exercise would correct some of the wine-induced feebleness, and would allow Dom Antonio to bestir his people. Certainly it would keep the fleet away from danger, which chimed with Elizabeth's protective warmth towards it – it was not to be risked in any dangerous enterprise. Of course the same was true of Essex, but he led the landing at Peniche, jumping into water that nearly swept him under in his armour, and recovering speedily to kill the first Spaniard. A force of 6,000 was landed in four hours, and despite some losses to the surf when Dom Antonio came ashore the Peniche garrison deserted, so he received the surrender of the castle the next day.

This allowed the march on Lisbon to begin, and a dismal toil it proved in weather far warmer than Englishmen were used to at this time of the year. Numbers were already down because, since La Coruña, another four ships had deserted to sail to La Rochelle with 400 men who latterly joined the Huguenot armies. Sickness reduced the number who went south under Norreys, and he had even to leave a company to guard the makeshift hospital at Peniche. Those who fell ill on the march were mostly left behind to be slaughtered by Spanish cavalry, and although Essex gave up his coach for some, the losses were mounting, and some estimated that by the time he reached Lisbon his fighting force was down to a meagre 4,000. Archduke Albert cannily avoided a pitched battle and had 5,000 Spanish infantry, the same number of Portuguese conscripts (who clearly regarded Dom Antonio as a wastrel), and even some cavalry. When Norreys got to Lisbon on the evening of 23 May his predicament became clear. Too few men, no heavy artillery, diminishing food supplies and a truly hopeless ally. Norreys made a brief pause to allow for the arrival of Drake; his army did what looting they could, and very soon Norreys in council decided to march on to Cascais, hoping to meet up with Drake. Despite some light opposition the road to Cascais was satisfactory, and the distance of 16 miles to join up with Drake was covered in a day.

Drake wrapped his failure to appear at Lisbon in excuses; sickness among his sailors, the wrong wind, the St Julian's fort too strong and the Tagus too frequented by Spanish galleys. In fact his attention to the main task had faltered on finding grain and naval stores on some sixty Hanseatic vessels and a cluster of French merchant vessels. When these were taken as prizes, it meant Philip II lost precious material for his traumatised fleet, but the intention had been to take Lisbon, and set against that failure the substitute prizes shrivelled. They returned upriver and looked hard at the fort of St Julian's, now heftily reinforced, and despite the issue by Essex of a challenge to personal combat the defenders saw off the invaders. Even at this late stage Norreys and Drake might have partially deemed themselves in Elizabeth's consideration, because on 20 May she had written again demanding the delayed attack on Santander. Unfortunately she allowed the possibility of sailing to the Azores after setting down Dom Antonio, and they fell on this to justify their own inclinations. Despite a smart rearguard effort put on by Archduke Albert, the fleet eventually got out of the Tagus with the welcome supply ships led by Captain Robert Crosse. But once again they were thwarted by Aeolus – southerly winds pushed them up the coast of Portugal, away from the Azores. By 19 June they were at Vigo, landing to find the townspeople fled with any item of value – except the wine barrels, which once again provoked an orgy of debilitating drunkenness. Then the long-suppressed pyromaniac instincts of Drake took over and the town was set ablaze.

The dual command of Drake and Norreys had been strained for some time, and while Drake's optimism about the Azores and the treasure fleet briefly flared again, Norreys led home the halt and the lame in ships and men. It was a sorry cluster that returned, some of the ships being reduced to a handful of able-bodied men to do the work of a full complement. By 2 July he reached Plymouth with twenty-five ships and found that the storm, which had lashed them outside Vigo, had presently driven back Drake to England. Waiting for them with some trepidation about his return to court was Essex, and he only departed for it on 4 July, when he had Anthony Ashley and Edward Norreys to answer interrogatives as well. These two were the representatives of the generals and had a letter for Walsingham that allowed that the mission had not been a total success. The intention was almost certain: Walsingham, with his exceptional diplomatic skills and mastery of 'spin', should prepare the Queen for the story of failure that would eventually emerge. There was a calm period before the inevitable, during which Elizabeth doled out praise, believing then that her fleet was unmaimed and able to take on another attempt on Santander. This notion was, of course, cruelly misplaced, and knowing it to be so Drake made no triumphant return to court. This signalled the truth to the Lord Admiral, who made no effort to hide his glee, and within a month, as the Privy Council set Ashley to head the prize commission, an exasperated Norreys told his brother Edward to reveal the ramshackle state of the returned ships. After that Santander as a target was deemed hopeless, and within months came a report that some sixty ships from there had reached Lisbon.

Thousands of apparently superfluous men had died. Nor were those with the strength, courage and luck to return home particularly well placed, and the discharged soldiers were about to become an aggressive, localised burden. Their generals had sourly neglected to provide clear answers about the state of the returned, and this drew a rebuke from the Privy Council. Their dereliction was sure to be costly, and the order came that they should focus on aiding the sick and getting the fleet refurbished. In late July Drake and Norreys were both summoned to London; the former proved much the more reluctant, no doubt feeling queasy that their financial accounts were going to be scrutinised by a special commission that included Sir John Hawkins and William Borough. By then London had seen a demonstration of people power in a hubbub at the Royal Exchange, a very well chosen public and merchant space guaranteed to get the attention of London's senior figures and the government. It may be that many who took part to claim their wages were indeed veterans, but they were infiltrated by 'lewd fellows', the thieves and professional beggars who saw an opportunity. By early August 1589 London was swamped by indigent hordes all claiming veteran status, and the hard-pressed Lord Mayor was ordered to give them a paper pass to go back to their former homes (more likely hovels). This diversion failed, and on 22 August a noisy mob in Westminster even took on the Queen, who responded by ordering the former Muster-Master, Ralph Lane, to look into their individual complaints. He and his assistants under the general direction of Norreys probably prevented an insurrection in London, and yet a clutch of hangings did not see off the problem, for the whole of the south-east and armed gangs on the roads remained to be dealt with.

The arrogance and cupidity of Norreys and Drake did not go unpunished, although we may think that they got off very lightly. No wonder that, on a list of senior men who might move to the war in the Low Countries, beside the name of Norreys, Walsingham wrote 'not in grace here', an opprobrium earned by the utterly botched Portugal expedition. By their actions the generals had even created an extra problem for Walsingham to try to sort out. It will be remembered that the Dutch had allowed sixty flyboats to go with the fleet, and on their return their captains had rejected grain instead of cash, which the Estates-General sought. This argument went on for months and each time the issue was broached the reputation of Norreys took a knock. As allies the English and Dutch presented an early political version of that famous childhood playground line: 'She's my best friend; I hate her.' There were many in England who felt, like Sir Thomas Wilkes, the English agent in the United Provinces, that the Dutch were 'as headstrong as so many bulls', provokingly ungrateful for all the men and money Elizabeth had allowed them, neglectful of regard and seriously wanting in judgement. This at a time after the Armada, when Parma's strategy was little changed: sit like a boa constrictor on the Dutch and endeavour to squeeze them to death. Early in September 1588 Bergen op Zoom in north Brabant (the town had joined the Union of Utrecht in 1579) became the targeted victim, and since the Dutch were themselves reluctant to respond when Willoughby pointed out that it would soon fall, Elizabeth acted with an almost unprecedented alacrity. As we have noted, Norreys went with 1,500 men on a combined military and diplomatic mission, and he arrived in time to see one of Parma's last assaults driven off. Campaigning for that year ended, and the next attack on Bergen by the Spanish army was delayed until 1597. Willoughby regarded Norreys with frank suspicion, and when the latter sought recruits for the Portugal expedition – men like Sir Thomas Baskerville, who later accompanied Drake on his last voyage to the Spanish Main – he was refused under pressure from Willoughby.

So now was the time of rivers freezing, trees swagged with frost, fingers and toes chilled. By the time Thomas Bodley went to the Netherlands in November 1588 with instructions to secure the support of John van Barneveldt, deputy of Holland to the Estates-General, Walsingham was mentally tired, and above all out of patience with the Dutch. The weather chimed with the chill on Anglo-Dutch relations, and Bodley the diplomat failed in his mission, reporting van Barneveldt as rude and inflexible, taking a real pleasure in thwarting English measures, however sensible.

Since the mild handling of shared concerns through diplomacy was without effect, Walsingham gave notice in March 1589, in a remonstrance to the Estates-General, that their general attitude to Elizabeth was seriously eroding their own cause. It would likely have been more potent if almost simultaneously Gertruidenberg, commanded by Sir John Wingfield (whose family were partisans of Norreys, but Sir John, the brother-in-law of Willoughby) had not been betrayed by others to the Spanish. The Dutch seem to have brought this on themselves by neglecting to pay the garrison. Yet they rashly and impertinently put out a public notice blaming Wingfield, Sir Francis Vere and even the honour and good name of Willoughby. Walsingham's reaction to this provocation was a canny one, and put to Bodley in a letter on 17 April 1589. If the Dutch placard was to be answered then Willoughby rather than the Queen should do it, but no response was better, since 'after the loss of the town thereby to hazard the loss also of her Majesty's favour, I know not what to think of them, but must conclude that . . . they have also lost their wits'.[6] No wonder Willoughby had sought and got a recall to England, and that English forces were now assigned to the leadership of a brilliant soldier, Sir Francis Vere, who was Sergeant-Major General and therefore not so elevated that he had to juggle diplomacy with fighting. It was Walsingham who was largely instrumental in getting this highly satisfactory employment of a man held in great esteem by the Dutch, and by the cadre of English officers he drew about himself. As for Vere, he certainly regarded even the perceptibly weary Walsingham as one of his best friends at court, and this appointment did much to shore up Anglo-Dutch relations after a contentious year. Vere managed to deal convivially with Prince Maurice of Nassau, so collaboration revived, and one further significant appointment was made: Robert Sidney was made Governor of Flushing – his instructions written by Walsingham.[7]

For those taken with the notion of symmetry it will seem appropriate that Walsingham's last months should have been so taken up with France, a country once again on the brink of confessional strife. It was the case that they had long wanted a full-on commitment to underpin the efforts of the protestant Henri of Navarre, a policy direction that because of its cost Elizabeth resisted. Instead she tried to support Henri III against the Guise and the League power base, who raged against her for the execution of Mary, Queen of Scots. But this was an interiorised response, and they did nothing to encourage James VI to believe that they would give him military aid if he took on Elizabeth. They had benefited from anti-Protestant anger in France, and Henri III had been pressed to denounce Anglo-French treaties. The buffeted French king, angry at Mary's execution, suffered further distress when his military push against Henri of Navarre failed in the summer of 1587, and his favourite and general, the Duke de Joyeuse, was killed – a very brief advantage to the Huguenots, who were routed a week later by Guise at Anneau, in a defeat that mangled any possible German assistance and left Henri III exposed even further, when he had prayed for the annihilation of the League. The pressure, renewed in 1588, came from the articles drawn up at Nancy, which demanded he accept counsel from the Guise and publish the decrees of the Council of Trent. Banned from Paris in April Guise defied his king and with an escort entered the city. The tumult of acclaim incensed Henri III, who responded with force to counter the manifestations. The resulting popular revolt led by the Guise and the *Seize*, the most militant urban faction, became known as the Day of the Barricades (12 May). Through Mendoza the Spanish did everything they could to give aid to their religious allies, and the unfortunate Henri III was forced to flee his capital the next day, never to return. His position was so much weaker, negotiation was inevitable, and the outcome of this was the July signing of the Edict of Union, in which the monarch gave in to the demands of the League on almost every matter of substance, and shortly after made Cardinal Charles de Bourbon his heir.

Some lightening of his weight of misery came with the defeat of the Spanish Armada – a flicker of strength revived. In October 1588 the convocation of the Estates General at Blois was still League-led, but Henri managed to find tender spots, rousing himself and his cohorts to action. On 23 December 1588 Guise and the Cardinal de Guise were assassinated. The reaction of the city of Paris was horrified shock and rage, because now the route to an alliance with Henri of Navarre was open. There were demonstrations before the Hôtel de Guise and leadership of the faction shifted to another brother, Charles de Lorraine, Duke of Mayenne. The University of Paris from within the Sorbonne, its theological faculty, declared Henri III a tyrant and to defend the Catholic religion called for an uprising against him – a decree endorsed by the Parliament, then under Leaguer sway. In March 1589 Henri of Navarre had published a manifesto for peace and national unity; yet in the same month the general council of the League made Mayenne the Lieutenant General of the Kingdom, and that same day he received the acclaim of the Rouen general assembly. With this haemorrhage of support to the enemy the two Henris were brought together at Plessis-les-Tours, and their key target after this had to be Paris. The preliminaries of the siege were underway when a fanatical monk got close enough to Henri III to assassinate him. On his deathbed the King named Navarre as his successor, and then, St Denis being held by the League, his body was escorted for temporary burial at Compiègne. To oppose Henri IV were enemies within, and also Spain. Early in September the Spanish Council of State declared its full military support for the League, and the ailing Parma was ordered to blanket the French frontier with all available troops. More than ever Henri IV needed English aid, and he got it: in the period 1589–95 some 20,000 troops went to France (8,000 to the Netherlands) while financial aid to him totalled £300,000 (if not more). The Dutch got £750,000 – all vastly more expensive than the naval operations, which were sideshows.[8]

Within two weeks of the political murder of Guise, Catherine de Medici was dead. In England the news of her natural demise was greeted with frank pleasure. Weighty in the political life of France, the English viewed them as tainted with innocent blood. Sir Edward Stafford in his last days as ambassador received a letter from Walsingham saying how Elizabeth's spirits had soared, and that Navarre (as he had been) would soon find an envoy from her at his court. By the time Christopher Marlowe wrote *The Massacre at Paris* (*c.* 1592) the reputation of Henri IV as a resistance leader was actually sliding into disrepute in England. Sensitive Elizabethans reviewing what had happened over decades in France were made fearful, struck as they were by the viciousness of mankind's nature; in the theatre such a thread of thought took fierce hold over the next two decades. While Henri had to be supported, he appears in Marlowe's play as he was in life – ambitious and self-interested.[9] The play avoids making him a hero, as if prophetically anticipating the pardon accorded him by the Pope in September 1595. With the deaths of Guise and Catherine, the anti-Huguenot war effort had taken palpable hits, and Walsingham felt the effect within his own deep reflections on diplomacy. At this time he looked to France for a close alliance against the powerful enemy Spain, and he even gave thought to inviting the Republic of Venice and other Italian courts into the Anglo-French détente.[10] Henri IV would continue to pelt Elizabeth with requests for aid since his succession was disputed by half of France, and Philip II was not without hope of placing his daughter by Elizabeth of Valois – the Infanta Isabella – on the French throne.[11] The newly appointed French envoy to England was Beauvoir la

Nocle, who solicited the cooperation of Walsingham and Burghley when putting forward his appeal to Elizabeth. Men, money and supplies he got in a startlingly short time. There was a royal loan of £20,000, and powder, munitions and soldiers were hurried across the Channel despite a sudden royal squall of nerves. It fell to Walsingham to do the detailed preparation for transport, victualling and paying for the 4,000 men sent under Willoughby, and Henri's victories at Arques (1589) and Ivry (March 1590) stemmed directly from English aid. He defeated a numerically superior enemy and on 20 October 1589 penned a fulsome letter to the exhausted Walsingham to acknowledge that the Secretary of State had been the pivotal figure in getting the resources out of Elizabeth: 'if my friendship can ever be fruitful to you, you will discover what a goodly share of it you have and will never regret what you have done to win it'.

In the last months of Walsingham's life there were two unrelated marriages for him to regard with deep satisfaction. The first was that of Anne of Denmark to James VI of Scotland, which was a union that might secure a Protestant successor to the ageing Elizabeth; the second that of his daughter Frances to the Earl of Essex, a remarkable leap up the social scale that shocked Elizabeth, but would not have troubled Walsingham, who in an essay penned around this time was startlingly dismissive of titles: 'As for titles, which at first were the marks of power and the rewards of virtue, they are now according to their name but like the titles of books, which for the most part the more glorious things they promise, let a man narrowly peruse them over, the less substance he shall find in them.' It was not an attitude that would have found favour with his new son-in-law, the moody, charismatic Earl longing to be in the battles that brought Henri IV closer to unifying France by defeating the League.

Chapter 25

DIGNITY, DUTY, DELIVERANCE

In his last days it is not unlikely that a weary Walsingham reviewed in his still formidable memory some of the compelling events in which he had had a direct involvement. Having been prepared by his political mentor William Cecil, Lord Burghley, for the post of Principal Secretary of State, he had shown a remarkable diligence, tenacity and resilience. His successes were delayed, often by Elizabeth tugging in the opposite direction, and his reputation as her most formidable minister has been somewhat overshadowed by his notoriety through centuries as a spymaster of legendary acumen. 'Political uncertainty over religion assisted the Romanists greatly', but by the 1590s Walsingham, Burghley, Leicester and their associates, good and bad, had seen off Catholic resistance. They were all dead by the time of that mad aberration in 1605 – the Gunpowder Plot.[1] The triumvirate had literally fought the papacy and its allies to a standstill, and they had done this under a Queen who was keen in public to suggest her piety – 'so good, godly and virtuous' – and yet had remained in private so opaque in her beliefs that the sense of her faking it lingers to tease the historian. Did she really believe she was 'God's handmaid'? In a long reign Elizabeth was only very rarely resisted by her Protestant subjects, even though by 1600 a good many thought her passing too long delayed. She had become a crabby bore, and by dying in 1590 Walsingham avoided the long, tasteless decline. He and like-minded men were never completely emasculated by her; there was struggle and resistance on both sides, and certainly points where his heroic patience was terribly eroded. Given the widely held conviction then that the monarchy was a 'ministry exercised under God and on his behalf', it is not surprising that in Walsingham's vast correspondence there are numberless sighs about Elizabeth's peevish and pinched inability to act decisively for the national good – there are numerous versions in his letters of the hope that God will open her eyes. In the event, the deity whose intervention Walsingham so craved allowed an improvement in Elizabeth's tunnel vision, and after the Babington Plot Walsingham was the impresario of Protestant England's advantage and triumph.

Walsingham died at around 1.00 a.m. on 6 April; remarkably he was 60, a martyr to ill-health, and yet by the reckoning of the day an old man. Without a son to settle his affairs and act as guardian of his archive and inheritance, it fell to Dame Ursula to bury her late husband in old St Paul's, not a great distance from their town house. There was no disagreement among Protestants that the 'fate of the soul was sealed at death'. Nothing done by the living could have any post-mortem effect, and the notion of ghosts was officially punctured. For all his strenuous engagement in public matters great and small – like being responsible for the freedom on bail in London of Sir John Southworth to live under the care of his son Thomas Southworth, who was a neighbour and friend of the Walsinghams – he had been a private man, quietly authoritative in his work and aloof from the frivolities of the court. His home was the safest refuge, and clearly as a house of state secrets it offered rich pickings for the seekers after maps, position papers, diplomatic correspondence and cipher letters of spies. The finding of such papers at Hatfield suggests that a primary pillager was Robert Cecil, an admiring opportunist who looked to learn much from the man he was being groomed to succeed at some future opportunity. Whoever undertook the raid on the house, it was done with extraordinary alacrity, perhaps even as the late minister's family and friends went to the night service and burial a day later. The dark man of the Elizabethan court (the Queen called him the 'Moor', and he had once himself referred to his 'Ethiop' appearance) who dressed in black – 'the hue of dungeons' – refused for himself the elaborate funeral to which he was entitled. His given reason in the will, probably dictated less than a year before, was that he had too many debts (not an inhibitor for the aristocracy), and feared 'the mean state I shall leave my wife and heirs in'.

The torchlight burial had been traditional in ancient Rome, but in England it was still exceptionally rare. There are a number of reasons why Walsingham chose this mode, apart from its antique associations. Cost was certainly one of them, and the night burial cut expenses by the very reduced amount of hired black cloth necessary to deck the church – in the case of old St Paul's this would have been huge.[2] Moreover, those who attended the funeral provided their own mourning garb, instead of the estate of the deceased paying for them. Another reason may have been family love, since by avoiding an heraldic funeral, which prevented any husband or wife from acting as mourner, Ursula Walsingham was not excluded as she grieved. Also a night burial meant the corpse was not handed over to embalmers for their peculiarly grisly ritual. Having dispensed with this aspect of the conventional funeral, did Walsingham also silence the sermon because generally this oration was in a critical condition? In the second half of the sixteenth century it became a topic that generated controversy, and the key question was whether in the Reformed church there could even be a sermon.[3] One formidable academic and preacher, Thomas Cartwright,[4] the Professor of Divinity at Cambridge until expelled by the university elders led by Whitgift, inveighed against what he regarded as a pre-Christian element to accompany the burial of the dead. Scripture made no reference to the sermon and, as Cartwright pointed out, the English Church at Geneva had junked it. In his brisk view it was tainted with Catholicism, and there were none in England 'more desirous of funeral sermons than the papists'. Among the church establishment Cartwright's fulminations were regarded as loopy, and according to his well-placed old enemy Whitgift there was a vast difference between a funeral sermon and superstitious ceremonies. Also, the argument was made then that sermons were not for the dead, but the living.

Praise for the manner in which the dead person had conducted their social negotiations was often abbreviated to a point that today we would find perfunctory and uncomfortable. At the funeral in 1586 of Sir Henry Sidney, the sermon offered the greatest praise of the deceased for his constant faith. The insinuation of Puritan bias into the funeral sermon came late in Elizabeth's reign, when 'English Puritans began to sense that they belonged to a tradition with its own saints and patriarchs'. Before Walsingham found his place in this hierarchy there had been his patron and contemporary Francis Russell, 2nd Earl of Bedford, a key supporter of Puritanism, whose funeral sermon in 1585 was delivered by Thomas Sparke and began with a long declaration of the saving power of faith, before declaring how this had been nobly exemplified by the late Earl. So perhaps the obsequies for Walsingham allowed a sermon. If not, the reason may have been that the prayerful listeners increasingly got to listen to something used 'to recall the godly equality of women'.[5]

The real duty of a testator in the making of a will was to transfer worldly goods in a godly fashion. 'The man who neglected to settle his estate had failed in his responsibility to God.'[6] Wills prepared for Walsinghams and their wives tended to be terse, and in the latter cases almost exclusively secular in content; that of his first wife, Anne, was a masterpiece of concision, simply listing the division of money and chattels; godly content: nil. Perhaps the key element was the positioning of Walsingham *vis-à-vis* his stepson, Christopher, who under the careful nurturing of his step-parents became an adventurous, humane, but not materially very successful individual, who late in life pawned all his plate for £400, but died before he could redeem it. In contrast to his first wife's will (which he may have drafted for her), Francis Walsingham's own will, dated 12 December 1589, put God first, in advance of 'our most gracious sovereign Lady Elizabeth' 'and offered thanks that his memory was unimpaired'. His first bequest was of his soul to the Holy Trinity, and because of his anticipation of a joyful resurrection it meant little that his funeral was speedily prepared for the day after his death. Three days before he died he sold property at Oxford and Chilton (Wiltshire), perhaps to cover the expenses. There were debts and legacies to be covered, an annuity for Frances, and the remainder passed to Dame Ursula. When she died in June 1602 the family plate and jewels went to Frances, now the widow of Sir Philip Sidney and the Earl of Essex (executed in 1601). This second Protestant hero of the people was widely mourned, and it was this esteem for him that led to criticism of her when she was finally persuaded to marry again in March 1603. Just who did the persuading? Her third and last husband was Richard Burke, Earl of Clanrickarde (born *c.* 1572), formerly impoverished, while an enthusiastic supporter of the English rule of Ireland, but now making his fortune through his evidently wealthy new wife. When Leicester had died the Queen had rewarded Walsingham with the Somerhill estate, an eminent seat in the parish of Tunbridge. When this passed to the Earl and his Countess he built a house there resembling Charlton House at Greenwich, and on his Irish lands he built Portumna Castle – two large building projects that suggest that Walsingham's efforts to pass wealth to his only surviving child had paid off handsomely for the Irishman, knighted in December 1601 after Lord Mountjoy's triumph at the battle of Kinsale, and said to look so very like the late second husband. Walsingham's granddaughter, Elizabeth Sidney (godchild of the Queen), married Roger Manners, 5th Earl of Rutland in 1599, and brought £4,000 to the union (*c.* £2,000,000 today), so the widely proclaimed poverty of the late Principal Secretary looks like a well-maintained barrier to the true state of his affairs. Elizabeth Sidney was the stepdaughter of Essex, but by 1599 his finances were genuinely in ruins and such a sizeable dowry quite beyond him. The countess of Rutland, a poet in her own right, died childless, and so did her stepbrother born in 1591, who would have been the first grandson of Walsingham to live. Robert Devereux, son of a philandering father who caused Frances Walsingham some misery, seems to have been impotent with two wives. His title of 3rd Earl of Essex was restored to him by King James, and he repaid the Stuarts by becoming a commander of the Parliamentary forces. So Sir Francis Walsingham who, with stoic rectitude, had underpinned the throne of the last Tudor, helped genetically to drive from that same throne the haughty, dwarfish Stuart monarch to whom death had accidentally and regrettably assigned it.

THE ICE-BREAKERS

In May 1553 a flotilla of three small ships sailed from English waters moving north-east to seek an unknown direct route to Cathay (China), and perhaps India. Two of the little vessels were destroyed in the coastal ice of Lapland, and the third, piloted by Richard Chancellor, ran aground in the estuary of the Dvina in August. Soon after this curtailment of the original plan, news of the surprise landing was carried to Moscow and Czar Ivan IV of the arrival of a 'strange nation of a singular gentleness and courtesy'. Their landing, it was eventually decided, was of great significance to the apparently landlocked throne of Muscovy; the Black Sea was out of reach as yet, the importance of the White Sea eluded advisers, and so the English adventurers got a hearty welcome. When they started on their journey home they took a request from Ivan IV for an English representative to be sent to Russia, and they had his full permission to trade freely with his empire. So the Muscovy Company was formed in London with a charter granted by Mary and her Spanish consort Philip in 1555, and confirmed later by Parliament. There was a broad social mix in its London membership that grew from a modest numerical base. As the purchase of Russian goods and sale of English commodities was in Russia itself, the centre of gravity of the Company was there too, with its interests under the guardianship of agents. These became pivotal figures, and the name of Russia actually had a specificity for him as an agent and as a resident who became embedded in the hitherto unfamiliar society. Agents too represented the Company to the Czar, upon whose despotic favour everyone depended. Like a school headmaster, the agent exercised a wide range of controls over the men doing company business, who lived together in a single dwelling. This made scrutiny easy, and if they ignored or struck out against the regulations on gambling, drunkenness, quarrelling and fighting, molesting women and abusive language, then they could be punished or expelled.

In the summer, mostly July, English merchants and merchandise would arrive on ships ranging in size from 100 to 160 tons, with ordinary goods for the quotidian lives of working people, luxuries for the court nobility, and above all military stores for the fighting Czar, all landed at Rose Island at the mouth of the Dvina. Then in August the ships would be loaded with naval stores, ships' tackle, tallow, tar, perhaps grain (though very much more came from Poland, which made it possible to avert famine riots and a Catholic uprising in England), wax and furs. By 1582 William Borough,

Comptroller of the Navy, felt convinced that the ropes and cables imported from Russia and used throughout the entire English fleet were indeed the best obtainable, so the Company would later claim some credit for the Armada triumph.[1] Charter investors did very well out of the first English joint stock company, with shares jumping in value by nearly 2,000 per cent within twenty years. This leap in value contributed to galloping optimism about other shareholdings, but the company that started so auspiciously could maintain itself for no more than half a century, and satisfactory profits dwindled over time. Some members chafed under the regulatory regime, and would do business unofficially with the Czar and his representatives. This was an *ad hoc* procedure that blunted what was otherwise a monopoly and helped not only to keep down the monopolistic prices but also secured for Russia, through free enterprise, types of goods – like armaments – which official regulations from time to time cut off.[2]

When Ivan IV died on 18 March 1584, the throne passed to his autistic (?) son Feodor, under the guardianship of five boyars led by his uncle, Nikita Yureyev, who chose as chief minister the chancellor, Andrei Shelkalov, the inveterate personal enemy of Elizabeth's ambassador, Sir Jerome Bowes – a very tall, good-looking, vain, quarrelsome Englishman slippery in negotiation. He was now in deep trouble, and the five met to discuss his permanent removal by execution, a fate apparently swept aside by the gusty Bowes in his claim that Elizabeth would not let his death go unavenged. After a shaky nine weeks Bowes got his marching orders, and he left feeling affronted despite a gift of sable skins from Boris Godunov. Feodor, under the control of the boyars, was now required to revoke the monopoly of the Company, but Jerome Horsey worked miracles to bring a clandestine trading cluster into operation, yoking his London allies, the brothers-in-law George Barne (II), Sir Francis Walsingham and Boris Godunov. Within two years this arrangement had undermined the Company so that its finances were in crisis. At the annual meeting of shareholders a move was made to censure the board of directors, who had benefited 'by liberality of Mr Horsey towards some of the chief dealers'. With a vote on a show of hands, 75 per cent of the Company debt was written off, and the refloated company with a new share issue, put power in the hands of just ten directors – the small men got squeezed out. The father of George Barne (II) was the Lord Mayor George Barne (I), for a short time in the early 1560s the father-in-law of Walsingham, and together they had privately traded with Russia. After 1587 Walsingham and George Barne (II) seem to have left such business to their associate Francis Cherry, who brought fairly large quantities of goods from Kola in 1589, having begun importing from there as early as 1579. This private trading was certainly known to the company's agent, Robert Peacock, who knew Horsey sufficiently well to write to Walsingham to warn that Horsey was getting meshed in debts to many people. The message to the Principal Secretary was essentially that he should always be vigilant in any dealings with him. As to the private trade, what Peacock knew the Company surely knew, but it mattered not a jot for it was heavily weighted towards men of Kent. Peacock declared to Walsingham that Russia would not corrupt him, but he could actually do very little to prevent venality among subordinates, including Anthony Marsh, a former agent who developed a substantial private trade in Russia.[3]

Elizabethan England was a kleptocracy. In prison in 1615 and resenting his fate, Ralegh bitterly noted in *The Prerogative of Parliaments in England* that Burghley, Leicester and Walsingham were all in the pocket of Thomas Smyth – that is, Mr Customer Smyth who had the farm of import duties in the London area from 1570 to 1589. The customs farm of the 'outports' was Walsingham's means to bolster his income through deputies in his service, in ports like Chester, Liverpool, Cardiff and Bristol, where Moses Crowe was collector.[4] It meant too that his passionate interest in exploration might bring something rare from the unknown. In October 1588 the Suffolk gentleman Thomas Cavendish returned to Plymouth, having experienced much as the second Englishman to sail around the world. Though rather overlooked, this was not a negligible achievement. On 8 October he wrote to Walsingham in appreciation of the courtesy shown to him by the customs officer there. He put the value of his personal acquisitions at £900 (*c.* £450,000 today).[5] 'There be some things which I have kept from their sight for special causes.' What could these be? Perhaps the detailed map of Cathay taken from a Portuguese prisoner called Rodrigo, who had lived in Canton. Whatever – these were things Cavendish wanted to present in person to Walsingham when he got to London. The secrets of the voyage were for the Principal Secretary's ears only.[6] Free of the ship at last were five boys, two from Japan and three from Manila, one of whom eventually found a place in service to Leicester's widowed countess. The age of the Filipino houseboy had begun.

Appendix B

THE LAND OF IRE

The Norman conquest of Ireland left a legacy of disturbance and hatred of the English ruling class that poisoned Anglo-Irish relations until the twentieth century. There were strange flourishes during this time, such as Perkin Warbeck's claim to the English throne in his assumed identity of the dead Richard, Duke of York, which began in Cork in 1491 and ended by 1499. Fifty years later the English Lordship in Ireland made an amoebic sweep from the coast facing the Isle of Man to Cork and to an outcrop on the Atlantic, Kerry between Dingle and Kilrush, and then separately around Galway. The Gaelic lordships were conquered between then and 1603, violence being an important political weapon for a Gaelic leader. Yet the English standing force in Ireland in 1560 was a paltry 1,500 men, and one Scottish lord, 5th Earl of Argyll, who was a force in lowland Scottish politics, offered the support of an expeditionary force of 3,000.[1] Argyll merits attention as a Protestant of strong conviction willing to support Mary, Queen of Scots in her struggle with the forces around her son. The ability of the Earl to raise forces far exceeded that of Elizabeth, whose position in Ireland was always shackled by cost. Military expenditure inexorably required two-thirds of her Irish budget, so that at the start of a crisis she would refuse the resources needed to deal with it, until it ran out of control, when to retrieve anything so would her costs.

As for private initiatives, settlement of the English in Ireland was all too often a shameless land-grab from an Irish owner. One who exercised his right to do this was Sir Thomas Smith, who in 1571 got a grant to settle the Ards peninsula in east Ulster, most of it ancestral lands of the Lord of Clandeboy, Sir Brian McPhelim O'Neill. Smith's illegitimate son led 100 men to settle in the Ards in 1572, but was defeated by Sir Brian and later gunned down by an assassin. Smith *père* reflected on this miserable outcome and imagined the walled city of *Elizabetha* – seeking to turn sycophantic rhetoric into stone. Under pressure from the Queen he failed, and transferred his rights to the 1st Earl of Essex, Walter Devereux, who was greedily anticipating triumph when the Queen lent him money (with his estates as security) on something that was not hers to give legitimately. Essex was 'a court-backed chancer' whose arrival in Antrim in 1573 pushed a bad situation towards the brink of calamity. Called governor of Ulster by Elizabeth, Essex launched a fierce campaign, invading Tyrone (central Ulster) and kidnapping Sir Brian, who saw the massacre of those about him before being sent with his wife and brother to be executed in Dublin. The Queen was hot to crush the O'Neills, but refused Essex important funding, so he resigned from his Ulster post. Tormented by failure and financial ruin he died soon of dysentery (possibly Crohn's disease). This led to court whispers that he had been poisoned by Leicester, who was besotted with the beauty of the Countess of Essex, Lettice Knollys.

By 1579 the Earl of Desmond, long detained in England, had been allowed home to a country in uproar. In considering the undisguised pressure on the traditional autonomy of his estates, Desmond could see no escape on any front, and so precipitated matters by sacking Youghal in southern Ireland. In addition, a force of 600 Spanish and Italian troops landed at Smerwick harbour on the Dingle peninsula. Despite defeats and the devastation of his estates, and the death of Sir John of Desmond in January 1583, the Earl fought doggedly until killed the following November. This left his huge appanage forfeited for treason, and also freed were the lands of those men of the nobility and lesser gentry of whom a startling number were dead. Here was land for the landless English courtier, a man like Ralegh, who was able to pile up the acreage, or Ralph Lane, an equerry of the great stable to the Master of the Horse – Leicester. Lane hoped that from military service in Munster he would be able to annex large areas, but his superiors there found him insufferable, just as Londoners detested Ralegh for his extravagant arrogance. There could be no greater contrast with this than the warm attitude of respect and admiration English Protestants felt for Walsingham, who was later widely mourned. Nor did he close his eyes to the Munster maelstrom, and in July 1580 Fulke Greville, his attentive junior aide, was there with Admiral Winter's naval force. By August Burghley himself was stirring, making his interest in Munster clear after the arrival of Lord Grey of Wilton in July, and Sir Henry Wallop was also alert, since the Lord Treasurer in London was trying to find evidence of fiscal improprieties by Ireland's vice-treasurer.[2]

In the hectic thrust and counter-thrust that ensued, one of Walsingham's friends lost ground. Various competing interests sought to reduce the power of the Earl of Ormonde, a cousin of Elizabeth. It was Walsingham who remained the security for Ormonde's heavy debts, but criticism of the Earl from men like Wallop was unsettling. It would have been more generous and obliging to put to Ormonde the accusations of military backsliding, and the Earl was entitled to feel much aggrieved by someone like Wallop, who wanted to trap him into a display of disloyalty to the crown.[3] Even a junior officer in the army felt empowered to join the fracas; Ralegh wrote to Walsingham to press the case for a substitute – his half-brother Sir Humphrey Gilbert. Walsingham evidently reviewed matters in the quiet of his room, thought the case made against Ormonde justified, and wrote to Grey of Wilton to relieve the Earl of his command. Ormonde and his advisers did try to resist this, but the former favourite of Elizabeth was pushed out of his post to save money. The gap he left seemed an open invitation to ruin, and Wallop quivered in dismay at the thought that Walsingham might nominate him. Irish aristocrats like Kildare and Ormonde and Desmond were harried out of suspicion and greed. Ormonde lost to the party of aggression, but they too were outflanked by a pseudo-policy of dawdling and hopping on the spot that was so much cheaper than war. And Walsingham was wedged and hemmed in by the fierce prejudices of those who looked to him as a voice of purpose in the Council. One of the obstacles to reform in Ireland was the lack of continuity in the office of Lord Deputy – they rarely held office for more than three or four years. The new Deputy found their predecessors' booby-trapped policy, so that the new man looked incompetent. Not only general policy but also personal fortunes could fluctuate with each change of incumbent, and it was not helpful that each Deputy could be over-ruled in London.

At the time of the Armada the Lord Deputy was Sir William Fitzwilliam, and his policy in time of crisis was a draconian one of systematic killing. Perhaps some 6,000 men from the remnant Armada fleet were shipwrecked off the west coast of Ireland, and although as many as 4,000 drowned, about 2,000 struggled ashore to surrender or be made captive. 'We authorize you to apprehend and execute all Spaniards. Torture may be used in prosecuting this inquiry.' So Fitzwilliam wrote to officers in the field, and with brutal alacrity some were killed by sword or noose. Yet one man of honour, brought from childhood to manhood in decency, resisted the pogrom. He risked his own reputation (maybe his life) to prevent the summary execution of prisoners. The man was Walsingham's stepson, Captain Christopher Carleill, who had fourteen prisoners in his charge in Ulster, refused to obey orders to execute them, and made it possible for them to escape to Scotland. The incident is known because the London-based contemporary historian Petruccio Ubaldino recorded it. An Italian immigrant who refused to speak a word of barbarous English, he noted that Carleill disliked rash and ill-considered cruelty – it was 'a thing which he hated'. Nor did Carleill want his nation to be regarded with scorn by observers in continental Europe.

NOTES

Abbreviations (also used in the Selected Bibliography)

AFR	Archiv für Reformationgeschichte
AHR	American History Review
AJH	American Jewish History
AoS	Annals of Science
BA	British Archaeology
BH	Business History
BL	British Library
BJRL	Bulletin of the John Rylands Library
BLJ	British Library Journal
CHR	Church History Review
CJH	Canadian Journal of History
CSPD	Calendar of State Papers, Domestic
CSPF	Calendar of State Papers, Foreign
CSPS	Calendar of State Papers, Scottish
CSPSp	Calendar of State Papers, Spanish
EEH	Explorations in Entrepreneurial History
EHR	English History Review
ELH	English Literary History
ER	Essex Review
ERC	Explorations in Renaissance Culture
HA	Historical Association
HJ	Historical Journal
HLQ	Huntington Library Quarterly
HT	History Today
JBS	Journal of British Studies
JEEH	Journal of English and European History
JHI	Journal of the History of Ideas
JMRS	Journal of Medieval and Renaissance Studies
M&L	Music & Letters
MLR	Modern Language Review
N&Q	Notes & Queries
P&P	Past and Present
PBA	Proceedings of the British Academy
PHFC	Proceedings of the Hampshire Field Club
PHR	Pacific History Review

PLL   *Papers on Language and Literature*
PRO   Public Record Office
SCJ   *Sixteenth Century Journal*
SEER   *Slavonic and East European Review*
SEL   *Studies in English Literature, 1500–1900*
T&C   *Technology & Culture*
TLS   *Times Literary Supplement*
TRHS   *Transactions of the Royal Historical Society*
WUS   *Washington University Studies*

Chapter 1

1   K.R. Bartlett, 'The Strangeness of Strangers, English Impressions of Italy in the Sixteenth Century', *Quaderni d'italianistica*, 1, 1, 1980, pp. 52–3
2   *Ibid.*, p. 53
3   *Ibid.*, p. 57

Chapter 2

1   G. Parker, 'The Place of Tudor England in the Messianic Vision of Philip II of Spain', *TRHS*, 12, 2002, pp. 192–3
2   *Ibid.*, pp. 216-7
3   *Ibid.*, pp. 199–200
4   *Ibid.*, p. 202
5   *Ibid.*, pp. 202–3
6   S.F.C. Moore, 'The Seizure of Brill by the "Sea Beggars"', *HT*, XXII, 5, 1972, p. 367

Chapter 3

1   J. Bossy, *Under the Molehill: an Elizabethan Spy Story*, 2001, pp. 55–6
2   Conyers Read, *Mr Secretary Walsingham and the Policy of Queen Elizabeth*, 3 vols. 1925, 1, p. 113
3   *Ibid.*, p. 127
4   *Ibid.*, p. 133
5   A matchlock weapon balanced for steadiness on a tripod. To ignite the gunpowder charge a burning match-cord was applied to the priming pan. Bullets could vary in size.
6   J. McDermott, *Martin Frobisher, Elizabethan Privateer*, 2001, p. 86
7   O.P. Grell, *Calvinist Exiles in Tudor and Stuart England*, 1996, pp. 100–3
8   Read, *Mr Secretary Walsingham*, 1, p. 229 n.1.

Chapter 4

1   D. Buisseret (ed.), *Monarchs, Ministers and Maps*, 1992, p. 68
2   *Ibid.*
3   D. Waters, *The Art of Navigation in England in Elizabethan and Early Stuart Times*, 1958, pp. 103–14
4   H. Wallis, 'England's Search', *Arctic*, 37, 4, 1984, p. 459
5   McDermott, *Martin Frobisher*, p. 109
6   J. Andrews, 'Industries in Kent, *c.* 1500–1640', pp. 132–3, in M. Zell (ed.), *Early Modern Kent*, 1999
7   J. Bower, 'Kent Towns, 1546–1640', p. 169, in M. Zell (ed.), op. cit.
8   G.B. Manhart, 'The English Search for a North-west Passage in the time of Queen Elizabeth', 1924, p. 162, in *Studies in English Commerce and Exploration in the reign of Elizabeth*

9   Michael Lok's nephew, Henry, was a career-servant to the earl for some twenty years.

10 Calendar reform was surely also discussed at this meeting. See Chapter 14.

11 R. Auger, 'Frobisher the Fraud', *BA*, 53, 6, 2000, p. 14

12 J. Bossy, *Giordano Bruno and the Embassy Affair*, 1991, p. 64

13 G.B. Parks, 'Hakluyt's Mission in France, 1583–8', *WUS*, Humanistic Studies, 9, 1922, p. 168

14 R. Trevelyan, *Sir Walter Raleigh*, 2002, pp. 61–2

15 Parkes, *Hakluyt's Mission*, pp. 171–2

16 N. Williams, *The Sea Dogs*, 1975, pp. 108–9

Chapter 5

1   A.G. Dickens. 'The Elizabethans and St Bartholomew', in A. Soman (ed.), *The Massacre of St Bartholomew, Reappraisals and Documents 1974*, pp. 62–3

2   SP 12/144/19, f. 46 r

3   P. Collinson, *Godly People*, 1983, pp. 247–59

4   C. Talbot (ed.), CRS Miscellanea 53

5   L.F. Parmalee, *Good Newes from Fraunce, French anti-League Propaganda in late Elizabethan England*, 1996, p. 31

6   S. Pears, *The Correspondence of Sir Philip Sidney and Hubert Languet*, 1845, pp. 75–6

7   B. Worden, *The Sound of Virtue: Philip Sidney's Arcadia and Elizabethan Politics*, 1996, p. 51

8   W.T. MacCaffery, 'The Anjou Match and the Making of English Foreign Policy', in P. Clark, A.G.T. Smith and N. Tyacke (eds), *The English Commonwealth, Essays in Politics and Society presented to Joel Hurstfield*, 1979, pp. 60–1

9   Dickens, 'The Elizabethans and St Bartholomew', p. 69

10 Worden, *Sound of Virtue*, p. 112

11 M.E. Lamb, *Gender and Authorship in the Sidney Circle*, 1990, p. 29

Chapter 6

1   Read, *Mr Secretary Walsingham*, pp. 316–17

2   M.M. Leimon, 'Sir Francis Walsingham and the Anjou Marriage Plan, 1574–81', unpublished Cambridge PhD thesis, 1989, p. 9

3   BL, Egerton Mss. 1694 f.3

4   Read, *Mr Secretary Walsingham*, pp. 336–7

5   Leimon, 'Sir Francis Walsingham and the Anjou Marriage Plan', p. 38

6   Read, *Mr Secretary Walsingham*, p. 356

7   R.J.W. Evans, *Rudolf II and his World*, 1973, p. 60

8   Read, *Mr Secretary Walsingham*, p. 358

Chapter 7

1   Leimon, 'Sir Francis Walsingham and the Anjou Marriage Plan', p. 31

2   *Ibid.*, p. 36

3   *Ibid.*, p. 39

4   *Ibid.*, p. 43

5   J. Gibson, 'Sidney's *Arcadias*, and Elizabethan Courtiership', *Essays in Criticism*, 52, 1, 2002, p. 37

6   Read, *Mr Secretary Walsingham*, p. 387

7   *Ibid.*, p. 391

8   Leimon, 'Sir Francis Walsingham

and the Anjou Marriage Plan',
p. 57

Chapter 8

1 P. Basing and D.E. Rhodes, 'English
   Plague Regulations and Italian
   Models', *BLJ*, 23, 1, 1997, p. 62
2 Bossy, *Giordano Bruno*, p. 59
3 L.E. Pearson, *The Elizabethans at
   Home*, p. 195
4 S. McMillin and S.-B. Maclean, *The
   Queen's Men and their Plays*, 1998,
   p. 23
5 *Ibid.*, p. 25
6 *Ibid.*
7 *Ibid.*, p. 27
8 Worden, *Sound of Virtue*, p. 50
9 J. Craig-McFeely, *English Lute
   Manuscripts and Scribes,
   1530–1630*, 2000, p. 23
10 S. Beek, *The First book of Consort
   Lessons, collected by T. Morley 1599
   and 1611*, 1959, p. 22
11 L. Ruff and D. Arnold Wilson, 'The
   Madrigal, the Lute Song and
   Elizabethan Politics', *P&P*, XLIV, 8,
   1969, p. 11
12 Hugh Paulet was a confidential
   messenger for his ambassador
   father, Sir Amias, and died in a
   Parisian street-fight aged about 22
   years (possibly in company with a
   brother or sister). Both the Queen
   and Walsingham wrote their
   condolences to Sir Amias.
13 I am most grateful to Mrs Maisie
   Brown for these details. Mary
   Walsingham died in June 1580.

Chapter 9

1 B. Lenman, *England's Colonial Wars:
   Conflicts, Empire and National
   Identity*, 2001, p. 75,

2 A. Lynn Martin, *Henry III and the
   Jesuit Politicians*, 1973, p. 66
3 Peter Ramus (Pierre de la Ramée)
   never fully accepted the Geneva
   church and its growing
   authoritarianism; Beza's power
   made him uneasy.
4 *Ibid.*, pp. 64–5
5 Rainolds led the opposition to
   academic plays performed in the
   universities.
6 G. Kilroy, 'Eternal Glory: Edmund
   Campion's Virgilian Epic', *TLS*, 8/3,
   2002, p.13
7 Bossy, *Giordano Bruno*, p. 19
8 D. Flynn, *John Donne and the
   Ancient Catholic Nobility*, 1995,
   p. 101
9 *Ibid.*, p. 108
10 J. Tedeschi, 'Tomasso Sassetti's
   Account of the St Bartholomew's
   Day Massacre', in A. Soman, (ed.),
   *The Massacre of St Bartholomew's,
   Reappraisals and Documents*, 1974,
   pp. 103–4
11 Read, *Mr Secretary Walsingham*,
   p. 263
12 Tedeschi, 'Tomasso Sassetti's
   Account', pp. 100–1
13 Flynn, *John Donne*, p. 123

Chapter 10

1 M. Graves, 'Thomas Norton, the
   Parliament Man: an Elizabethan
   MP', *HJ*, 23, 1, 1980, p. 18
2 Martin, *Henry III and the Jesuit
   Politicians*, p. 112
3 *Ibid.*
4 P. Collinson, 'The Monarchical
   Republic of Elizabeth I', *BJRL*, 69,
   1986, p. 416
5 G. Parker and M. Leimon, 'Treason
   and Plot in Elizabethan Diplomacy:

The "Fame" of Sir Edward Stafford Reconsidered', *EHR*, CXI, 1996, pp. 1136–7

6   M. Questier, 'Practical anti-Papistry during the reign of Elizabeth I', *JBS*, 36, 1997, p. 388

7   *CSPD*, Elizabeth, vol. CLVII, no. 51

8   A. Haynes, *The Elizabethan Secret Services, 1570–1603*, 2000; 2004, pp. 37–8

9   Flynn, *John Donne*, p. 95

10   *Ibid.*, p. 136

11   Parker and Leimon, 'Treason and Plot', p. 1142

Chapter 11

1   BL Add Mss, 32091, f. 262

2   Read, *Mr Secretary Walsingham, II*, p. 203

3   *Ibid.*, p. 209

4   *Ibid.*, p. 215

5   *CSPS* 1584–5, p. 257

6   Read, *Mr Secretary Walsingham*, p. 237

7   Hamilton papers, Ii, pp. 673–4

8   *Ibid.*, pp. 704–5

Chapter 12

1   Bossy, *Giordano Bruno*, p. 67

2   C. Nicholl, *The Reckoning: The Murder of Christopher Marlowe*, 1992, p. 141

3   C. Winn, *The Pouletts of Hinton St George*, 1977, p. 11

4   *Ibid.*, p. 13

5   C. Meyers, 'Lawsuits in Elizabethan Courts of Law: the Adventures of Dr Hector Nunes', *JEEH*, 25, 1, 1996, pp. 157–68,

6   *Ibid.*

7   C. Nicholl, *The Creature in the Map*, 1996

8   PRO: E 351/542, f. 92v

Chapter 13

1   P.E. McCullough, *Sermons at Court: Politics and Religion in Elizabethan and Jacobean Preaching*, 1998, p. 56

2   A King's College tribute to Bucer after his death, volumes of Greek and Latin verse edited by John Cheke, Walter Haddon and Thomas Wilson, had a contribution by William Temple, an exile to Basle during Mary's reign, who seems to have kept company with Walsingham while there.

3   McCullough, *Sermons at Court*, p. 56

4   L.M. Higgs, *Godliness and Governance in Tudor Colchester*, 1998, p. 239

5   *Ibid.*, p. 248

6   J. McConica, 'Humanism and Aristotle in Tudor Oxford', *EHR*, 94, 1979, pp. 302–9

7   Higgs, *Godliness and Governance*, p. 324

8   P. Clark, *English Provincial Society from Reformation to Revolution, Religion, Politics and Society in Kent, 1500–1640*, 1977, p. 150

9   *Ibid.*, p. 137

10   *Ibid.*, p. 439, n. 61

11   *Ibid.*, pp. 169–70

12   Father of a daughter baptised More-fruit

Chapter 14

1   L. Stone, *Family and Fortune: Studies in Aristocratic Finance in the Sixteenth and Seventeenth Centuries*, 1973, p. 211

2   E. Ash, 'A Perfect and Absolute Work: Expertise, Authority and the Rebuilding of Dover Harbor, 1579–83', *T&C*, 41, 2, 2000, pp. 239–68

3   Leonard Digges was a friend of Sir

Nicholas Bacon, and Thomas recalled their long chats about science.

4   S. Johnson, 'Mathematical Practitioners and Instruments in Elizabethan England', *AoS*, 48, 1991, p. 323

5   *Ibid.*, pp. 322–3

6   R. Poole, 'John Dee and the English Calendar: Science, Religion and Empire', in R. Poole, *Time's Alteration: Calendar Reform in Early Modern England*, 1998

7   *Ibid.*

Chapter 15

1   R.B. Merriman, 'Some Notes on the Treatment of the English Catholics in the reign of Elizabeth', *AJH*, XIII, 3, 1908, pp. 484–5

2   Bossy, *Giordano Bruno*, pp. 26–7

3   G. Grassl, 'Joachim Gans of Prague, the First Jew in English America', *AJH*, 86, 2, 1998, p. 204

4   M. Christian, 'Elizabeth's Preachers and the Government of Women: Defining and Correcting a Queen', *SCJ*, XXIV, 3, 1993, p. 571

5   Collinson, *The Monarchical Republic*, p. 409

6   Eventually the Queen grudgingly forgave the offence. Two and a half years later she rode from Richmond to London to be godmother to the Sidney daughter, but offered no gift. Yet the nurse and midwife got to share £5, and the child was called Elizabeth.

7   Lenman, *England's Colonial Wars*, p. 221

Chapter 16

1   Nicholl, *The Reckoning*, p. 131

2   *Ibid.*

3   E.C. Butler, 'Dr William Gifford in 1586', *The Month*, CIII, 1904, pp. 245–9.

4   Winn, *The Pouletts of Hinton St George*, p. 18.

5   *Ibid.*, p. 26.

6   A. Kenny, 'A Martyr Manqué, The Early Life of Anthony Tyrrell', *Clergy Review*. Also C. Devlin, 'An Unwilling Apostate', *The Month*, XII, 1951

Chapter 17

1   Bossy, *Giordano Bruno*, p. 19

2   P. Roberts, 'The Studious Artizan: Christopher Marlowe, Canterbury and Cambridge', in P. Roberts and D. Grantley (eds), *Christopher Marlowe and English Renaissance Culture*, 1996, p. 29

3   P. Lake and M. Questier, *The Anti-Christ's Lewd Hat*, 2002, p. 199

4   J.D. Alsop, 'Sir Philip Sidney's Tax Debts, 1585–6', *N&Q*, 44, 1997, December Pt 4, p. 470

5   Read, II, p. 29

6   M.G. Richings, *Espionage*, 1934, p. 146

7   Nicholl, p. 155

8   *CSPS* 1585–6, p. 531

Chapter 18

1   Read, II p. 35

2   *Ibid.*, p. 47

3   BL Cotton, Mss. App. 1, f. 143

4   Nicholl, pp. 157–8

5   T. Maclean 'The Recusant Legend: Chideock Tichborne', *HT*, 32, 5, 1982, p. 13

6   C. Devlin, *Robert Southwell*, 1956, p. 121

7   A.G. Smith, *The Babington Plot*, 1936, p. 87

8   S. Doran, 'Revenge her Foul and

Most Unnatural Murder? The impact of Mary Stewart's Execution on Anglo-Scottish Relations', *History*, 85, 2000, 280, p. 591

9   D. Hickman, 'Religious Belief and Pious Practice among London's Elizabethan Elite', *HJ*, 42, 4, 1999, p. 949

Chapter 19

1   A. Heisch, 'Arguments for an Execution: Queen Elizabeth's "White Paper", and Lord Burghley's "Blue Pencil",' *Albion*, 24, 4, 1992, p. 591

2   Doran, 'Revenge her Foul and most Unnatural Murder', p. 597

3   *Ibid.*, p. 596

4   *Ibid.*, p. 609

5   *Ibid.*, p. 602

Chapter 20

1   Stephen Le Sieur late in 1585 fetched up in prison in Dunkirk, and Walsingham's former payment to him of £50 needed augmentation if he was to be freed.

2   Parker and Leimon, 'Treason and Plot', p. 1139

3   The wardship lasted from 1569 to 1577

4   Bossy, *Giordano Bruno*, p. 63

5   Parker and Leimon, 'Treason and Plot', pp. 1138–9

6   Doran, 'Revenge her Foul and most Unnatural Murder', p. 601

7   Flynn, *John Donne*, p.130

8   J.-P. Desprat and J. Thibau, *Henri IV, Le règne de la tolerance*, 2001, p. 44

9   A. Tenenti, *Piracy and the Decline of Venice, 1550–1615*, 1967, p. 62

10   I. Seymour, 'The Political Magic of John Dee', *HT*, 39, 7, 1989, p. 34

11   V. Stern, *Sir Stephen Powle of Court and Country*, p. 87

12   *Ibid.*, p. 93

Chapter 21

1   M. Hay, *The Life of Robert Sidney, Earl of Leicester*, 1984, p. 53

2   *Arcadia* was a century-long bestseller and the first work of English fiction to be translated into other languages.

3   Read, op. cit. iii, p. 232

4   R. Boucard, *Les dessous de l'espionnage anglais*, 1936; also Haynes, op. cit. p. 103

5   Read, op. cit. p. 242

6   What other court in Europe would have allowed a mere sugar factor into the Presence Chamber?

7   A. Haynes, *The White Bear: Robert Dudley, Elizabethan Earl of Leicester*, 1987, p. 184

8   P. Jorgenson, 'Theoretical Views of War in Elizabethan England', *JHI*, 13, 1952, p. 480

9   BL Cotton Ms Galba D.i.f.244

10   *CSPD*, ccvi, 2, 2/12, 1587

11   SP Spain iii, 4, 1588

Chapter 22

1   P. Croft, 'Trading with the Enemy', *HJ*, 32, 2, 1989, p. 284

2   BL Harleian Ms 6994.f.76

3   *Ibid.*

4   Relatively new to English war preparations, a petronel was fired from chest-height like a carbine with a curved butt.

5   J. Tincey, *The Spanish Armada*, 1988, p. 9

Chapter 23

1   R.W. Kenny, *Elizabeth's Admiral*, 1970, pp. 144–5
2   Read, op. cit. III, pp. 317–18
3   *Ibid.*, p. 324
4   *Ibid.*
5   *Ibid.*, pp. 325–6

Chapter 24

1   J.S. Nolan, *Sir John Norreys and the Elizabethan Military World*, pp. 126–7, 1997
2   *Ibid.*, p. 10
3   Noue died in July 1591 from injuries occasioned by his fall from his horse – itself caused by a bullet lodging in his head.
4   *Ibid.*, p. 15
5   *Ibid.*, p. 101
6   *Ibid.*, p. 128
7   BL Galba D. iv, f. 175
8   Hay, op. cit. p. 73
9   J.R. Green, 'The Martyrdom of Ramus', in Marlowe's *The Massacre at Paris*, *PLL*, 9, 4, 1973
10 Read, op.cit. III, p. 368
11 Rowse, *Expansion*, p. 407

Chapter 25

1   A.J. Haynes, *The Gunpowder Plot: Faith in Rebellion*, 1994
2   A night funeral in this great church would still not have been cheap. The timing caused disruption so fees were doubled.
3   F.B. Tromly, '"According to sounde religion": The Elizabethan controversy over the funeral sermon', *JMRS*, 13, 2, Fall 1983, p. 293
4   Cartright's *Confutation* of the works of English Jesuits was written with financial assistance from Walsingham.
5   J. Morgan, *Godly Learning: Puritan Attitudes towards Reason, Learning and Education, 1560–1640*, 1986, p. 39
6   C. Marsh, 'In the name of God? Will-making and Faith in Early Modern England', in G.H. Martin & P. Spufford (eds), *The Records of the Nation*, 1990, p. 200

Appendix A

1   R. Wilson, 'Visible Bullets: Tamburlaine the Great and Ivan the Terrible', *ELH*, 62, 1, p. 48
2   W. Kirchner, 'Entrepreneurial Activity in Russo-Western Relations', *EEH* (1st ser.), 8, 4, 1956, pp. 250–1
3   S.H. Baron, 'Ivan the Terrible, Giles Fletcher and the Muscovite Merchantry: A Reconsideration', *SEER*, 56, 4, 10/78, p. 579
4   PRO E 122/24/41
5   N.Williams, *The Sea Dogs, Privateers, Plunder and Piracy in the Elizabethan Age*, 1975, p. 198
6   BL Harleian Mss 286 f. 161

Appendix B

1   Lenman, *England's Colonial Wars*, p. 50
2   Leimon, 'Sir Francis Walsingham and the Anjou Marriage Plan', p. 194
3   *Ibid.*, p. 197

SELECTED BIBLIOGRAPHY

To his magisterial study *Mr Secretary Walsingham and the Policy of Queen Elizabeth*, 3 vols, 1925, Conyers Read appended a 27-page bibliographical review of archival and printed material. I commend this to any serious student of the life and times of the Principal Secretary, and I see no point in trying to improve on it.

However, I can add books and articles published since 1925 which endorse, expand, enhance or even correct Read. The place of publication for books is London unless otherwise indicated.

Books

Agrell, W and Huldt, B., *Clio Goes Spying* (Lund), 1983

Andrews, K.R., *The Spanish Caribbean, Trade and Plunder, 1530–1630*

Baumgartner, F.J., *Radical Reactionaries: The Political Thought of the French Catholic League* (Geneva), 1975

Bellamy, J., *The Tudor Law of Treason* (Toronto), 1979

Benedict, P., *Rouen during the Wars of Religion*, 1981

Berkowitz, D.S., *Humanist Scholarship and Public Order* (Washington, DC), 1984

Berry, L.E. (ed.), John Stubbs' *Gaping Gulf*, Folger Documents Series (Virginia), 1968

Blayney, P., *The Bookshops in Paul's Cross Churchyard*, 1990

Bossy, J., *Giordano Bruno and the Embassy Affair*, 1991

—, *Under the Molehill: An Elizabethan Spy Story*, 2001

Boucard, R., *Les dessous de l'espionnage anglais* (Milan), 1936

Breight, C., *Surveillance, Militarism and Drama in Elizabethan England*, 1996

Brooks, E. St John, *Sir Christopher Hatton*, 1946

Brown, C., *Patronage, Politics and Literary Tradition in England, 1588–1658* (Detroit), 1991

Buisseret, D. (ed.), *Monarchs, Ministers and Maps*, Chapters by Peter Barber (Chicago), 1992

Burn, M., *The Debatable Land*, 1970

Caraman, P., *The Other Face, Catholic Life under Elizabeth I*, 1960

Champion, P., *Charles IX: la France et le contrôle de l'Espagne*, 2 vols (Paris), 1939

Charteris, R., *Alfonso Ferrabosco the Elder* (NY), 1984

Clark, P., *English Provincial Society from Reformation to Revolution: Religion, Politics and Society in Kent, 1500–1640*, 1977

Clegg, C.B., *Press Censorship in Elizabethan England*, 1997

Cliffe, J.T., *The Puritan Gentry*, 1984

Code, J.B., *Queen Elizabeth and the English Catholic Historians* (Louvain), 1935

Collinson, P., *The Elizabethan Puritan Movement*, 1967

— *Godly People*, 1983

— *The English Captivity of Mary, Queen of Scots* (Sheffield), 1987

— *Elizabethan Essays*, 1994

Cooper, N., *Houses of the Gentry, 1480–1680*

Cooper, W.R., *Notices of Anthony Babington*, 1862

Craig-McFeely, J., *English Lute Manuscripts and Scribes 1530–1630*, 2000

Crockett, B., *The Play of the Paradox* (Philadelphia), 1995

Cross, C., *The Puritan Earl, Henry Hastings, 3rd Earl of Huntingdon*, 1966

D'Amico, J., *The Moor in English Renaissance Drama* (Tampa, Fl.), 1991

Davies, C.S.L., *Peace, Print and Protestantism*, 1976

Dean, D., *Law Making and Society in Late Elizabethan England*, 1996

Desprat, J-P. and Thibau, J., *Henri IV, Le règne de la tolerance*, 2001

Devlin, C. *The Life of Robert Southwell; Poet and Martyr*, 1956

Du Maurier, D., *Golden Lads, Anthony Bacon, Francis and their Friends*, 1975

Edmond, M., *Hilliard and Oliver*, 1983

Edwards, F., *Robert Persons: the biography of an Elizabethan Jesuit* (St Louis), 1995

—, *The Marvellous Chance*, 1968

Evans, F.M.G., *The Principal Secretary of State* (Manchester), 1923

Evans, R.J.W., *Rudolf II and his World*, 1973

Flynn, D., *John Donne and the Ancient Catholic Nobility* (Bloomington, Ind.), 1995

Friedman, A., *House and Household in Elizabethan England* (Chicago), 1989

Gallagher, L., *Medusa's Gaze: Casuistry and Conscience in the Renaissance* (Stanford), 1991

Garrett, C.H., *The Marian Exiles, 1553–9* (Cambridge), 1938

Gittings, C., *Death, Burial and the Individual in Early Modern England*, 1984

Graves, M., *Thomas Norton, The Parliament Man* (Oxford), 1994

Greg, W.W., *Some Aspects and Problems of London Printing, 1550–1650* (Oxford), 1956

Grell, O., *Calvinist Exiles in Tudor and Stuart England* (Aldershot), 1996

Handover, P.M., *Printing in London, from 1476 to Modern Times*, 1960

Harrison, B., *A Tudor Journal: The Diary of a Priest in the Tower*, 2000

Hart, A.T., *The Man in the Pew, 1558–1660* (NY), 1966

Hasenson, A., *The History of Dover Harbour*, 1980

Haynes, A., (Original title) *Invisible Power: The Elizabethan Secret Services, 1570–1603*, 1992

    Now, *The Elizabethan Secret Services* (Stroud), 2000

Hicks, L., *An Elizabethan Problem*, 1964

Higgs, L., *Godliness and Governance in Tudor Colchester* (Ann Arbor, Mich.), 1998

Holmes, P., *Resistance and Compromise: The Political thought of the Elizabethan Catholics*, 1982

Holt, M., *The Duke of Anjou and the Politique Struggle during the Wars of Religion*, 1986

Hudson, W., *The Cambridge Connection and the Elizabethan Settlement of 1559* (Durham), 1980

Hume, M., *Treason and Plot*, 1908

Jensen, DeL., *Diplomacy and Dogmatism: Bernardino de Mendoza and the French Catholic League*, 1964

Kahn, D., *The Codebreakers*, 1963

Kay, D., *Melodious Tears: The English Funeral Elegy from Spenser to Milton*, 1990

Kenny, R.W., *Elizabeth's Admiral*, 1970

Kingdon, R., *Myths about the St Bartholomew's Day Massacres 1572–76* (Cambridge, Mass.), 1988

Lake, P. and Questier, M., *The Anti-Christ's Lewd Hat*, 2002

Lamb, M.E., *Gender and Authorship in the Sidney Circle* (Madison), 1990

Lehmberg, S.E., *Sir Walter Mildmay and Tudor Government* (Austin, Tex.), 1964

Lenman, B., *England's Colonial Wars 1550–1688, Conflicts, Empire and National Identity*, 2001

Lezra, J., *Unspeakable Subjects, The Genealogy of the Event in Early Modern Europe* (Stanford), 1997

Llewellyn, N., *Signs of Life*, 1997

Loades, D.M., *The Reign of Mary Tudor*, 1979

Loomie, A.J., *The Spanish Elizabethans*, 1963

Lynn, Martin, A., *Henry III and the Jesuit Politicians* (Geneva), 1973

MacCaffery, W., *Queen Elizabeth and the Making of Policy*, 1981

Maclean, J., *Memoirs of the Family of Poyntz*, 1886

Manhart, G.B., *The English Search for a North-West Passage*, 1924 (Reprinted 1968)

McCullough, P.E., *Sermons at Court; Politics and Religion in Elizabethan and Jacobean Preaching*, 1998

McDermott, J., *Martin Frobisher, Elizabethan Privateer*, 2001

Meadows, D., *Elizabethan Quintet*, 1956

Miller, A., *Sir Henry Killigrew* (Leicester), 1963

Morgan, J., *Godly Learning, Puritan Attitudes towards Reason, Learning, Education 1500–1640*, 1986

Morris, J., *The Letter-books of Sir Amias Paulet*, 1874

Nelson, A. H., *Monstrous Adversary, The Life of Edward de Vere, 17th Earl of Oxford* (Liverpool), 2003

Nicholl, C., *The Reckoning: The Murder of Christopher Marlowe*, 1992

Osborn, J., *Young Philip Sidney*, 1972

Parmalee, L.F., *Good Newes from Fraunce, French Anti-League Propaganda in late Elizabethan England* (Rochester), 1996

Peck, D.C. (ed.), *Leicester's Commonwealth and related documents* (Athens, Ohio), 1985

Poole, R., *Time's Alteration: Calendar Reform in Early Modern England*, 1998

Questier, M., *Conversion, Politics and Religion in England 1580–1625*

Raab, F., *The English Face of Machiavelli*, 1964

Rees, J., *Fulke Greville, Lord Brooke 1554–1628*, 1971

Richings, M.G., *Espionage*, 1934

Roberts, P. and Grantley, D., *Christopher Marlowe and English Renaissance Culture*, 1996

Ronan, M., *The Reformation in Ireland under Elizabeth, 1558–1801*, 1930

Rosenberg, E., *Leicester, Patron of Letters* (NY), 1955

Sargent, R., *The Life and Lyrics of Sir Edward Dyer*, 1968

Sissons, C.J., *Thomas Lodge and other Elizabethans* (NY), 1966

Soman, A. (ed.), *The Massacre of St Bartholomew's: Reappraisals and Documents* (The Hague), 1974

Smith, L.B., *Treason in Tudor England; Politics and Paranoia*, 1986

Stern, S.M., *Documents from Islamic Chanceries*, 1965

Stern, V., *Sir Stephen Powle of Court and Country* (Selinsgrove), 1992

Stone, L., *An Elizabethan: Sir Horatio Palavicino*, 1956

Symons, T.H.B., *Meta Incognita: A Discourse of Discovery* (Hull, Quebec), 1998

Taylor, E.G.R., *The Mathematical Practitioners of Tudor and Stuart England*, 1954

Thomson, D., *Renaissance Paris*, 1984

Tincey, J., *The Spanish Armada*, 1988

Tittler, R., *Nicholas Bacon: The Makings of a Tudor Statesman*, 1976

Trimble, W.R., *The Catholic Laity in Elizabethan England*, 1964

Trinkaus, C., *Adversity's Noblemen* (NY), 1940

Wegg, J., *The Decline of Antwerp under Philip of Spain*, 1924

Wernham, R.B., *The Making of English Foreign Policy, 1558–1603* (Berkley, Cal.), 1980

Williams, N., *The Sea Dogs* (NY), 1975

Wilson, C., *Queen Elizabeth I and the Revolt of the Netherlands*, 1970

Woolfson, J., *Padua and the Tudors, English Students in Italy, 1485–1603* (Cambridge), 1999

Worden, B., *The Sound of Virtue, Philip Sidney's Arcadia and Elizabethan Politics*, 1996

Wright, N. and McGregor, F. (eds), *European History and its Historians* (Adelaide), 1977

Zell, M. (ed.), *Early Modern Kent* (Woodbridge), 1999

ARTICLES

Adams, R.P. 'Depotism, Censorship and Mirrors of Power Politics in Late Elizabethan Times', *SCJ*, X, 3, 1979

Alsop, D.D. 'Sir Philip Sidney's Tax Debts, 1585–6', *N&Q*, 44, 12 (4), 1997

Ash, E. 'A Perfect and an Absolute Work. Expertise, Authority and the rebuilding of Dover Harbour, 1579–1583', *T&C*, 41, 2, 2000

Auger, R. 'Frobisher the Fraud', *BA*, 53, 6, 2000

Baron, S.H. 'Ivan the Terrible, Giles Fletcher and the Muscovite Merchantry', *SEER*, 56, 4, 1978

Bartlett, K.R. 'The Strangeness of Strangers, English Impressions of Italy in the Sixteenth Century', *Quaderni d'italianistica*, 1, 1, 1990

Basing, P. and Rhodes, D.E. 'English Plague Regulations and Italian Models', *BLJ*, 23, 1, 1997

Baughan, D.E. 'Sir Philip Sidney and the Matchmakers', *MLR*, October 1938

Bossy, J. 'The Character of English Catholicism', *P&P*, 21, 1962

Bowler, G. 'An Axe or an Acte. The Parliament of 1572 and Resistance Theory in Early Elizabethan England', *CJH*, XIX, 3, 1984

Christian, M. 'Elizabeth's Preachers and the Government of Women: Defining and Correcting a Queen', *SCJ*, XXIV, 3, 1993

Collinson, P. 'The Elizabethan Exclusion Crisis and the Elizabethan Polity', *PBA*, 84, 1994

— 'The Monarchical Republic of Queen Elizabeth I', *BJRL*, LXIX, 1987. Reprinted in *Elizabethan Essays*

Craig, H. 'The Geneva Bible as a Political Document', *PHR*, VII, 1938

Cressy, D. 'Binding the Nation: The Bonds of Association, 1584 and 1696', in D.J. Garth & J.W. McKenna (eds), *Tudor Rule and Revolution, Essays for G.R. Elton*, 1982

Croft, P. 'Trading with the Enemy, 1585–1604', *HJ*, 32, 2, 1989

Dawson, J.E.A. 'Revolutionary Conclusions: The Case of the Marian Exiles', *HPT*, 11, 1990

Doran, S. 'Revenge her Foul and most Unnatural Murder? The Impact of Mary Stewart's Execution on Anglo-Scottish Relations', *HA*, 85, 2000

Edwards, W. 'The Walsingham Consort Books', *M&L*, LV, 1974

Gibson, J. 'Sidney's *Arcadias* and Elizabethan Courtiership', *Essays in Criticism*, 52, 1, 2002

Glenn, J.R. 'The Martyrdom of Ramus in Marlowe's "The Massacre at Paris"', *PLL*, 9, 4, 1973

Grassl, G.C. 'Joachim Gans of Prague, The First Jew in English America', *AJH*, 86, 2, 1998

Graves, M. 'Thomas Norton, the Parliament Man: An Elizabethan MP', *HJ*, 23, 1, 1980

Heisch, A. 'Arguments for an Execution: Queen Elizabeth's "White Paper" and Lord Burghley's "Blue Pencil"', *Albion*, 24, 4, Winter 1992

Jenkins, G. 'Ways and Means of Elizabethan Propaganda', *History* (n.s.), 26, 1941

Johnston, S. 'Mathematical Practitioners and Instruments in Elizabethan England', *AoS*, 48, 1991

Jorgensen, P.A. 'Theoretical Views of War in Elizabethan England', *JHI*, 13, 1952

Kilroy, G. 'Eternal Glory, Edmund Campion's Virgilian Epic', *TLS*, 8 March 2002

Kirchner, W. 'Entrepreneurial Activity in Russo-Western Relations', *EEH* (1st ser.), 8, 4, 1956

Leimon, M. and Parker, G. 'Treason and Plot in Elizabethan Diplomacy. The "Fame" of Sir Edward Stafford Reconsidered', *EHR*, CXI, 1996

Lock, J. 'How Many Tercios has the Pope? The Spanish War and the Sublimation of Elizabethan anti-Popery', *History*, 81, 1996

Lowe, B. 'Religious Wars and the Anglican Anti-War Sentiment in Elizabethan England', *Albion*, 28, 1996

Maclean, T. 'The Recusant Legend : Chideock Tichborne', *HT*, 31, 5, 1982

Martin, R. 'Anne Dowriche's "The French History", Christopher Marlowe and Machiavellian Agency', *SEL*, 39, 1, 1999

McBride, G.K. 'Elizabethan Foreign Policy', *Albion*, 5, 3, 1973

McConica, J. 'Humanism and Aristotle in Tudor Oxford', *EHR*, 94, 4, 1979

McCoog, T.M. 'The English Jesuit Mission and the French Match, 1577–81', *CHR*, 87, 2 2001

Mears, N. 'Love-making and Diplomacy', *History*, 86, 2001

Merriman, R.B. 'Some Notes on the Treatment of English Catholics in the Reign of Elizabeth', *AHR*, XIII, 3, 1908

Meyers, C. 'Lawsuits in Elizabethan Courts of Law', *JEEH*, 25, 1, Spring pages, 1996

Moore, S.F.C. 'The Seizure of Brill by the Sea Beggars', *HT*, XXII, 5, 1972

Parker, G. 'The Place of Tudor England in the Messianic Vision of Philip II of Spain', *TRHS*, 12 (6th ser.), 2002

Parks, G.B. 'Hakluyt's Mission in France, 1583–88', *WUS*, 9, 1922, Humanistic Studies

Peck, D. 'Raleigh, Sidney, Oxford and the Catholics 1579', *N&Q* (n.s), 23, 5–6, Oct 1978

Phillips, J.E. 'Renaissance Concepts of Justice and the Structure of the Faerie Queene Book V', *HLQ*, 33, 1970

Questier, M. 'Practical Anti-Papistry during the Reign of Elizabeth I', *JBS*, 36, 1997

Read, C. 'The Fame of Sir Edward Stafford', *AHR*, 20, 1915

Ritchie, J. Ewing. 'James Morice, MP for Colchester', *ER*, 2, 1895

Ruff, L. and Wilson, D. Arnold. 'The Madrigal, Lute Song and Elizabethan Politics', *P&P*, XLIV, 8, 1969

Seymour, I. 'The Political Magic of John Dee', *HT*, XXXIX, 1, 1989

Shammas, C. 'The "Invisible Merchant" and Property Rights. The Misadventures of an Elizabethan Joint-Stock Company', *BH*, 17, 2, 1975

Steggle, M. 'Charles Chester and Richard Hakluyt', *SEL*, 1500–1900, 43, 1, 2003

Sutherland, N.M. 'The Marian Exiles and the Establishment of the Elizabethan Regime', *AFR*, 78, 1987

Tromly, F. 'According to Sounde Religion: the Elizabethan Controversy over the Funeral Service', *JMRS*, 13, 1983

Wallis, H. 'England's Search', *Arctic*, 37, 4, 1984

White, P.W.W. 'Calvinist and Puritan Attitudes towards the Stage in Renaissance England', *ERC*, 14, 1988

Whitehead, J.L. 'An Inventory of the Goods and Chattels of Sir Richard Worsley of Appuldurcombe', AD 1566, *PHFC*, 5, 1904–6

Wilson, R. 'Visible Bullets: Tamburlaine the Great and Ivan the Terrible', *ELH*, 62, 1, 1995

Woodhouse, J.R. 'Honourable Dissimulation: Some Italian Advice for the Renaissance Diplomat', *PBA*, 84, 1994

Unpublished Theses

M.M. Leimon, 'Sir Francis Walsingham and the Anjou Marriage Plan, 1574–81', Cambridge PhD, 1989

J.C. Weaver, 'The concept of ethos in Tudor rhetorical theory and practice', Purdue PhD, 1993

INDEX